TITANIC'S
LAST SECRETS

TITANIC'S
LAST SECRETS

THE FURTHER ADVENTURES

OF *SHADOW DIVERS*

JOHN CHATTERTON AND RICHIE KOHLER

BRAD MATSEN

NEW YORK BOSTON

TWELVE

Twelve
Hachette Book Group USA
237 Park Avenue
New York, NY 10017

Visit our Web site at www.HachetteBookGroupUSA.com.

Twelve is an imprint of Grand Central Publishing.
The Twelve name and logo are trademarks of Hachette Book Group USA, Inc.

Book design by Fearn Cutler deVicq
Printed in the United States of America

First Edition: October 2008
10 9 8 7 6 5 4 3 2 1

Library of Congress Cataloging-in-Publication Data
Matsen, Bradford.
   Titanic's last secrets : the further adventures of shadow divers John Chatterton
and Richie Kohler / by Brad Matsen.—1ˢᵗ ed.
      p. cm.
   ISBN-13: 978-0-446-58205-6
   ISBN-10: 0-446-58205-0
   1. Titanic (Steamship). 2. Shipwrecks—North Atlantic Ocean. 3. Underwater ar-
chaeology—North Atlantic Ocean. 4. Chatterton, John. 5. Kohler, Richie. I. Title.
   G530.T6M345 2008
   910.9163'4 22

2008003193

for Diane

CONTENTS

CONTENTS

EPILOGUE

SHIPWRECK

HISTORY

A late-night highway phone call was the beginning of it. When John Chatterton's BlackBerry chirped, he was northbound on the New Jersey Turnpike with the cruise control set at seventy-two, eighties rock on the radio, and a box of fried chicken thighs on the seat next to him. He was staying awake on pure willpower after a long day, knowing that waking up the next morning with his wife on the coast of Maine would be a hell of a lot better than waking up alone in a motel room.

As much as he liked being home, Chatterton had no complaints about the time he was spending on the road. He had always seen his life as an album of before and after pictures. Before Vietnam, after Vietnam. Before his first wife, after his first wife. Especially, before *U-869*, and after *U-869*. Since 1997, when Chatterton and Richie Kohler had identified a U-boat they'd found off the coast of New Jersey, exploring shipwrecks was no longer just Chatterton's obsession, it was his job. He and Kohler were the stars of a PBS documentary and a television series, *Deep Sea Detectives*, diving and getting paid generously to do what they loved to do.

Since the U-boat, there had been other before-and-afters in Chatterton's life, but the shocker was cancer. A squamous cell carcinoma had announced itself as an odd ripple in the familiar terrain of his neck on an otherwise ordinary morning shaving at the bathroom sink. That discovery had propelled Chatterton into the world of Big Medicine, which offended him even more than the cancer, but four years after the numbing litany of chemo, surgery, and radiation, he was still alive.

Chatterton picked up his BlackBerry as the sodium-vapor glare of the turnpike rest area north of Newark flashed by on his left.

John, it's David Concannon. Got a minute to talk?

For you, lots of minutes, Chatterton said.

Concannon was a lawyer in Philadelphia who had hired Chatterton as an expert witness in a lawsuit involving the death of a scuba diver. It had been dragging on for more than a year. One of the skills Chatterton had picked up after *U-869* was interacting with clients without being disingenuous or getting too close. Concannon wasn't a friend, so Chatterton didn't really know him, but he had checked the lawyer out before agreeing to work with him. Concannon was big on the Explorers Club, went to meetings, was the president of his chapter in Philly, and was one of the club's lawyers. Concannon ran a company that gave advice to explorers putting expeditions together. He seemed like a nice enough guy.

So, I've got an idea for you, Concannon said.

Chatterton was used to this part of life after *U-869*, too. Everybody had an idea for *Deep Sea Detectives*. The premise of the series was simple: Every shipwreck presented a mystery; he and Richie Kohler solved it. Chatterton listened to people who called him with ideas because some of them panned out, and some were just good stories.

Let's hear it, Chatterton said.

The Big *T*, Concannon said. The words hung in cellphone space.

The Big *T*? Chatterton couldn't figure out what Concannon was talking about.

Titanic, Concannon said, breaking the awkward silence. He went on to say that he had been an adviser to an expedition in 2000 that had been picking up *Titanic* artifacts for a museum exhibit, and something had been nagging at him ever since. At the end of his last dive in a *Mir* research sub, he saw ribbons of steel that looked like they had been peeled from the bottom of a ship. Scattered around them, there was debris—shoes, suitcases, trunks—that might have come from a cargo hold. Concannon had talked about the ribbons of steel with others who had been to the wreck of *Titanic*, but none of them had seen anything like them.

Where are the pictures? Chatterton asked.

No pictures, Concannon said. It was at the end of a five-hour dive and we were out of video tape.

What about stills?

No stills. I shot some, but the film wasn't advancing in the camera.

Chatterton's bullshit detector went off. It wasn't just the coincidence of both video and still cameras going kaput at the same time. Things like that happened. Something in the lawyer's voice—a little too much eagerness, maybe—put Chatterton on alert. At the same time, Concannon's story presented him with a classic reward-versus-risk situation. As the potential reward increased, greater risks—whether of life or money—became more and more tolerable.

No underwater mystery in the world upped the stakes like *Titanic*. After countless ill-fated voyages of ships, it was the most famous wreck of all. Almost a hundred years after *Titanic* sank, it still captivated people everywhere. When Chatterton and his wife, Carla, were touring Asia on motorcycles, they took a break in a village whose residents rarely saw Westerners, and stood against a hut for the shade. It had no door, so Chatterton stole a glance inside. A single room, no furniture, dirt floor. The only thing on the wall was a three-by-five-foot poster of Kate Winslet and Leonardo DiCaprio, with *Titanic* steaming head-on between them.

Chatterton knew only the outlines of *Titanic*'s brief life and unforgettable death. The ship was as long as four city blocks, as wide as a freeway, and as tall as a nine-story building. The Harland and Wolff shipyard in Belfast built it. The White Star Line owned it. J. P. Morgan owned the White Star Line. *Titanic* hit an iceberg on its maiden voyage, and sank a couple of hours later in the early morning of April 15, 1912. People were still arguing about exactly how the ship sank. It had been built with watertight compartments, which should have kept it afloat until help arrived. But they didn't. There were only half enough lifeboats for the 2,200 passengers and crew, and many lifeboats were less than full when they were launched. More than 1,500 people died. Chatterton believed there were three kinds of history: what really happened; what most people think happened; and what people in power wanted future generations to think happened, which is 90 percent of the history in books.

Concannon was still talking.

John, I saw something that might make a difference in what the world knows about how that ship sank, he said. I can take you right to it. I wrote the coordinates in my notebook.

Who else has seen these ribbons of steel? Chatterton asked.

Concannon told him that neither the sub pilot, Anatoly Sagalevich, nor the other man, one of the expedition leaders, paid any attention to them.

Why not? Chatterton thought. What he said was Let me think about it, Dave.

Concannon told Chatterton he needed a decision right away. The Russians who owned the mothership, *Keldysh*, and the two *Mir* subs were provisioning for the whole summer of *Titanic* charters that very week. They had to know if Chatterton wanted the last slot of the year in August. Concannon sounded like a telemarketer trying to close a deal.

Chatterton said he would be in touch and hung up.

There was something not quite right about Concannon, but another voice was telling Chatterton that if he and Kohler found out what had happened to *Titanic*, their discovery and identification of *U-869* would pale by comparison.

Without taking his eyes from the road, Chatterton punched his speed dial to call Kirk Wolfinger, a documentary filmmaker with whom he had been working since the U-boat movie. In 1996, Wolfinger had been scouting for a good story about World War II German submarines and running into one crackpot after another. At the same time—an insane coincidence—Richie Kohler called *Nova* to ask if the series producers might be interested in the U-boat that he and another diver had found but not yet identified. *Nova* referred him to Wolfinger. Wolfinger said U-boat leads were like UFO sightings, so how about some proof? A week later, Kohler showed up at the *Nova* office in Boston carrying a dinner plate.

This came from a submarine off the coast of New Jersey, Kohler said. Nobody suspected it was there before John Chatterton and I found it. Nobody knows *why* the sub was there. We intend to find out. Kohler flipped over the plate, revealing the swastika embossed on the bottom. We do know it was a Nazi U-boat.

The *Nova* boss actually gasped. We'll do it, she said.

Four years later, "Hitler's Lost Sub" aired on PBS; a literary agent in New York put Chatterton and Kohler together with a writer who turned their story into a bestselling book; and Wolfinger, Chatterton, and Kohler parlayed "Hitler's Lost Sub" into *Deep Sea Detectives*.

Kirk, my man, Chatterton said when Wolfinger answered the call. What do you know about *Titanic*?

What do you have there, John? A sunken treasure story? How about a conspiracy theory that it didn't really sink? Wolfinger said.

Very funny, Chatterton continued. Anyway, this guy—his name is Concannon—says he went to the wreck in a submarine and saw pieces of steel that looked like they had been peeled from the bottom of the ship. Didn't you do something on *Titanic*?

Wolfinger told Chatterton that he had made a film about *Titanic*'s sister ship, *Britannic*—which sank after hitting a mine during World War I—and had learned a lot about *Titanic* in the process. The American and British investigations into the *Titanic* disaster took testimony from hundreds of surviving crew and passengers. Half of the survivors seemed to be either lying or describing what they had imagined when they were in shock. Some said the boilers exploded; some said they didn't. Some said the stern of the ship rose high into the night sky before plunging straight down; some said it sank without a ripple. The Americans concluded that *Titanic* had hit the iceberg, flooded, and sunk in one piece. The British said about the same thing. Both blamed only the captain. In 1985, when Bob Ballard and Jean-Louis Michel found *Titanic* on the bottom in two widely separated pieces, they proved that the official conclusion that it had sunk in one piece was wrong. The current theory, Wolfinger said, was that the ship sideswiped the iceberg and tore a gash about three hundred feet long in the hull. The bow flooded, the stern rose at a thirty-five- or forty-five-degree angle, and the ship broke and finally came to rest on the bottom in two big pieces. A lot of people disagreed with all or part of that scenario.

Chatterton interrupted: "Who's a lot of people?"

Wolfinger laughed. When he was researching *Britannic*, he had dipped into the subculture of men and women he called Titaniacs—model builders, artists, the Society of Naval Architects and Marine Engineers forensics panel, complete amateurs with too much time on their hands, lunatics, and conspiracy theorists—who endlessly debated the events of the early morning hours of April 15, 1912. They argued about everything from the color of the drapes in the second-class smoking room, to the number of rivets in the ship, to the possibility that everything after the moment of impact was one big cover-up.

The real questions revolved around the extent of the damage from the iceberg, the flooding of the ship, and why it went down so fast. One faction thought that if the ship had grounded on part of the iceberg instead of sideswiping it, the bottom of the hull could have ripped open, which would explain why *Titanic* sank so fast. The first rescue ship, *Carpathia*, got there a couple of hours after *Titanic* went down. If *Titanic* had stayed afloat for just a little longer, fifteen hundred people who died screaming in the frigid North Atlantic would still have been alive when help arrived.

At that moment, Chatterton crossed the point of no return. He could not believe that the real story of the world's most notorious shipping disaster was still his to tell. If there was even a fifty-fifty chance that Concannon's ribbons of steel really were pieces of *Titanic*'s bottom, he had to do everything within his power to find them. Chatterton was dead sure that Richie Kohler would agree with him.

———

The fallout from *U-869* had spun Richie Kohler out of the comfortable orbits of running his glass contracting company, holding his family together, and diving on shipwrecks when he had the time and money. After "Hitler's Lost Sub," he had tiptoed into the world of television with Chatterton, not entirely sure it was a reasonable way to make a living, but willing to give it a try. A few episodes of *Deep Sea Detectives* convinced Kohler that he couldn't make enough money at it to support his family, so he said the hell with it. He had gotten a divorce, had married again, and was raising his two children. He couldn't take the chance of losing his glass business. Then the book about *U-869*, *Shadow Divers*, became a bestseller, and Kohler had enough money in the bank to gamble on diving for a living again.

The changes in Kohler's life after *U-869* weren't only about making a living. Just before he and Chatterton finally put the pieces of the puzzle in the right places to identify the U-boat, Richie Kohler—formerly known as the Tonnage King—was transformed. His two-story house on a suburban lane in Brick, New Jersey, is a museum of portholes mounted on varnished wood plaques, china etched with shipping-line crests, silverware, crockery, bottles, sextants, gauges, chronometers, helms, wheels, engine telegraphs, compasses, binnacles, bells, and builder's plates. Loot. But the exploration of *U-869* had the unintended consequence of transporting Kohler into the lives of the men who died on the sub, and his motivation for exploring wrecks changed forever. He still craved the thrill of surfacing with an artifact from a sunken ship, but people had become more important to him than loot.

Deep Sea Detectives was in its third year, and he and Chatterton were thriving together even though they didn't necessarily get along all the time. They never had. Chatterton was ten years older than Kohler. Maybe that was the chasm that separated the two men; maybe it was that each of them had gotten used to filling up a room on his own. Kohler and Chatterton were like a couple of big dogs of different breeds rescued from the pound by a generous family and installed in the same nice house with plenty to eat. They were never really going to enjoy each other's company, but each of them knew he was better off steering clear of the other's food dish than sitting in a cage waiting for the needle.

Kohler always answered his phone when he saw it was Chatterton calling.

So, this guy just called me, Chatterton began without introduction. A lawyer named David Concannon . . .

He talked for five minutes, shouted, really, as he usually did when he was excited. Ribbons of steel. No film. Kirk says maybe a documentary deal but nothing for sure. We have to decide soon. Might mean we each have to put up $100,000 or so. Nobody knows why that ship sank so fast. Lots of theories. We're wreck divers, right? *Titanic* is the wreck to end all wrecks.

What if this lawyer is totally fugazy, John?

I've been thinking about that. I can't come up with a good reason to figure he's making it up, Chatterton said.

Not to put too fine a point on it, but if we push all that cash into the pot and come up empty, it won't just be the money we're losing. We fall on our asses, a lot of people are going to know about it.

I hear you, Richie.

How long do I have to think about it? Kohler asked.

Chatterton picked up the hesitation in his partner's voice. He had a deep respect for Kohler's caution, not only because Kohler had kids, a family business, and a new wife, but also because Chatterton knew himself to sometimes err on the side of impulse.

We won't actually start writing checks for a couple of weeks.

Okay, Kohler said. Let's do whatever's next.

RIBBONS OF STEEL

T en weeks later, as if they had been fired from a cartoon cannon by that flurry of phone calls in May, Chatterton and Kohler landed on the waterfront in St. John's, Newfoundland. They had drained their bank accounts, pulled some equity out of their houses, and wired $256,000 in cash to the company that brokered the charter for the Russians. The package included eight days on the 400-foot *Keldysh*, its crew of seventy-five, and the two *Mir* submersibles for four dives each.

Wolfinger had not been able to make a firm deal for a film to underwrite the expedition, but if they found pieces of steel that had been peeled from *Titanic*'s hull, he knew he'd have plenty of buyers for the story and the pictures.

Concannon had grown increasingly believable. He had gone through his notes and found the exact coordinates of the tantalizing wreckage he had seen in 2000. He had the location of other debris that could be equally sensational—pieces of the grand staircase, and trunks and suitcases that might have come from a cargo hold. He seemed less like someone going off half-cocked to feed his own ego and more like a genuine explorer hungry for the truth.

Even without a contract for a movie deal, Wolfinger fronted the cost of high-definition cameras, a cameraman, and a soundman. For the underwater photography, he arranged for the most experienced *Titanic* cinematographer, Ralph White, and an equally experienced deep-ocean imaging technician, Billy Lange, to join the crew. Wolfinger also hired naval architect Roger Long, with whom he had worked on earlier films about shipwrecks. Long designed and built ships, but more important to the investigation into the ribbons of steel, he had two decades of experience in maritime forensics and ship stability. Simon Mills, an English historian who had been studying the *Olympic*-class ships for most of his life, signed up. Bob Blumberg, the U.S. State Department's specialist on shipwrecks and salvage treaties, was coming along as an observer. Joe Porter, the editor of *Wreck Diving Magazine*, joined the expedition as its photographer and reporter.

Keldysh sailed at dusk on August 10, 2005. After sunset, when the spectacular granite bluffs of Newfoundland had faded to slivers on the western horizon, Anatoly Sagalevich's voice crackled over the intercom. Everyone was to assemble in the main conference room for a briefing. Captain Yuri Gorbach ran the ship, but Sagalevich, whom everybody called Tolya, was in charge of the diving.

For anyone who knew the history of deep-ocean exploration, being in a room with Anatoly Sagalevich was the equivalent of an audience with Neil Armstrong. As a young man, Sagalevich had worked as a professional basketball player and jazz musician, then enrolled in college to become an electrical engineer. For thirty-five years, he had been the head of the P. P. Shirshov Institute of Oceanology, where he'd helped design the two *Mir* submersibles. Sagalevich had published more than three hundred scientific papers, written twelve books, and spent more than three thousand hours piloting the *Mir*s.

The key members of the expedition team, along with a few others, assembled around Sagalevich. Kohler had brought his wife, Carrie, a qualified wreck diver who was hoping for a seat on one of the *Mir* dives. Concannon had his new wife, Donna, with him, along with a friend who ran a dive shop in Pennsylvania, Tom Maddux, and Maddux's son.

Wolfinger and his crew moved around the conference room, dipping for camera angles and swinging the microphone boom to record conversations. The first gathering of an expedition, whether in a hotel, a tent, or this room on the world's biggest research ship, was known as the meet and greet. These meetings were all the same. Hellos for old friends, introductions to new ones, and the camaraderie of the optimistic moment at the beginning of an expedition when a great discovery seems like a sure thing.

Sagalevich opened with a joke. *Mir* translates to the English word "peace," he said, and the name of the mother ship, *Akademik Mstislav Keldysh*, honors a Soviet cold-war rocket scientist who built ICBMs. He laughed. Everybody else laughed.

Then he announced that he had good news and bad news. The storm of the past week was leaving. By the time they reached the wreck, in two days, they should have calm seas for launching and retrieving the subs. The bad news, he said, was that a bigger storm was on the way. They would have to leave a day earlier than planned to make it safely back to St. John's. That meant three days of diving, instead of four. To punctuate what he had just said, Sagalevich looked at Captain Gorbach, seated at the table in his dress white uniform, who nodded.

Kohler and Chatterton locked eyes, both of them thinking the same thing: We just lost 25 percent of our bottom time. They'd finally come to believe that Concannon had definitely seen pieces of metal peeled from *Titanic*'s hull. With forty years of feeling around in the underwater dark between them, they knew how hard it would be to find the ribbons of steel if Concannon's coordinates were wrong.

Despite Sagalevich's bombshell, the mood of the expedition remained high. The blend of skill and expertise they had assembled was a lot better than Chatterton and Kohler had counted on when they'd made their decision to go two months earlier. Few people knew the wreck of *Titanic* better than Bill Lange and Ralph White. Nobody knew the *Olympic* class of ships better than Simon Mills. And Roger Long was the perfect choice to lead the forensic investigation once they found new evidence. Long had been fascinated with *Titanic* all his life but had remained outside the circle of bickering theorists. As an outsider, he would bring original thinking to his interpretation of any new evidence.

———

For Chatterton and Kohler, there was no reason to make a dive unless they had a job to do. They appreciated the beauty of the sea, its creatures, its shipwrecks, and the dance of light underwater, but recreational diving was simply not in them. Neither of them, however, had ever been in a deep submersible. Even with the hoary fear of failure pinging away inside their heads, anticipating a ride in a *Mir* made them as giddy as the goofiest tourist.

All wreck divers are gearheads, and a *Mir* submersible is the ultimate gear. No vehicle can take a human being deeper into the sea. As *Keldysh* steamed southeast, Sagalevich led the expedition team on a tour of his subs. White, Concannon, and Lange were *Mir* veterans, but for the others it was an introduction to the most amazing machine any of them had ever seen.

The two identical *Mir*s were built in 1987 in Finland, but they had been completely overhauled every five years, most recently in 2004. They could dive to a depth of 19,680 feet, which allowed them to reach the bottom of 98 percent of the world's oceans.

Each *Mir* is 25.6 feet long, 11.8 feet wide, and 9.8 feet high, most of that made up of aluminum sheathing. The pressure hull—what keeps the crew alive—is a much smaller nickel-steel sphere with an inside diameter of 6.9 feet. Each *Mir* weighs 40,920 pounds. It can carry a payload of 640 pounds, which allows for one pilot and two observers. There are three viewing ports. The one in the middle, for the pilot, is 7.5 inches in diameter. On each side, the ports are 4.5 inches in diameter. All are Plexiglas 7 inches thick.

Electric power comes from oil-filled nickel-cadmium batteries. The top speed forward is 5 knots. Communication on the surface is by radio; underwater, by hydroacoustic telephone, which sends sound waves through water instead of air. For navigation, an array of transponders is anchored to the sea floor at known locations determined by GPS. The transponders send out a code, and onboard receivers triangulate precise locations from those signals. The subs also have a gyro compass, a depth sounder, and an echo sounder that can acquire targets as far away as 3,280 feet. For observation and research, each *Mir* is equipped with side-scanning sonar with a range of 820 feet, still and television cameras, and halogen lights.

Inside a *Mir*, divers are in a one-atmosphere environment,

the same pressure as on the surface. Breathable air is produced as it is in a spacecraft, with lithium hydroxide scrubbers to remove carbon dioxide, and oxygen replaced from tanks. One *Mir* can sustain three people for about three and a half days. The *Mir*s have made more than 720 dives between them, and have never had to make an emergency ascent.

Sagalevich announced the dive plan for the next day, which he had worked out with Chatterton and Kohler. In *Mir-1* would be John Chatterton and David Concannon. Sagalevich made eye contact with each man as he spoke his name. Sagalevich would pilot *Mir-1*. In *Mir-2* would be Richie Kohler and Ralph White, with Genya Cherniaev as pilot. The subs will carry a light meal of sandwiches and drinking water, Sagalevich said, adding: They have no toilets. There are piss bottles for emergencies, but it's better to drink nothing for six hours before diving.

———

At midmorning, two and a half days after leaving St. John's, Chatterton and Kohler were hunched over the bottom chart of the wreck, reviewing their dive plan, when they felt the pulse of *Keldysh*'s engines slow from the steady throb of cruising speed. Once *Titanic* had been found, global positioning satellites took all the guesswork out of finding it again. As *Keldysh* coasted to a stop, Chatterton and Kohler knew they were hovering precisely over the wreck.

Mir divers wear blue fireproof coveralls intended to give them an extra few seconds to put out an electrical blaze before it ignites the oxygen-rich air in the sub. Just before noon, Richie Kohler walked hand in hand with Carrie across the deck to *Mir-2*. The night before, when they'd put the coveralls on for the first time, Chatterton had called them hero suits.

Kohler didn't feel like a hero, but he knew he was about to enjoy one of the greatest days of his life. He waved to no one in particular, kissed Carrie, smiled, and stepped onto the ladder leading to the hatch on top of *Mir-2*.

The instruments, the controls, and the cramped cockpit of the *Mir* spelled spacecraft to Kohler. He fought it off for a few seconds, but he couldn't temper the sense of pride he felt. He was making a voyage to another world, realizing a dream that had captured him as a boy watching the television coverage of the first *Apollo* moon mission. The Saturn rocket riding a plume of fire through the sky over Florida and out into the blackness of space was the climax of the launch, but to Kohler, it was when the three men in white suits and helmets smiled and slipped into the gumdrop on top of the rocket that represented the moment of truth. For years, the courage it took to do that stuck in Kohler's mind as the epitome of what it meant to be a man.

In *Mir-1*, the hatch slammed shut above Chatterton's head. Nothing settled him down more than knowing he was in a place that would forgive no mistakes. He felt the lurch of the crane lifting the sub out of its cradle, then looked out his viewport and saw two dozen people lining the rail, waving and applauding. He was amazed at how clear they appeared through seven inches of Plexiglas.

Sagalevich toggled switches to sound test alarms, lit up the instrument panel, and triggered the whir of fans and pumps. Concannon talked on the radio to the launch crew on *Keldysh*, checking the communication circuits. Chatterton made sure the audio and video recorders inside and outside the sub were rolling. Every word spoken during the dive would be on tape.

The subs seemed to fall rather than settle into the sea, and began rolling in the leftover chop of the departing storm.

Chatterton heard a clamor on the top of *Mir-1*; Sagalevich looked at him, and with his fingers made a hook leaving a circle. A crewman was releasing the crane cable. The sub bobbed free, rolling and lurching, then descended into the calmer water beneath the surface.

Chatterton lay on his side, pressed his forehead against a pad above the viewport, and watched the colors disappear from the spectrum. Red was gone at 50 feet; orange at 100; green at 400. In five minutes, the *Mir* passed 450 feet. Chatterton was deeper into the ocean than he had ever been on scuba. At 800 feet, he saw for the first time the strange, iridescent blue that was left after the wavelengths of the other colors had been blocked by the density of the water. At 2,000 feet, that hardy blue was gone, too, and he looked out into the eternal darkness of the sea beyond sunlight. Galaxies of bioluminescent animals flashed in the absolute darkness— chains of neon jellies; fish flashing yellow, blue, and red lights to lure prey and frighten predators; and phosphorescent plankton. Okay, Chatterton thought. Okay. There's definitely something not right about Concannon, but at least he got me here.

In *Mir-2*, Kohler was glued to his viewport for most of the two-and-a-half-hour trip to the bottom. The dive plan called for Chatterton and Concannon to land near the stern to begin looking for the ribbons of steel immediately. Kohler and White would land near the bow section and photograph it to document its condition. Microscopic organisms that feed on rusting metal were devouring the hull, and it was only a matter of time before nothing would be left of *Titanic* but a dark stain on the seafloor. The question was, How much time? There wasn't anything anybody could do about it, but *Titanic* offered a rare opportunity to measure the phenomenon. After surveying the bow section, Kohler and White would explore the debris field around it with whatever was left of their five hours of bottom time.

Kohler marveled at the descent into darkness, and the bioluminescent light show on the other side of the Plexiglas. But he couldn't stop thinking about *Titanic* making the same plunge. The final plunge of a sinking ship was the most powerful bridge between life and death he could imagine. Kohler also knew that death by shipwreck was not instantaneous. *Titanic*, like most sinking ships, had gone down with pockets of air trapped inside the hull. People in them could breathe for a while, and would experience the most horrific terror until the water pressure in the depths killed them.

There was no point in wasting electricity on the *Mir*'s outside lights during the descent. Inside, only the glow from the instruments gave firm dimensions to the surfaces of the sphere. Conversation in *Mir-2* petered out after a half hour. To Kohler, it was a little bit like the endless hours of hanging on a rope underwater during decompression after a deep scuba dive. He entertained himself with unuttered thoughts, glancing up every once in a while to watch the orange numbers on the depth sounder tick over.

Mir-2 was a Russian sub, so the numbers read out in meters. At 3,500 Genya Cherniaev lit up a part of his instrument panel that had been dark. He was fine-tuning his position and trimming the sub for landing. He flicked on the floodlights. The bottom was fifty feet below, and closing.

After two and a half hours in the dark, the brown muck of the seafloor was entertainment enough for Kohler. His eyes adjusted to the brightness. The bottom was littered with unnatural objects, none of them particularly significant; they just didn't belong there. Cherniaev nursed *Mir-2* forward.

The lumps and hummocks became coal, jagged bits of steel, wire, and other debris that to Kohler's experienced eyes virtually shouted "shipwreck."

The lights of the sub swept through the darkness like a yellowish flashlight beam on a night trail. New terrain snapped into view as the abrupt edges of the beam reached it, then faded to black as the *Mir* moved on. Suddenly, without the fanfare that should have accompanied so astonishing a spectacle, the weird light fell on the bow of *Titanic*.

"Oh, my God," Kohler said, abandoning all pretense that he, one of the most experienced wreck divers who had ever lived, was not overcome with awe. "Unbelievable. Unbelievable. Look at that. Oh, man."

It was the railing that rendered *Titanic*'s bow so powerful an image, not because of the "king of the world" scene in the movie but because it humanized the wreck. Rails were there to keep people from falling off the ship. People had stood at the rails, waved good-bye, stared out at the sea. Kohler could see them. And the spare anchor! Right there on the foredeck under the arm of the still-standing crane. Ready to go. *Mir-2* glided over the remains of the navigation bridge, and there were the stanchions of the helm and engine telegraphs. Cherniaev had witnessed the moment of first encounter with the bow of *Titanic* many times before, and he knew just where to go next for maximum effect. He gave a squirt on his tail thruster and said, "Captain Smith's stateroom."

Through the ruptured ceiling of the deckhouse, Kohler saw the glimmering white ceramic rim of Smith's bathtub. Though he knew the absurdity of his next thought, he couldn't keep it out of his head. Kohler longed to be swimming free with a tank of gas on his back. Just to be able to touch the ship.

———

In *Mir-1*, Sagalevich turned on his lights. After the long, passive descent, the sub was alive. They were a half mile south of the bow section, with the wreckage of the stern coming up a couple of hundred feet ahead of them. As the sub settled slowly, the bottom resolved itself as a carpet of brown mud studded with hard-looking debris. Coal. Bits of metal. Sagalevich steered *Mir-1* toward the massive target dead ahead that was pinging on his sonar screen.

The wreck that greeted Chatterton and Concannon was not as sensational as the intact structures of the bow, but it was far more disturbing. It looked as if three hundred feet of a ship—the hull, superstructure, engine room, propellers, and shafts—had been thrown off a two-and-a-half-mile-high mountain onto solid concrete. Every surface sagged toward the bottom from the force of the impact, leaving only the solid steel girders of the two main engines standing in anywhere near their original shapes. The engine frames—as high as five-story buildings—loomed over *Mir-1* as Sagalevich steered past the enormous pile of scrap. Finally, Chatterton saw the proof that the mess outside was really a ship: A gigantic propeller, half its diameter buried in the ancient mud of the seafloor, materialized in his viewport.

Like Cherniaev, Sagalevich knew what the customers wanted. He gingerly nosed *Mir-1* closer, until the lights fell full on one of the propeller blades, still a yellowish bronze nearly a century after it turned its last revolution. On the blade, Chatterton saw numbers gradually coming into focus. The three numbers made one figure: 401. Every wreck diver searched for positive identification of a ship—an engraved bell, a name etched into the steel of its bow, a builder's plaque. Chatterton knew that he was looking at the builder's hull number for one ship and one ship only.

"I'm ready to leave here, Tolya," Chatterton said. "You ready, Dave?"

"Let's go do what we came to do," Concannon said.

Sagalevich reset his sonar receiver with the coordinates Concannon had given him the night before. He did not get an immediate return from a target, but he adjusted his dead-reckoning course in the direction of the spot he estimated to be another half mile to the southeast. "Fifteen minutes," Sagalevich said.

Chatterton and Concannon remained at their viewports the whole time. They talked out of the sides of their mouths to keep from fogging the Plexiglas. Sagalevich sounded pleased when he announced that he had acquired a target: "Not big, not small. Two hundred meters."

Then: "One hundred meters."

Mir-1 was ten feet above the bottom, moving forward at 3 knots.

"Fifty meters."

"We're right where we should be," Concannon said. "And . . . there's the hill. There's the hill. There's dishes on the hill."

Ahead of *Mir-1*, the bottom wrinkled in a hummock that could have resulted from the impact of something heavy. Chatterton saw the tracings in the mud left by the skids of a previous *Mir* landing and, on the gently sloping flank of the hummock, the white blips of crockery. In every direction, coal was scattered like black confetti. Then he saw the shoes.

"Oh, man," Chatterton said. "Look at all those shoes.

The research ship *Akademik Mstislav Keldysh* at the dock in St. Johns, Newfoundland. (Photograph by Joe Porter/*Wreck Diving Magazine.*)

John Chatterton (*left*) and David Concannon before their first dive to *Titanic*.
(Photograph by Joe Porter/*Wreck Diving Magazine*.)

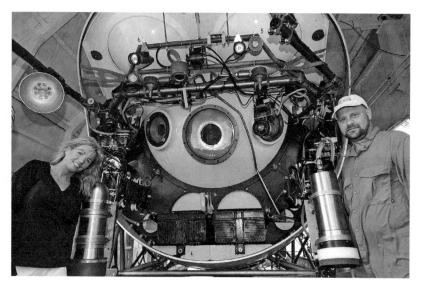

Carrie and Richie Kohler. (Photograph by Joe Porter/*Wreck Diving Magazine*.)

From left: Richie Kohler, John Chatterton, Bill Lange, David Concannon, Ralph White. (Photograph by Joe Porter/*Wreck Diving Magazine*.)

John Chatterton boarding *Mir-1* for his first dive to *Titanic*.
(Photograph by Joe Porter/*Wreck Diving Magazine*.)

Richie Kohler's view from *Mir-2*. (Photograph by Richie Kohler.)

Mir-2, carrying Richie Kohler and Ralph White, dive one.
(Photograph by Joe Porter/*Wreck Diving Magazine.*)

Launch crew "Cowboy" frees *Mir-2* from its cable.
(Photograph by Joe Porter/*Wreck Diving Magazine.*)

Dr. Anatoly Sagalevich (*standing in hatch*) boarding *Mir-1*
for the first dive of the 2005 expedition to *Titanic*.

(Photograph by Joe Porter/*Wreck Diving Magazine.*)

Kohler and Chatterton, after their first dives to the wreck.
(Photograph by Joe Porter/*Wreck Diving Magazine.*)

Planning for dives two and three.
(Photograph by Joe Porter/*Wreck Diving Magazine.*)

Ralph White videotaping Roger Long as he boards the *Mir*.

(Photograph by Joe Porter/*Wreck Diving Magazine*.)

Richie Kohler in the *Mir*. (Photograph by John Chatterton.)

John Chatterton in the *Mir*. (Photograph by Richie Kohler.)

Bob Blumberg (*left*) and Kirk Wolfinger, after their successful dive on the final day. (Photograph by Joe Porter/*Wreck Diving Magazine*.)

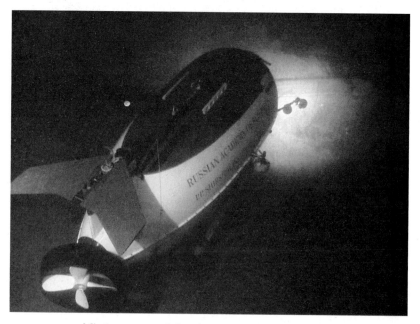

Mir-1 over one of the giant pieces of *Titanic*'s bottom.
(Photograph courtesy of Lone Wolf Documentary Group.)

A section of one of *Titanic*'s two bilge keels. (Photograph courtesy of Lone Wolf Documentary Group.)

Titanic's keel, the steel bar running diagonally through the frame.
(Photograph courtesy of Lone Wolf Documentary Group.)

The edge of one of the newly discovered pieces of *Titanic*, showing the double bottom and the edges of the torn and compressed steel plating.
(Photograph courtesy of Lone Wolf Documentary Group.)

Titanic 2005 expedition photo. *From left*: Joe Porter, Kirk Wolfinger, John Chatterton, Ralph White, Valerie Moore, Simon Mills, Evan Kovacs, Jason Maddux, Sean Glenn, Richie Kohler, Carrie Kohler, Rush DeNooyer, Bill Lange, Dr. Scott Williams, Donna Concannon, Tom Maddux, David Concannon. (Photograph by Joe Porter/*Wreck Diving Magazine*.)

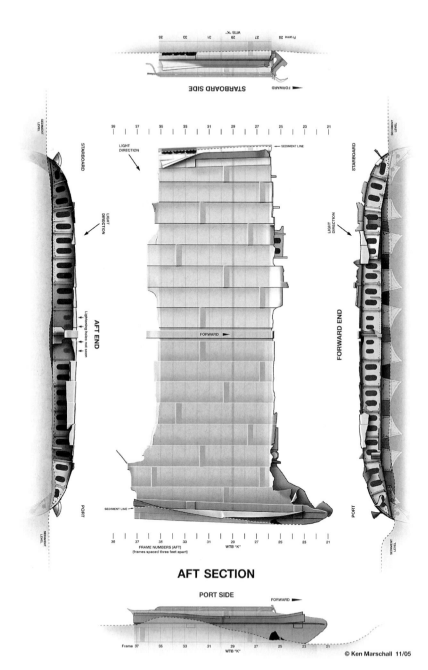

Drawing of the aft bottom piece, by Ken Marschall, that helped Roger Long visualize the damage to *Titanic*. (Rendering © Ken Marschall/KenMarschall.com.)

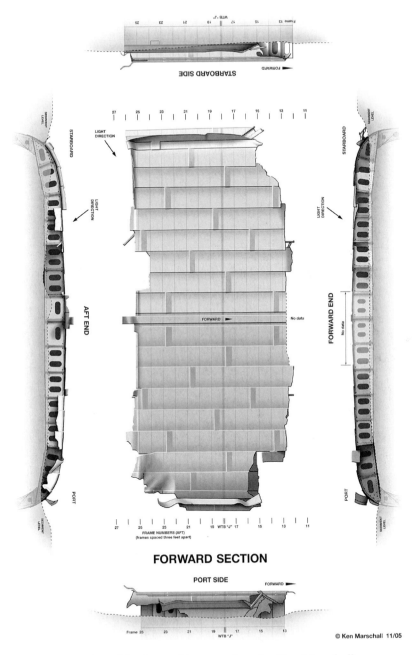

Drawing of the forward bottom piece, by Ken Marschall.

(Rendering © Ken Marschall/KenMarschall.com.)

Tom and Sylvia McCluskie, after Queen Elizabeth II made him a Member of the Order of the British Empire for his service to shipbuilding.
(Photograph courtesy of Tom McCluskie.)

You've got all kinds of stuff here. This is a bona fide debris field."

Concannon said, "Oh yeah, I remember this. I remember all that coal right there. Yeah. This is right. Keep going, keep going."

Chatterton loved nothing more than an all-or-nothing moment.

"We've got some steel over here," he announced. "What's this?"

"Yeah. A piece of steel," Sagalevich said, breaking his usual silence. He had taken so many tourists to do nothing but sightsee on *Titanic* that he had been swept into the exhilaration of perhaps discovering something new.

"This is it. This is right where we were," Concannon said. "I remember that the sand and mud were all humped up like that. We found it. Yeah, baby!" he shouted. "There's a big piece of steel."

Concannon drew back from his viewport, reached around Sagalevich, and offered his hand to Chatterton for a high five.

Chatterton didn't move. What he saw outside looked nothing at all like ribbons of steel.

"I was not crazy," Concannon went on. "This is the big boy. This is what I was thinking. It's right where I said it was. But what is it?"

"It looks like a box beam of some sort," Chatterton snapped. "It's definitely not pieces of the bottom."

Sagelevich maneuvered the sub to slowly sweep the debris with the searchlights. The dull metal was a few feet long, flaking with rust—maybe a piece of ducting. There were some smaller pieces that looked like wire or cable. Beyond them, the men saw only the desolate seafloor reaching to the edge of the light and disappearing into the darkness.

"*Mir-1*, this is *Mir-2*. John?" Kohler's voice burbled over the acoustic telephone.

"Richie. This is John. Can you hear me?"

"Yeah, John. I read you loud and clear. You know I'm dying to hear. Did you find the ribbons of steel? Did you find the ribbons of steel?"

On an acoustic phone, audio waves travel through water instead of through air or a wire. When no voice is being transmitted, the static sounds just like the ocean when you put a conch shell to your ear. For an interminable ten seconds, that was all Kohler heard.

"Negative, negative, negative," Chatterton said.

TITANIACS

When the *Keldysh* crew popped the hatches on the *Mirs*, nothing was more important to the divers than getting to a toilet. Everybody worked hard at being graceful, but that was the deal. Afterward, Kohler tracked down Chatterton, who was in the galley eating a sandwich. It was after ten. Sagalevich had announced that they would dive the next day, take a day off for maintenance, then make the third and final dives the day after.

John, we have to talk, Kohler said.

Oh, great, Chatterton answered. The four worst words in the English language.

One of Chatterton's coping behaviors for containing rage was sarcastic humor. Kohler had seen it enough times to know when his partner required careful handling. He led the way to a secluded spot on the stern. They leaned on the rail, staring out into the darkness instead of looking at each other. The clanks and voices of the crew recharging and stowing the *Mirs* filtered up from the hangar deck.

I want to throw that son of a bitch over the side, Chatterton snarled. This has turned into the most expensive sport-diving charter in history.

Kohler felt the same way, but Concannon and the ribbons of steel were already old news. Even worse than what had happened that day was not knowing what they would do next. They had endless experience investigating sunken ships with scuba gear, which allowed them to return to a wreck again and again. Four *Mir* dives—representing a total of eight seats—were the last they and the members of their expedition would ever make to *Titanic*.

They knew that their best bet was to try to find evidence that *Titanic* had grounded on the iceberg. That scenario still made more sense to them than the sideswipe theory. They had looked at dozens of pictures of icebergs, most of which showed shelves of ice protruding from the nine-tenths of the berg that was underwater. There had to be some reason why *Titanic* went down so quickly, and grounding on the iceberg explained it.

Apart from the practical reality of figuring out what to do next, the first dives had transformed their relationship with *Titanic*. This had happened to both of them many times before. Until they dove on a shipwreck, it was just a name, a rumor, numbers on a chart, and a pile of rotting wood and metal on the bottom of the ocean. After they had been there, they were as involved as if they had boarded the ship at its last port of call before it disappeared into the sea.

Chatterton and Kohler decided that they would take the next day off, and use it and the following maintenance day to study the tapes from the first dives in hopes of coming up with a solid plan for the final dives. They had promised two of the eight remaining *Mir* seats to Tom Maddux and Carrie Kohler, both experienced wreck divers who would know how to conduct a search and run the cameras. They could get the beauty shots of the wreck—the bow, navigation bridge, decks, cabins, portholes—that would be essential if they found enough new evidence to justify making a film.

Roger Long was the obvious choice for one of the seats on the second day of diving. He could take a look at Concannon's ribbons of steel and come up with a second opinion. Most of all, he would know how to interpret other damage that might indicate that *Titanic* had grounded. The bottom of both large pieces of the hull had never been seen because they were buried in the mud. But on each side of the ship where the flank of the hull joined the double bottom were stabilizers called bilge keels. Each of these was three hundred feet long and angled downward to reduce the rolling of the ship in heavy seas. If *Titanic* had grounded on the iceberg, the bilge keels should have been damaged. Most of the length of the bilge keels was buried in the mud, but a few feet, Chatterton and Kohler figured, should be visible just ahead of where the ship broke in two. More than anyone else, Long would know what to look for. Ralph White, who had made more dives to *Titanic* than anyone but the *Mir* pilots, would accompany Long. White knew every inch of the wreck and would be able to quickly orient Long to what he was looking at in the narrow beams of the searchlights.

This plan gave Chatterton and Kohler thirty-six hours to decide how to use their last four *Mir* seats on the final day of diving. If Long found even the slightest evidence that *Titanic* had grounded, they would stick with that. If not, they were back to zero.

———

Roger Long had been one of those funny kids who flunked everything in school, but in seventh grade, he designed an electric combination lock for a cigar box. He built the relays, circuits, and a keypad, turned it on, and it worked. The box wouldn't open unless he pushed the three buttons in the right order. His father was a professor of Christian ethics at Oberlin College; his mother's life revolved around Roger and his two younger brothers.

Long slogged through prep school in Massachusetts and lived for tinkering and fixing things. He reminded himself of the goofy, curious kid in the Sherman and Peabody cartoons. During his teenage summers on Queechy Lake, in upstate New York, Long learned to sail in a 7-foot boat. He redesigned the little sloop into a traditional catboat, then moved on in high school to designing an 18-foot cruising sloop in meticulous detail. The elegant process of drawing, lofting, and shaping a boat felt better to Long than anything he had ever done. In college, where he still wasn't able to mesh with academic routines, he spent most of his spare time designing another boat.

In 1970, Long walked into the Boston office of naval architect Philip Rhodes and asked for a job. Rhodes, who needed a draftsman, hired him that day. Long had planned to go back to school and become a social worker, but thirty-five years later, he was a naval architect without a college degree. He had learned his trade by working with some of the most respected designers and marine engineers in New England: Chetley Rittall, Paul Luke, and John Gilbert. It was with Gilbert that Long became more interested in designing boats with jobs to do than pleasure boats. He still worked on a few yachts on his own time, but his day job was designing fishing boats and other working craft.

When Wolfinger had approached Long about joining the expedition, he'd sworn Long to secrecy, then told him about the ribbons of steel. There was no question in Long's mind that pieces of steel torn from *Titanic*'s bottom would change everything about what the world thought had happened to its most notorious wreck. But August was sailing season; he had just bought a new sailboat and was planning cruises with his sons.

Wolfinger left Long with transcripts of his conversations and interviews with Concannon. He also gave him a stack of magazines from the Titanic Historical Society; a book by theorist David Brown, who championed the grounding theory; and a list of URLs of Internet discussion forums.

As they were parting, Wolfinger said, Roger, you are not going to believe how crazy some of these people are over that ship.

Long was not a complete stranger to the subculture of men, women, and children whose lives revolve around *Titanic*. He was a student of shipwrecks and a marine forensics investigator, and there were no greater maritime mysteries than those surrounding the Ship of Dreams.

Long dove into the arcane, passionate, and often absurd lives of the Titaniacs. There were complete lunatics, harmless crackpots, playful reenacters who belonged to clubs, rabid archivists, list makers, artifact curators, amateur sleuths, and highly credible engineers and naval architects.

William Barnes, for example, insisted that, under hypnosis, he became *Titanic*'s designer, Thomas Andrews, and he wrote a book about the sinking from Andrews's point of view.

Another man believed he was the reincarnation of Captain E. J. Smith. He announced it one night at dinner at the home of White Star historian Paul Louden-Brown and his wife, who started laughing. Their guest burst into tears, and sobbed his way through his story of his terrible death in the icy water, the cries of the dying, the guilt he felt at letting them perish.

Though rarely so oddly, fantasy played an enormous part in the lives of the members of the twelve *Titanic* historical societies in England, Northern Ireland, Ireland, Scotland, South Africa, Switzerland, Germany, Canada, and the United States. All of them had their beginnings as groups of survivors who wanted to get together, preserve their memorabilia, and honor the memories of the dead.

The Titanic Historical Society, with its headquarters and museum in Indian Orchard, Massachusetts, for instance, was born in the teenage mind of Edward Kamuda. His father owned the lone movie theater in the village on the outskirts of Springfield. When the Academy Award–winning movie *Titanic*, starring Clifton Webb, Barbara Stanwyck, and Audrey Dalton, played at the theater in 1953, Twentieth Century Fox sent a promotional package with the film. Ed's father put up the posters and photographs of the cast in the lobby and gave the rest of the material to him. The first showing of *Titanic* touched something deep inside Ed Kamuda. Afterward, he spent hours poring over movie reviews, background stories about the real *Titanic*, and, especially, the list of the names and addresses of passengers and crew members who were still alive. After *Titanic* left Indian Orchard, Ed started writing letters.

Ten years later, Kamuda and dozens of *Titanic* survivors had become regular correspondents. As the number of living survivors moved inexorably toward zero, many asked Kamuda to set up a museum in which their menus, silverware, tickets, postcards, photographs, diaries, and other memorabilia would have a permanent home. Kamuda agreed. He founded the historical society and set up the museum in the back room of the jewelry store he owned, across the street from the theater where Webb, Stanwyck, and *Titanic* had changed his life. In the mid-1970s, Kamuda and his equally passionate *Titanic* aficionado wife, Karen, started publishing a magazine with articles about the ship, the White Star Line, survivors' accounts, theories about the sinking, and biographies of the passengers and crew. Wolfinger had left Roger Long a few issues of the Titanic *Commutator*.

Thumbing through an issue of the *Commutator*, Long turned to an ad for the *Titanic* Launch and Gala Dinner Weekend. It was the highlight of the year for the society, an annual event for which members dressed in period costumes, ate meals from *Titanic*'s first-, second-, and third-class menus, and danced to a ragtime string band. Ed Kamuda always came in uniform as Captain E. J. Smith. Months before the event he started growing a beard, which itched and irritated him to distraction. The day after the closing ceremony, Kamuda shaved off the beard.

Prominently in the center of the ad for the annual gala, the society's Internet address directed members and prospects to its Web site. There, from an online store, a visitor could order tickets to the gala, join the society, read about its history, read dozens of articles from the *Commutator*, and buy any of thousands of items, including *Titanic* T-shirts, baseball hats, and coffee mugs; CDs of selections from the White Star Line music book; and 70-millimeter film cels from James Cameron's movie.

The release of Cameron's *Titanic* had coincided with the blooming of the Internet in the mid-1990s, and the film threw the world of the Titaniacs into an entirely new dimension of speed and obsession. Soon *Titanic* discussion forums, historical Web sites, diatribes by conspiracy theorists, thousands of photographs, and auctions of memorabilia were a mouse click away. There were hundreds of discussions about the sinking of the ship, and everyone expected to be taken seriously.

The wreck had inspired some conspiracy theories that would not die. According to one of them that circulated among Irish Catholics, the Protestant owners at Harland and Wolff and White Star had cursed the ship by naming it *Titanic*. Reflected in the water under just the right conditions, the Catholics said, the name *Titanic* read as "No Pope Here" in Gaelic.

A second theory involving religious fanaticism was the Jesuit conspiracy, built around a lunatic fringe that claimed the Jesuits had been in charge of all the significant events in the world for hundreds of years. In 1910, they said, J. P. Morgan—who they claimed was in secret a Jesuit—held a meeting on an island off Georgia to unite his empire with those of the Rockefellers and the Rothschilds to establish a powerful central bank and guarantee funding for Jesuit schemes and wars. Three extremely rich and powerful Americans opposed Morgan's grand plan: Benjamin Guggenheim; Isidor Straus; and John Jacob Astor. *Titanic* was then nearing completion at the Protestant stronghold of Belfast. To eliminate the opposition, the Jesuits commanded Morgan to make sure Guggenheim, Straus, and Astor were aboard *Titanic* for a voyage to America that they would never complete. The next part of the plan was to order Captain E. J. Smith—also a secret Jesuit—to arrange the accidental sinking by running at full speed through a known ice field. *Titanic*, its passengers, and its crew would be sacrificed to get rid of three men.

Another theory drew far more attention than "No Pope Here" and the Jesuit conspiracy. The Switch, which inspired several books, endless threads of blather on the Internet, and a movie, proposed that *Titanic* was really *Olympic*. Even after the wreck was discovered and positively identified, thousands of people contended that a collision with HMS *Hawke* had fatally damaged *Olympic*. Repairing *Olympic* would have taken months, maybe years, and cost more than the hull and machinery insurance would cover. So White Star secretly switched the ships, sank *Olympic* as *Titanic*, and collected the insurance. In 2004, the most recently published book on this theory—Olympic *and* Titanic: *The Truth Behind the Conspiracy*—debunked the theory. The authors spent two hundred pages doing it.

Long moved on from the absurd. He dove into the thicket of theories on the sinking that he found in hundreds of Internet discussion threads and more books than he could possibly read. Everyone agreed on only two facts: *Titanic* had hit an iceberg; it was totally gone two hours and twenty-three minutes later. Everything else about the disaster was debatable.

Most of the arguments revolved around the extent of the damage and depended upon the testimony of the men in the forward stokeholds who were the only eyewitnesses to the first rush of water. But even they would not have seen what happened to the outer bottom of the ship, since it was separated from the inner bottom by five feet. It was entirely possible that part of the outer bottom was peeled off, water flooded the space between it and the inner bottom, and nobody knew about it.

Some theorists believed the iceberg punched holes in the first three of the sixteen watertight compartments. Others said the first four compartments were affected, the first five, or even the first six. *Titanic* was built to stay afloat with up to four compartments flooded, but not with five.

Nobody had proved anything conclusively about how badly the iceberg damaged the ship. When *Titanic*'s bow plowed into the bottom of the ocean, it was moving at about 35 knots—faster than it had ever gone on the surface. The impact drove the front three hundred feet of the ship into the ancient mud of the sea floor, all the way up to the anchors. There was no way to see the damage caused to the bow by the iceberg.

In the summer of 1996, an electronics technician, Paul Matthias, scanned the wreck with a sonic imager that could penetrate the bottom sediments. He saw what might have been evidence of iceberg damage below the waterline in six compartments. But when he scanned the port side as a control, he found similar damage. More than likely, the lines on the scanner that he interpreted as damage from the iceberg happened when *Titanic* hit the bottom.

In the absence of hard evidence about the damage caused by the iceberg, the Titaniacs had three theories regarding the impact itself. *Titanic* either sideswiped the iceberg, grounded on the iceberg, or both. There were two subsets to the sideswipe scenario. The Big Gash theory held that the iceberg tore open the steel or popped rivets along three hundred feet of *Titanic*'s side, from the first compartment, called the peak tank, back to Boiler Room 5. A few theorists, who were marginalized by the others, supported the Even Bigger Gash theory, which damaged the ship back to Boiler Room 4. Small Gash theorists claimed that the damage extended only as far as Boiler Room 6, the one closest to the bow.

In the beginning, when the Americans and British kicked off a century of investigation with their official inquiries, fortunes rode on the determination of how much damage the iceberg had done to *Titanic*. If the ship had sustained massive damage—the Big Gash—there was only the bad luck of hitting the iceberg, and Captain Smith, to blame for the deaths of 1,504 people. If it had suffered only minor damage, flooding four or fewer compartments, then it should not have sunk so quickly. That would have introduced the disturbing and expensive possibility that the disaster involved negligence on the part of the White Star Line or Harland and Wolff.

The grounding theory was a wild card. If the ship ran over an underwater shelf that tore open part of the outer bottom, there would have been flooding but *Titanic* should have been able to stay afloat on its inner bottom. If the ice tore open both inner and outer bottoms of four or more compartments, that would explain why the ship sank so fast.

Among the proponents of the grounding theory Long discovered a charter boat captain, boatbuilder, and obsessed *Titanic* historian named David G. Brown. Like millions of people, Brown had tumbled into the *Titanic* whirlpool because of James Cameron's movie. He was moved by the beauty of the ship and the human tragedy. But Brown instinctively doubted the dramatic scenes in the movie in which the stern rises to a forty-five-degree angle before the ship breaks in half.

Brown painstakingly constructed a second-by-second chronology of the disaster based on the testimony and accounts of survivors. He studied diagrams of the ship until he was as familiar with it as he was with the floor plan of his house in Ohio. Brown studied the accounts of the collision, testimony about the damage by officers and crew, and came up with a combination of the Small Gash and the grounding theories. But he did not think the damage was anywhere near as severe as commonly assumed. *Titanic*, Brown believed, sank far more quickly than it should have. He was, of course, jeered by those Titaniacs who disagreed with his theory. And he jeered back at them.

What interested Roger Long most about Brown's contrarian perspective was his concentration on the behavior of the ship's officers, crew, and passengers in the hours after the impact. Brown insisted that for two hours, they did not act like men who thought they were on a sinking ship—except for its captain, E. J. Smith, its designer, Thomas Andrews, and its owner, J. Bruce Ismay, who behaved as if the ship had been doomed even before they finished inspecting it for damage. What did they know that no one else aboard *Titanic* knew?

Long pulled himself out of a spiral of supposition. Brown was a Titaniac, he reminded himself. But as a contrarian himself, Long was inclined to believe that Brown might be on to something.

Long was more skeptical of the hidebound theory of the sinking that had been published by the Society of Naval Architects and Marine Engineers in 1995. SNAME, founded twenty years before *Titanic* went down, policed its profession by reviewing papers, books, and licensing exams and creating panels for advancing the interests of marine engineering.

Long had a copy of the forensic panel's paper "The *Titanic* and *Lusitania*: A Final Forensic Analysis." The lead author was William Garzke, a member of Gibbs & Cox, a naval architecture firm that had designed, among hundreds of other ships, the last great transatlantic ocean liner, SS *United States*.

Garzke and his coauthors based their conclusions on videographic evidence and observations from expeditions to the wreck in 1985, 1986, 1991, 1993, and 1994. They said that the three-hundred-foot gash could not have happened, as claimed by Edward Wilding, the Harland and Wolff engineer who testified at the British inquiry. Wilding had calculated the weight of the water required to sink the ship, the size of an opening required to admit enough water to match that weight, and determined the total size of the opening to be twelve square feet. That would require a tear in the hull three-quarters of an inch wide and three hundred feet long.

The Garzke report quoted the pilot of the submersible *Alvin*, with which the wreck was first explored: "No metal sword known, much less a sword of ice, could make a continuous ¾-inch-wide slice in 1-inch-thick steel without dulling or breaking."

"We now conclude that the gash is non-existent, and should be considered as folklore," Garzke wrote. But the report offered only speculation as to what kind of hole, gash, string of popped rivets, or other opening could flood the ship fast enough to sink it in two hours and twenty-three minutes.

Garzke and his coauthors calculated the effects of flooding the bow in the time between the impact and sinking and offered their most sensational conclusion: The stern of *Titanic* had risen out of the water at a forty-five-degree angle before either breaking on the surface or following the bow down and breaking off during the fatal plunge.

Now, Long thought, I see where James Cameron found his most terrifying scene for the movie. As it had been with everyone who saw *Titanic*, the horrible specter of the man falling hundreds of feet from the stern into the propeller was indelibly etched into Long's mind.

The Garzke report was interesting, but Long did not see any hard evidence to validate its authors' conclusions. The extent of the damage was critical, and nobody really knew how badly the hull was breached, or how the ship had broken and sank.

Long decided right then that the best thing he could do to bring an open mind to the investigation was to read as much as he could from moderately credible theorists such as Brown and Garzke and stay out of the forums on the Web. But after his sojourn through the world of Titaniacs, he knew that if there was even the slightest chance that he could contribute to understanding why those people died, he had no choice but to join the expedition.

When Chatterton and Kohler asked him to make a *Mir* dive to *Titanic*, Long felt like an audience member suddenly dragged onstage during a magic act. They had told him it was extremely unlikely that he would make a dive. But the vanishing ribbons of steel changed everything. They needed his eyes on the bottom, Chatterton and Kohler said.

As Chatterton talked, Long felt reluctance building inside him. When he'd worked at the Woods Hole Oceanographic Institution, he'd shared an office with an *Alvin* pilot who'd told him chilling stories about getting tangled in a shipwreck, and the impossibility of rescue. The pilot said that the stream of water from a pinhole rupture under 350 atmospheres of pressure would cut you in half. And when Sagalevich had briefed the expedition on the *Mir*s, Long had concluded that there was no Russian word for "redundancy." They were proven submersibles, Long thought, but very primitive.

We need you down there, Roger, Chatterton said.

Okay. Long paused. But I told my wife I wasn't going down in the sub.

No worries, said Kohler. We won't tell her.

———

The next day, Long's restless night of predive jitters vanished when he reached the top of the ladder, took off his shoes, put them in the yellow dry box a crewman held next to the open hatch, and lowered himself into *Mir-1*. He made conversation with Ralph White and the pilot, Genya Cherniaev, for a half hour, then fell asleep.

Two hours later, Genya woke him, turned on the lights, and did a radio check with *Mir-2*. Long lay on his belly, his forehead against the leather pad over his viewport, his face an inch from the Plexiglas. He was right where Chatterton and Kohler wanted him to be, looking at the torn metal at the broken end of the stern section. Long directed White in videotaping the edges of the steel at the points of separation between the two sections, capturing the patterns of fracturing, tension, and compression. He was not exactly sure what he was looking for, but if there was a story to tell, the steel would tell it.

After an hour of nosing around the frightening, jagged gash where *Titanic* had come apart during its death throes, Long asked Genya to take him to the starboard side for a look at the bilge keel. Genya steered well away from the hull to avoid cables and tangles of debris, then approached slowly, the skids of the sub just two feet above the bottom. The side of the ship appeared first as a black blot against the brown mud; then Long could make out the overlapping steel of the hull plating. There. Right in front of him. The bilge keel. Long could clearly see the two-foot-wide slab of red-painted steel protruding from the side of the hull right where it met the bottom. He asked Genya to take the sub slowly toward the bow at the same height. Long was hoping to see rumpled and torn steel on the bilge keel to take the grounding theory from the realm of supposition to possible reality. But no. From the point of the break in the hull until the bilge keel disappeared into the mud as the bow dug into the seafloor, its red antifouling paint wasn't even scratched.

For another two hours, they cruised over a strange part of the seafloor etched with canyons thirty feet deep, then over a debris field that was interesting but nothing new, and finally over Concannon's junk. Still junk, Long concluded. Some kind of box beam or ducting. And definitely not a piece of the bottom of *Titanic*.

FOUR

THE EYES OF BILLY LANGE

The day after Roger Long surfaced with the dismal news that the grounding theory was impossible to prove, Chatterton and Kohler sulked around the ship. While the *Keldysh* crew used the day to check out the *Mir*s, they sat in front of the video monitors and watched the film of the worthless debris from the first dives and the disappointing images of the pristine bilge keel from the second. They looked at them a second time, like poker players squeezing their cards and hoping that when they peeked again, the deuce of clubs would have become a heart to make the flush. Even the third time through the tape, the box beam or whatever it was still wasn't ribbons of steel, and the bilge keel still looked like it had just come out of the shipyard.

The voice of self-recrimination in Kohler's head never stopped. How could he have missed the obvious fact that he was risking a small fortune on the word of one man he'd never even met before? He made snap decisions all the time; he was used to paying off when he was wrong. But this one sent a jolt to a part of his self-image that had been propped up with hubris. He had gotten very used to being right. Way too used to being a hero all the time.

Chatterton, too, blamed himself. He understood that when you were looking for things no one had ever found, sometimes you didn't find them either. But he should have known better than to trust an eager, chatty lawyer instead of his own gut. Like Kohler, he had to admit that pride had reached out to slap him down.

———

Billy Lange, the imaging technician from Woods Hole Wolfinger had hired for the underwater camera work, had seen plenty of deep-ocean expeditions implode under the pressure of runaway egos, poor planning, and bad luck. Expeditions had pecking orders. What Lange had just witnessed was a shuffling of that order because the man who was on the top—on whose word others had spent a small fortune—had been demoted in the harshest possible way. The expedition was about to get ugly.

Lange was a compact man, graying as he approached fifty, carrying the extra weight of age on a sturdy frame with a low center of gravity. He moved with the efficiency of someone who thought about what he was going to do before he did it, and he spoke with the same restraint. For twenty-five years, Lange had worked at Woods Hole building underwater cameras and imaging equipment for exploring the deep ocean. He and a small cadre of other inventive men and women designed and built instruments that took the place of eyes where humans could not go. Until Lange's generation of engineers had intersected with the technology to shield instruments from the deadly pressure, the abyss had hidden its secrets for all of the two hundred thousand years *Homo sapiens* had existed.

Attempts to find out what was under the surface of the sea began the first time human beings stuck their heads into the water and opened their eyes. Alexander the Great had himself lowered a few feet into the Mediterranean in a glass barrel on the end of a rope. In 1690, Edmond Halley, who discovered the comet that bears his name, invented a chamber that could be lowered into the water to depths of forty feet and resupplied with air ferried down in skin bladders. Free divers held their breath, swam sixty feet to the bottom, and, for a minute or two, looked around for oysters that might yield pearls. Divers in heavy copper helmets couldn't go much farther than the pearl divers, but they could stay down and walk on the bottom as long as someone on the surface pumped air through a hose to them. For millennia, the unfathomable mysteries of water pressure, compressed gas, and the limitations of muscle power defeated attempts to dive deeper.

Then, in 1934, William Beebe and Otis Barton had themselves sealed into a four-and-a-half-foot-diameter, half-inch-thick steel sphere with three quartz glass portholes, and dropped at the end of a cable into the Atlantic off Bermuda. Their first dive took them to 800 feet and made them international heroes, celebrated on the front pages of newspapers as stupendously brave travelers to another world. Four years later, they reached a depth of 3,028 feet. In the primitive craft they called a bathysphere, they became the first humans to go beyond sunlight into the eternal darkness of the deep ocean.

In 1960, Don Walsh and Jacques Piccard dove the submersible *Trieste* down to the deepest place in the ocean, a depth of seven miles. In 1964, Woods Hole built the highly maneuverable, three-person sub *Alvin*, which could reach a depth of 14,764 feet.

For the expedition to *Titanic*, Lange brought two high-resolution Sony studio cameras he had modified to fit into six-inch-diameter titanium housings. The cables from the cameras went to high-speed digital tape recorders inside the sphere. With high-intensity TV lights mounted on arms outside the sub, it was a straightforward, simple system. Even someone running the cameras for the first time was likely to get it right.

Lange usually worked quietly in the background. He was content with tinkering, preparing, making sure that every camera he sent into the depths at enormous cost and risk of life worked perfectly. He went to planning meetings but tuned out anything that did not relate to imaging. There was nothing sweeter to him than an important discovery that happened because of his wires, cameras, and steel.

In 1985, however, Billy Lange had moved to center stage during an expedition to search for *Titanic*. It was the latest in a succession of attempts to reach the wreck, the first of which had been announced on April 20, 1912, five days after the disaster. Vincent Astor, the son of John Jacob Astor, who had been aboard *Titanic* and was presumed dead, said he would return to the scene immediately, blow up the wreck with high explosives, and recover his father's body when it floated to the surface. The following day, the steamer *Mackay-Bennett* found the frozen body of J. J. Astor in his life jacket among hundreds of his fellow passengers and crew, and Vincent canceled his expedition.

Fifty years passed before a team of British adventurers chartered a salvage ship named *Help* and tried to find *Titanic* using an array of explosions that were supposed to create a profile of the ship on the bottom. They were at *Titanic*'s last reported position, but their bombs returned no shapes of a ship to the sonar receivers, and no debris floated to the surface.

For most of the 1970s, Douglas Woolley, a young English-man, dominated the search for *Titanic* with his plan to find it, photograph it, raise it, and bring it to Liverpool to become a floating museum. He claimed salvage rights to the wreck and raised millions from investors, to whom he promised shares of a half-billion-dollar fortune in gold, diamonds, and vintage wine. Woolley vanished in 1977, never having found *Titanic*.

Soon after Woolley's escapade collapsed in a heap of law-suits and bad press, oceanographer Robert Ballard of the Woods Hole Oceanographic Institution proposed a venture with the more modest goal of simply finding the wreck.

Ballard talked the Aluminum Company of America into loaning him its drilling ship, *Alcoa Seaprobe*. He would lower 12,400 feet of pipe in sixty-foot lengths; at the end of the pipe, instead of a drill bit, would be a heavy steel pod loaded with side-looking sonar, still cameras, and television cameras. With the pod a few feet from the bottom, the ship would tow it and the connecting pipe through the water. Ballard told the institution that his search for *Titanic* would serve as a test of what could become a revolutionary system for studying the floor of the deep ocean for the first time.

Ballard sailed from Woods Hole on schedule in October 1977, confident that ten or twelve days of searching with the *Alcoa Seaprobe* pod would be all he'd need to find *Titanic*. He was testing the system in shallower water when a coupling broke, sending three thousand feet of pipe, weighing sixty-one thousand pounds, to the bottom.

Ballard didn't give up on *Titanic*, but instead of pipe, he next decided to use a camera and sensing pod towed along the ocean bottom at the end of a cable. He formed a company called Seaonics International to raise money to build deep-towed sensing and imaging equipment. For a while, Ballard had Roy Disney, Walt's brother, interested, but he backed out at the last minute. A Texas oilman, Jack Grimm, offered to buy into the venture, but Ballard didn't like Grimm; he turned him down even though it meant he was stalled in his quest to become the man who found *Titanic*.

Grimm tried again with some other scientists but failed to find the wreck on three expeditions plagued by rough seas, equipment failures, and bad blood. They found hard targets with their towed sonars but couldn't confirm any of them as wreckage from a ship. Grimm pushed the scientists to announce that they had discovered *Titanic*. They refused, saying only that they were pretty sure there was something wrong with the last position of the ship reported by its radiotelegraph operator.

———

On the night of September 1, 1985, Bill Lange and another imaging technician, Stu Harris, were an hour into their watch in the control room aboard *Knorr*, the mother ship of the Ballard-Michel expedition to find *Titanic*. They sat side by side, staring into television monitors at images from a camera on *Argo*, a contraption that carried cameras in pressure-proof housings they had built themselves. Towed on a cable behind *Knorr*, *Argo* was gliding a few feet over the bottom 12,400 feet below, its lights shining on a few hundred square yards of rocks and muck.

Knorr's around-the-clock watches had been combing the bottom with their robot eyes for five weeks, checking out targets from earlier sonar scans of the area, and searching the area in a systematic grid pattern. They had seen only numbingly monotonous images of the desolate seafloor. In the control room with Lange and Harris, Michel piloted *Argo* with a joystick, keeping it level and on course for each transect, turning the ship and the camera sled at the end of each run. Ballard was off duty, reading in his cabin.

After more than a month of nothing, the team's edge of anticipation had long worn off. It was entirely possible, they knew, that earthquakes or underwater landslides had completely covered the wreck and they would never find it. They maintained their concentration as well-trained pros, but "boring" had begun turning up more frequently in log entries on their watches. They played music. They amused themselves by predicting the exact time they would find the wreck on a particular watch. They sat quietly. They fought to stay awake.

There's something, Harris said, shortly before one A.M.

It would not have been the first false alarm or practical joke for the tired crew. Lange looked over Harris's shoulder and saw shapes on the screen that were definitely man-made.

Wreckage! Lange shouted.

A moment later, a technician monitoring *Argo*'s sonar signals said he had a hard contact. Then nothing. Some boulders slid under the camera. They had seen plenty of those.

A minute later, more shapes jumped out from the natural patterns of the seafloor. Harris was in charge of the watch. He decided to wake up cinematographer Ralph White to begin filming the debris.

Then they saw it: a circle in the mud. Nature rarely made perfect circles. Harris switched cameras, leaving the forward view and moving to the higher resolution of a camera pointed straight down at the bottom. They saw three smaller circles in part of the arc of the larger one. There was no question. It was a ship's boiler, identical to those in a photograph they had of the boilers on *Titanic*. Minutes later, the pictures streaming up from *Argo* showed enormous pieces of the wreck.

Word of the discovery spread through the ship. The control van was jammed with people slapping each other on the back and drinking paper cups of Mateus wine. White was commanding *Argo* to snap still pictures every eight seconds, sending a spectacular montage of the wreck flashing across the screens.

After twenty minutes, Ballard announced that he was going back to the fantail of the ship for a moment of commemoration. Everyone who was not busy keeping *Argo* alive and on course followed him. Just after two A.M.—at about the same time of the night that *Titanic* disappeared into the sea— Ballard unfolded a red-and-white flag, clipped it to the stern-post lanyard, and let it fly into the breeze over the North Atlantic. In the center of the flag were the gold initials *H* and *W* against a black diamond. The emblem of Harland and Wolff.

———

Late in the day, Chatterton and Kohler had calmed down enough to get everyone together to figure out what to do on their last dives. When they walked into the meeting, they didn't have even the most embryonic of ideas. It was obvious that the best bet for making a new discovery was to go where nobody had gone before. But after two decades of exploration, there wasn't much of the wreck that had not been seen by somebody.

"Roger, is there anything more we can learn from looking at the main wreckage?" Chatterton asked.

"Maybe more shots of the edges," Long said, shaking his head. "The best evidence of what might have happened to that ship will be in the steel. The more we see, the better. But, hell, guys, I really don't know what to tell you."

"Anybody else?" Kohler asked.

Kohler looked at Chatterton. Chatterton looked away and caught Wolfinger's eyes. Wolfinger shook his head and looked at Concannon. Nothing.

Bill Lange's voice had a gentleness to it, as though he wanted to say something to ease the distress that he could easily read in the body language of the people around him. They had their arms folded across their chests, their shoulders hunched. Most of them fidgeted with their fingers or swung their legs. Their eyes were dull, their faces slack.

"There's a lot of heavy debris to the east of the stern," Lange said.

Lange didn't often give advice on make-or-break decisions. He was a hired hand, there to take care of the gear. But he liked Chatterton and Kohler because they were so passionate about finding something new about the wreck. Lange had been on a lot of expeditions whose purpose was commerce of one sort or another—making a movie, collecting artifacts for exhibits, charging tourists for seats on the subs. He was glad to be on one whose goal was trying to answer some real questions.

"There are some large holes in the '85 and '86 surveys in that area," Lange went on. "I mean big enough to hold some major pieces. Even though that area was surveyed with side-scan sonar, it's not complete."

Lange said he had a vague recollection that divers on a French expedition with the *Nautile* submersible a decade earlier might have actually seen big pieces of debris, but nobody had paid much attention to the discovery. They had never been photographed in detail, never been studied for their forensic value.

"He might be right," Long said, relieved that his own dismal speculation was not the last word of advice on what to do next. "Judging from what's left of the bow and stern sections, there are big pieces of that ship somewhere down there."

In all their lives Chatteron and Kohler had never been so glad to be handed a long shot.

———

At eight o'clock the next morning, with a freshening breeze slapping the first swells of the approaching storm against *Keldysh*'s sides, Chatterton and Kohler shoehorned themselves into *Mir-1*. Both of them had performed the mental gymnastics necessary for embarking on a near-hopeless quest. They simply assumed they had already lost everything. They had failed. They were already dead. If, by some incredibly slim chance, *Titanic* dropped a miracle on them, they would be grateful. But having nothing to lose was the only way to get through the next ten hours together in a titanium sphere the size of a Volkswagen Bug.

Chatterton and Kohler had decided to send both of the *Mir*s into the darkness to the east. They gained nothing by combing wreckage and debris that had been seen over and over again. Two *Mir*s in one place doubled their chances. They would land together far from the stern and fan out a hundred feet apart from there.

Just aft of *Mir-1*, Kirk Wolfinger and Bob Blumberg boarded *Mir-2*. Blumberg had a bad hip and trouble sleeping, and, with his sixty-one-year-old bladder and digestive system, was a little bit skittish about spending ten hours in the sub. But he was determined to take a look at the shipwreck that had consumed him for the better part of three years.

A career State Department officer from McLean, Virginia, Blumberg had helped draft a treaty that named *Titanic* as an international maritime memorial. Ratification by the United States, Britain, France, and Canada was years away, and they were still trying to get the Russians to sign on. Blumberg knew the treaty wasn't perfect. Treaties never were. But just stopping hard landings on the decks and deterring poachers from chipping away at the badly deteriorating hull would preserve the wreck longer for careful research. Most of all, Blumberg thought, the treaty made *Titanic* a sacred place. A tomb.

Two and a half hours in the dark seemed like an eternity. In *Mir-1*, Chatterton and Kohler did what they had done in similar straits time and again: They talked each other into believing they were on the right track. Of course there were more pieces of the ship out there somewhere. The bow and stern sections accounted for only three-quarters or so of its length. The rest of the hull had to have landed somewhere. It could not have just vanished.

In *Mir-2*, Blumberg dozed, woke himself up snoring, apologized, dozed some more, snored some more. Wolfinger screwed his iPod buds into his ears and prayed that he would find something that might save his ass. Two thoughts repeated themselves over and over in his mind: How long can I go before I have to grab a piss bottle and fill it up while I'm shoulder to shoulder with two grown men? and If this thing springs a leak, we'll all be chowder in a split second.

The audiophone burbled as *Mir-1* and *Mir-2* made communications checks with each other and up to the surface. Roger Long was standing by in the radio room on *Keldysh*. If they found something, they would describe it to him. He would tell them what to shoot with the cameras.

After the radio checks, Wolfinger pressed his face to the viewport. As with all first-time visitors to the bottom of the ocean, just seeing the boulder-pocked muck was thrilling. And then he could not believe his eyes.

"Bob. Bob. Do you see what I see?"

"Where? What?" Blumberg answered.

"Look to the right, about twenty feet out in front."

There, as though brought in by a waiter on a tray, six champagne bottles stood straight up on the bottom. The wood of the crate that had once held them had long since been eaten away, leaving them in two perfect rows.

In *Mir-1*, pilot Victor Nischeta swung onto an easterly course, reached up, and tapped on the screen of the sonar receiver.

"Big target. Ten minutes."

Could it be this easy? Chatterton wondered. He looked at Kohler, whose eyes were as wide as saucers in the reddish haze of the instrument lights.

"A hundred meters to target," Nischeta said. "Very big. Hard."

Chatterton had been through the same moment with Concannon. He willed that memory out of his mind. The only sounds were the whine of the thrusters and the whirring fan of the carbon dioxide scrubber. Nischeta maneuvered three feet above the bottom.

"Right over here we got something," Chatterton said, drawing the last word out the way he did when he went on alert.

Kohler thought, I haven't heard that John for a couple of days.

"You see object?" Nischeta asked. He was as interested in finding something as Chatterton and Kohler. But he was most interested in not running into it.

"Oh, yeah," Kohler said. "I see something now."

"Yes," Chatterton said.

"Yeah. Look at that, huh." Kohler's words came out in the wavelengths of awe.

Not only were the shapes beyond their viewports not natural to the desolate sea bottom, they were clearly pieces of steel that had been riveted together.

"Is that part of the bilge keel?" Chatterton said.

"I don't know, John. I can't see out of my port yet."

"I think it is," Chatterton said. "Yes. Yes. Yes!"

"I see it, John. I see it. We're looking at the bottom of the ship!"

"Yeah. Absolutely."

"Unbelievable!"

"Yes. Yes. Yes. Yes. That's double hull."

"Oh, man. Look at this. Wow."

The plates were covered with slime and rust, but the red of the bottom paint showed clearly. The sub hovered three feet above the wreckage, moving slowly across the steel plain below. From their viewports, Chatterton and Kohler saw nothing but the bottom of *Titanic* in every direction. They reached the edge of the steel and could discern the five-foot gap between the inner and outer bottoms.

Chatterton began to laugh, a throaty cackle that he snapped off after a few seconds.

"We want to document this thing as well as we can," he said.

At the same moment, he and Kohler pulled away from their viewports to make sure the recorders for the TV cameras were running.

"The question is," Kohler said, "how big is this thing?"

Thirty seconds later, they reached the edge on the other side.

"Richie. That's bilge keel."

"What are you saying? That we're looking at the entire bottom?"

"Yeah."

"The only way we're going to prove that is to go back over to the other side," Kohler said. "Okay?"

"Okay. Yeah. Let's follow it around."

Nischeta steered *Mir-1* back over the plain of steel.

"There's the keel!" Kohler shouted. They were crossing what looked like a steel strap that rose an inch above the plating. "Oh, my God, John. That's the keel. This is the keel of *Titanic!*"

They kept going.

"Wait. Wait. Wait. Wait," Kohler said. "It's coming into focus. There's the other bilge keel."

"We've got all the double hull here," Chatterton said.

"It's a section of the entire bottom from port to starboard and, what, thirty feet wide?"

"Right, Richie. Right." Chatterton slipped into the trance of concentration at his viewport that was so much of what he loved about looking at a shipwreck.

No one had ever seen even a fragment of *Titanic's* bottom, the rest of which was deeply buried in the mud. If Chatterton and Kohler found nothing else, this was enough. There was no question that the discovery would make a sensational contribution to what the world understood about the doomed ship. Relief flooded into *Mir-1*.

Kohler radioed the news of their discovery to Roger Long on *Keldysh*. Then he called the other sub.

"*Mir-2*, this is *Mir-1*, over."

"Roger, *Mir-1*. Kirk here."

"You are not going to believe this," Kohler said. "We found an entire section of the bottom, bottom-up on the seafloor."

"You're not going to believe this," Wolfinger came back. "So did we."

No way, Chatterton and Kohler thought. They've got to be on the same piece as us. They asked Nischeta to find the other sub with his sonar. The hard targets of *Mir-2* and some large debris returned a signal from a hundred yards away. Wolfinger and Blumberg had found a second piece of the bottom that ran bilge keel to bilge keel and was thirty feet long.

"We're going to film every inch of these things," Kohler told Long. "Is there anything you want us to concentrate on?"

"Definitely," Long said on an open circuit to both subs. "Shoot the edges of the steel on the ends of the sections of the double bottom where it broke. That's where we'll be able to see the patterns of tension and compression that have not changed since the night the ship sank. And be sure to give me shots of the tops of the pieces so we can see if and how they fit together."

For two hours, the *Mir*s crisscrossed the red rusting plates, hovered at the edges, and painstakingly recorded the jagged steel that had once been joined to the rest of the ship.

"*Mir-1*, this is *Mir-2*."

"Go," Kohler said. He hated to pull away from his viewport for even a few seconds. He was in the relatively comfortable confines of the *Mir* instead of swimming around in the dark, silty murk of a shipwreck on scuba. But Kohler knew only one way to focus: completely.

"I think we've got it all," Wolfinger said. "This is once-in-a-lifetime stuff here, Richie."

"You got it, man."

"We're going to go take a look at the bow, then maybe the stern. Bob and I don't want to have come all this way and not see what it looks like."

"Good idea, Kirk. John and I are going to finish up here, then scout around some more."

"It's a plan, Richie. *Mir-2* out."

A half hour later, Chatterton and Kohler decided they had every square inch of their piece of *Titanic*'s bottom on tape.

———

On *Mir-2*, Wolfinger was savoring his reward. He had taken chances before, but nothing like this. Now he was going to get a look at one of the wonders of the world. The bow of *Titanic*. Ship of Dreams. The lights of the sub were on, sweeping over something big and black. He heard the thrusters roar. Up. They were going up. There it was, the bow rail. The lights swept over the foredeck. There was the crane. The anchor. He could see the navigation bridge. The wreck metamorphosed into the magnificent ship it once had been, as his mind added white paint, glass in the windows, passengers on deck.

A singsong muttering broke Wolfinger's reverie. Bob. He hoped he wasn't sick. He'd been pretty uncomfortable, used the bottle a few times, but stayed game. Wolfinger looked a few feet across the darkness of the sphere. There was Bob, his head back a foot or so from the viewport, his eyes closed. But he wasn't sick. He was praying. In Hebrew. Wolfinger wasn't religious, but somewhere from the distant past, his memory matched what he was hearing. Kaddish. The Jewish prayer for the dead.

———

The trip back to St. John's was two days of relief and exhilaration. The storm that cost the expedition its fourth day of dives to *Titanic* built steadily to the south, but with a following sea it was a comfortable ride. They spent their time eating, resting, and enjoying the leisurely pace of an ocean crossing that is the most delicious reward of travelers on comfortable ships. After a vodka-soaked celebratory dinner, Sagalevich called the divers to the head of the table one at a time and presented them with jacket patches, signifying that they had made a *Mir* descent into the abyss. Billy Lange got a standing ovation.

They watched videotape of the new debris, making sketches of various scenarios in which the pieces they found might have fallen through two and a half miles of water and come to rest on the seafloor so far from the main wreck. They wondered what could possibly have happened during *Titanic*'s final moments that had separated hundreds of tons of steel from the bottom of the ship. Roger Long wouldn't risk a guess. Without a time machine, Long said, there was no way to know for sure what had happened that night, but he should have some answers—or at least some new questions—in about a month.

DREAMS

PIRRIE

Pirrie has built more ships and bigger ships than any man since the days of Noah. Not only does he build them but he owns them, directs them, controls them on all the seas of the world.

—William T. Stead, journalist
Born July 5, 1849, died April 15, 1912
From a character sketch, March 1912

W illiam Pirrie wasn't at all sure why, but in the summer of 1899, when he was fifty-two years old, he let his wife, Margaret, talk him into a palm reading. Cheiromancy, astrology, and séances were fairground attractions, but she had convinced him that the man who called himself Cheiro—of all things—was on the level. He had read the Prince of Wales's palm, she said. And Mark Twain's, Oscar Wilde's, Sarah Bernhardt's, William Stead's, and those of most of London and New York society. He had predicted the Boer War, which was clearly going to ignite at any moment. And recently, to everyone's consternation, he had forecast the death of Queen Victoria, which had not yet occurred. His readings just make you think more clearly about the future, his wife said. It would be better, Pirrie told her when he capitulated, if Cheiro told him the date of the next foundry strike so he could buy steel before it started.

On a muggy, sooty Friday in August 1899, Pirrie clattered across London in his one-horse trap to the West End, delighted as he always was to be pleasing Margaret. As the chairman of Britain's biggest shipyard, Harland and Wolff, Pirrie was used to a little bowing and scraping, but when he reached Cheiro's rooms, a receptionist told him to expect a long wait. Three women in day gowns, hats, and gloves were perched on a red velour settee. Two men stood against a silk-covered wall opposite them with their hands clasped at their belts. Pirrie had a mind to walk out, but he hated the idea of leaving once he had decided to do something. He nodded in the direction of the men, then settled against his own patch of the wall. A half hour dragged by as the door to an even more dimly lit chamber opened every few minutes to discharge a visibly shaken man or woman and admit another from the waiting room.

Finally, Pirrie sat at a black-lacquered table lit by a single candle across from a beefy man with dark, wavy hair who appeared to be wearing face powder and stage makeup. The man had smiled at Pirrie as he'd walked into the muggy little room, after which his face had seemed frozen except for the movement of his rouged lips.

You have the hands of a child, Cheiro said. And you began your life far from home. Pirrie watched the palmist study his reaction, gauging whether his guess was right. In fact, Pirrie had been born in Canada to parents who'd left Belfast for the New World. If he had not been born abroad, Pirrie knew, Cheiro would have detected a tic or some other sign of denial and retreated to a figurative rather than literal interpretation of the idea of far from home.

Pirrie nodded. Right you are, he said. From those three words, Cheiro knew that Pirrie was Irish, and told him so. He knew from his well-cut hacking jacket, whipcord trousers, white linen shirt, and flat black cravat that his subject was not a man adrift. Cheiro put him to work in Belfast's most famous industry, shipbuilding, because he recognized the broad-shouldered, heavy-crowned features of his ancestry. The ship-yards of Belfast were dominated by migrants from the Clyde River valley in Scotland.

Even an amateur seer would have recognized the scent of the ocean on Pirrie, a blend of confidence and humility that rose from a man who knew the terror and magnificence of the sea. Cheiro said he saw a long voyage in Pirrie's past. Pirrie nodded, thinking of his grandfather, a celebrated mariner who had raised him after his father died young of cholera, leaving him, his older sister, and his mother alone in the fortress city of Quebec. The Pirries had endured a stormy eastbound voyage home to Belfast, which William had never forgotten.

Pirrie never believed that Cheiro was summoning his past from the lines in his hand, but he appreciated the bravura exhibition of observational power. It was not unlike what he used himself in negotiations with shipping companies, and he knew he was in the presence of a master. Pirrie felt a kind-ness for the palm reader and began making things even easier for him with more nods of his head to confirm his increas-ingly more accurate guesses. Yes, his mother had bought him a gentleman's apprenticeship at a shipyard in Belfast when he was fifteen. Yes, he had moved up directly into management. (Cheiro had noticed that Pirrie's hands were not only small but unblemished by calluses.) Yes, he was now a partner in the company. (Otherwise, he would be back in Belfast hard at work during the good-weather building months.)

And tomorrow? Pirrie said when Cheiro fell silent for a few seconds.

You are about to be honored in some way, the palmist said.

And . . . , Pirrie coaxed.

And you will soon find yourself in a fight for your life, Cheiro whispered. His first impressions about the tidy, compact man across the table from him had been wrong. He was no easy mark but a shrewd and powerful predator. It was not much of a reach for Cheiro to assume that a man in the notoriously volatile business of ships and shipping would be in some kind of a fight for survival in the not too distant future.

A month after his palm reading, Pirrie wrote Cheiro a letter to congratulate him and invite him to tour the shipyard if he was ever in Belfast. Pirrie had received word that the Royal University of Ireland in Dublin was awarding him an honorary law degree in recognition of his achievement in shipbuilding, and he mentioned it to Cheiro as proof that he had been right. What's more, he had heard rumors that J. P. Morgan was about to make an attempt to take control of the North Atlantic shipping industry.

John Pierpont Morgan's financial empire was built on United States Steel, a syndicate that included every iron ore mine, coal mine, steel mill, and foundry in America and owned more land than the states of Massachusetts, Vermont, and Rhode Island combined. According to the prevailing wisdom in maritime circles, he was leery of investing in things that depended upon the sea. In late autumn, however, a surge in shipping profits driven by the Spanish-American War began to roll in, and Morgan changed his mind about ships and shipping. With Clement Griscom, a Philadelphia railroad baron,

Morgan bought a controlling interest in the only two American shipping companies serving the North Atlantic. He also bought a majority stake in Leyland, a leading British freight line. Since just those three companies couldn't control enough traffic to set prices for passenger tickets and cargo, it was clear that Morgan wasn't done. Nobody was sure where he would strike next.

Pirrie dug deeper and found that Morgan had the backing of the United States government for his plan to create an American shipping monopoly. After making his deal with Griscom, Morgan had gone to Washington and called in a big favor. In 1895, his banks had loaned the government millions of dollars to keep the nation out of bankruptcy. Though the nascent trust-busting movement was gaining momentum, President Teddy Roosevelt and a loyal cadre of big-business supporters beat the drum for Morgan's navy. Congress created the American merchant marine and subsidized the operation of every ship that flew the American flag. Pirrie had no doubt that with such deep pockets, Morgan was about to make a move on one or both of England's celebrated shipping lines, Cunard and White Star. Morgan called his new combine International Mercantile Marine.

———

Pirrie couldn't help but remember Cheiro's final prediction from two years earlier. Harland and Wolff built ships for every company Morgan controlled, as well as all White Star ships. If Morgan took his business elsewhere, it would bankrupt the company that was a second skin to Pirrie.

Pirrie had gone to work at the shipyard when he was a teenage boy. His mother, Eliza, had not remarried after her husband's death in Canada. In the summer of 1862, she had paid Edward Harland one hundred guineas to train her son as a shipbuilder.

The fifteen-year-old Willie Pirrie rented a room in a row house a short walk from the shipyard gate and settled into the demanding routines of his apprenticeship. He worked as a messenger, painter's assistant, and parts runner before moving into the drawing office to begin his climb up the ladder into management. From the drawing office, Harland moved him around through the chores of timekeeper, assistant manager, scribe, and ledgerkeeper.

Pirrie thought Harland's, as everyone called the company, was paradise. Hard work produced fair rewards. Solving the puzzles of designing and building a ship came naturally to him, and every few weeks a ship he'd helped build splashed into the river Lagan like a round of applause. He had seen ships born from Belfast yards all his life, but a month after he went to work at Harland's he watched his first as a shipbuilder. Pirrie hadn't had much to do with it, just some deliveries to some of the foremen who were working on it, but at eleven o'clock on the morning of July 15, he heard the pop of the launchway arresting cables letting go. He ran out of the paint shed, where he was assigned that day, and watched a mass of steel, wood, and rivets that was no more graceful than a warehouse on land groan down the slipway and transform itself into the 240-foot steamship *Catalonian*, afloat and alive on the river.

Edward Harland remained aloof from the energetic apprentice, but he knew very well that the boy's pedigree made him a good prospect for the shipbuilder's life. Pirrie's grandfather had dredged the sandbars of the river Lagan to help transform Belfast shipbuilding from a desperate local enterprise into an industrial powerhouse. Harland also noticed Pirrie because he showed talent not only in ship design and engineering but in finance, and he made a point of extending the boy's time with the company bookkeeper, John Bailey. After Pirrie proved out, Harland sent him back to the drawing office as a journeyman draftsman, but Bailey left his door open to the young man, who continued to devour the complexities of shipbuilding contracts. In 1874, Harland and Wolff offered the twenty-seven-year-old Pirrie a share of the company. With money from his mother, and his own savings from five years on the job, he bought in for £13,000. Over dinner aboard the liner *Adriatic* a few years later, Gustav Wolff toasted what quickly became a powerful collaboration: "Edward Harland builds the ships; Mr. Pirrie makes the speeches; and I smoke the cigars."

By 1890, Harland and Wolff had pulled most of their time and money from the shipyard, leaving Pirrie as the majority shareholder and chairman of the company. The first thing he did as the man in charge was to open the books of what was known as the Commission Club of preferred customers. With the details stored only in his head, Pirrie negotiated a schedule of costs and fixed commissions with a dozen shipping companies. He sweetened the deals by taking more stock instead of some of the cash, guaranteed that he would repair their ships for labor, materials, and a 5 percent commission, and promised to have a dry dock available for those repairs. All he asked was that they give him their business and allow him to equip the ships with furniture, fittings, rigging, and anything else he could manufacture himself, making a profit on each of those sales. Six months after expanding the Commission Club during a depression that wiped out half the shipbuilders in Great Britain, Pirrie had twenty-three steamship orders on the books, and Harland and Wolff survived until the economy recovered in the mid-1890s.

William Pirrie loved selling ships, but he loved building them even more. During the next decade, he launched more than a hundred for the members of his Commission Club and the occasional drop-in customers who simply wanted a Harland and Wolff liner and were willing to pay top price. The amount of coal required to propel a single 10,000-ton ship across the ocean was far less than the amount required to drive two 5,000-ton ships across the same distance. No one on the waterfronts of the North Atlantic failed to notice that Pirrie was leading the way in building ships of steadily increasing tonnage, which translated into more freight, livestock, grain, and passengers per voyage. In July 1901, Harland and Wolff broke the 20,000-ton barrier with the delivery of the biggest ship in the world to the White Star Line. *Celtic* was 680 feet long, could carry 2,859 passengers and hundreds of tons of cargo from Liverpool to New York in less than eight days, had two of the largest steam engines ever built, and was by far the most luxurious ocean liner afloat. Until its christening, *Celtic*'s nickname in the British press was *Gigantic*, and its instant commercial success convinced Pirrie and other insiders that the world would soon see 50,000-ton ships a thousand feet long. There was absolutely no question that bigger was better for crossing the ocean. In the meantime, White Star ordered three sister ships immediately, to be named *Adriatic*, *Baltic*, and *Cedric*.

At about the same time as *Celtic* inaugurated its Liverpool–to–New York service, J. P. Morgan pounced on its owner, the Oceanic Steam Navigation Company. Better known by the nickname derived from its swallow-tailed red burgee with a white star, the White Star Line had been founded in 1868 by Thomas Ismay. His first ship was the 172-foot, 580-ton iron sailing bark *Broughton*, built by Edward Harland. Ismay paid Harland with shares in the White Star Line, and for the rest of his life, he built all of his ships at Harland and Wolff.

Morgan learned that the late Thomas Ismay had been a

canny dealmaker who probably would have seen the wisdom of joining his syndicate. His son Bruce, White Star's largest surviving shareholder, was a socially clumsy, brooding, conservative man who wouldn't even quote a price for his company. As Morgan's men cast around England trying to seduce either White Star or the other great passenger line, Cunard, to give his combine a chance to succeed, the shipping industry was struggling for survival.

In October 1901, Pirrie painted a dismal picture for the Harland and Wolff directors at their board meeting. Over four million tons of ships had been launched between 1896 and 1900 because owners had followed their typical but foolhardy pattern of building new ships at the end of a boom, since that was when they had the money. To make matters worse, Pirrie said, all the ships that had been pressed into admiralty service during the recently ended Boer War were now back in commerce; and if that wasn't enough, a depression was crippling Europe, the American corn crop had failed, and immigration to the United States had fallen off sharply. Price wars had flared up that chopped freight revenues by 30 percent and passenger ticket sales by 50 percent. Nobody was ordering new ships. Orders for dozens of ships had been canceled. Two old-line yards, Earle's of Hull and Maudslay of London, had already failed. If something didn't happen to stop the collapse of freight and passenger revenues, Pirrie told his board, Harland and Wolff would not be far behind them.

What Pirrie knew but did not tell his directors was that he had secretly been sending out feelers to J. P. Morgan with a plan to save Harland and Wolff. Without White Star, Morgan's combine didn't have a prayer of competing on the vital routes between North America and Europe, let alone controlling prices for freight and passengers. Cunard had rejected Morgan's offer after convincing the British government to cough up enough money to prevent the American from hijacking control of the North Atlantic sea-lanes. In return, Cunard had agreed to build fast ships with fittings for guns and armor that could be turned into Royal Navy men-of-war when needed.

Stymied by Bruce Ismay's refusal to even begin negotiations, Morgan took a last-ditch shot at White Star through its second-largest shareholder, William Pirrie. A month after delivering his gloomy forecast to his directors, Pirrie met Morgan across the matched walnut panels of a conference table in the offices of the American's London bank. Except for a stenographer to take notes, the men were alone. Morgan spoke first.

I hate Cunard, he said, and then spent five minutes on a bitter account of being stranded with his family on a Liverpool dock on Christmas Day a few years earlier when the crew of the Cunard liner on which they had just crossed the ocean bolted for home without making sure their first-class passengers were on the boat train.

It took us two days to get to London, Morgan sputtered. How much do you want for White Star?

Pirrie stayed right with Morgan's abrupt change of gears from small talk to negotiation. Our shares are not publicly traded, as you know, Pirrie said, thinking he was beginning what would be many parries in a fencing match. White Star is worth whatever we say it is worth.

How about ten times your 1900 earnings? Morgan said. Call it $32 million—$24 million in preferred stock in the combine, $8 million in cash.

How could J. P. Morgan, the most celebrated dealmaker on earth, not know that White Star's profit in 1900 was a record for the half-century-old company? Ten times earnings was a standard estimate of a company's value that was used for only the most cursory analysis of its real worth. But a price based on 1900's profit was wildly inflated, and it would make the White Star shareholders, including Harland and Wolff, rich beyond their wildest expectations. What it did to Morgan's grand plan was another matter, Pirrie thought as he sorted methodically through the nuances of the offer. Once the deal was done, the combine, of which he and Ismay would be part owners if they accepted shares as partial payment, would have to keep up payments on the stock dividends and interest. Overpaying for White Star was bound to make a huge dent in profits for the combine.

Pirrie dragged out his silence. He studied the American, amazed that so unattractive a man could have accumulated so much power and confidence. Morgan was dressed in a perfectly cut chalk-stripe three-piece suit with a wide maroon cravat, but despite the expensive tailoring he looked rumpled. And worse, the poor man was afflicted with rhinophyma, a skin disease that had turned his nose into a dreadful, swollen purple knob. Before the meeting, Pirrie had read everything about Morgan he could get his hands on and had come across one story that he thought was terribly sad but that gave him a subtle upper hand. Morgan had gone to an afternoon social at the home of a banker and his wife, who had coached their daughter to avoid staring at Morgan's nose when she served the tea. The girl dutifully brought in the silver service and biscuits and left the room. Her mother, breathing a sigh of relief that the moment had passed, said, "Mr. Morgan, do you take one lump or two in your nose?"

As I understand it, Pirrie finally said, you already own Griscom's International Navigation and Atlantic Transport, Leyland, and the Dominion Line. I also understand that the British ships will continue to fly the Union Jack, and that the combine will have British as well as American directors.

Correct, Mr. Pirrie, Morgan said. And I hope you and Mr. Ismay will consider serving on the board.

I would be delighted, and I will propose the seat to Mr. Ismay, Pirrie said. I must tell you that Ismay thinks the whole thing is a swindle and a humbug, he added, dropping his voice and leaning ever so slightly toward Morgan. But I'll take your offer to him if you include this in the terms of the combine.

Pirrie played his real cards now. The White Star deal, as good as it was, meant nothing to him compared to saving his shipyard. As Morgan brightened visibly, Pirrie pushed across the table a piece of cockle-finish onionskin on which, in the elegant hand of a Victorian bookkeeper, was a single paragraph.

Builder's Agreement

All orders for new vessels and for heavy repairs, requiring to be done at a shipyard of the United Kingdom, are to be given to Harland & Wolff, but nothing herein contained shall prevent the purchasers from placing orders for new steamers and repairs at shipyards in the United States. In return Harland & Wolff agree not to build ships for any persons not in the combination, except the Hamburg-American company, so long as orders from the combination keep the builders' works busy. Harland & Wolff are to be paid the cost of the work plus 5 percent on new ships, 10 percent on new machinery in old vessels, and 15 percent on repairs. This agreement runs for ten years and is terminable thereafter only on five years' notice from either side.

Morgan read it in a minute. Done, he said.

Pirrie said, I'll take care of Ismay.

ISMAY

Pirrie delivered Morgan's offer to Bruce Ismay on a frosty January morning when the ancient Liverpool docks seemed to begrudge the prospect of yet another windy, freezing day. The cobbles and timbers were slippery with the night's coating of rime, and the bad footing slowed the men as they picked their way among the sheds, chandleries, and tally shacks on the wharves. The first hour of a cold day working outside was brutal, but the effort of stowing cargo, coaling, watering, mucking out ballast, and manhandling mooring hawsers banished the chill by the time dawn marked the peaks of the buildings on the fringe of the waterfront. The new White Star office on the corner of James Street and the riverfront Strand where Bruce Ismay waited for Pirrie was among the first to catch the rays of the sun winking over the upper Mersey to the southeast. It was an eight-story ocher-and-white layer cake of brick and limestone set on a hulking granite base, ornamented with turrets and wrought-iron balconies, and topped with three oversized chimneys already flinging their dark smudges of coal smoke into the brightening sky.

James Street, as the White Star headquarters was known in the company, was a radical departure from the stately Victorian pile of the nearby Royal Liver Assurance headquarters, the blocky Cunard building, and the surrounding warehouses. Some called it "a slice of New Scotland Yard" because its architect, Richard Shaw, had also designed the famous police headquarters in London and seemed to be merely repeating himself in Liverpool. Scotland Yard was originally going to be an opera house, but its owners ran out of money; Shaw inherited the two floors of granite already in place and a smaller budget to complete the building for the Metropolitan Police. He finished it with six stories of alternating brick and limestone, transforming a stalled project into a curious masterpiece. Twelve years before getting the White Star job, Shaw had also designed Thomas Ismay's mansion, Dawpool, a drafty monstrosity with primitive plumbing that was impossible to heat because the place filled with smoke from the chimneys no matter which way the wind blew. Some people wondered why Ismay stuck with the architect for James Street. Others, who knew him better, understood that the last thing Ismay would do would be to admit to failure as a judge of character.

The public office on the ground floor of James Street was as austere as a mausoleum, furnished in stark oak, its high walls sparsely decorated with two paintings of *Teutonic*, the first White Star liner with twin engines and no sails, a portrait of Thomas Ismay, and, in a glass case in the central aisle, the builder's model of *Afric*, a 12,000-ton colonial service ship delivered in 1899 to carry livestock, frozen meat, and passengers on the Australian routes. The marble porter's lodge opened into a cavernous ticketing room in which clerks managed sales, bills of lading, and customs declarations. Every sound—a stamp snapping against its pad, a cash drawer clicking shut, the ratchet of a Comptometer—ricocheted off the granite walls, giving the hall the efficient but chilly feel of a railway station.

Pirrie was fairly certain he would be able to talk Bruce Ismay into selling to Morgan, but he knew from experience that convincing his younger partner of anything was much easier if he treated him with the respect of an equal. Bruce's father, Thomas Henry Ismay, or T.H., as he was known, had been dead for two years, after a cascade of heart attacks. Pirrie sensed that Bruce was not entirely unhappy about his father's departure. T.H. had subscribed to the philosophy that boys will not become men unless they are browbeaten, criticized, and subjugated; the elder of his two sons had caught the worst of it.

Bruce Ismay still cringed every time he thought of the day he went to work as an apprentice in the early autumn of 1880. The old White Star offices on Water Street were ripe with memories from visits arranged by his mother to remind him and his younger brother, James, that as surely as beavers built a dam, they were destined to run a shipping company. The bite of stale tobacco, the thuds, clatters, and shouting on the wharves, and the mystical presence of the great ships outside were as familiar to him as his childhood nursery. Wearing a black vested suit, he had followed a pace behind his identically dressed father through the freight bins on the ground floor, up two flights of stairs, and into a room full of men at high-legged ledger tables, each of whom muttered, Morning, Mr. Ismay, Master Ismay, without looking up from their books.

Thomas Ismay's office overlooked the Mersey River, fully a mile across at that point in its journey from the middle of England to the Irish Sea, alive with ships, lighters, ferryboats, and smacks attending one another and the docks on the Liverpool side. T.H. walked to a leaded bay window and lit a cigarette. He stood with his back to his waiting son, scanning the waterfront below where one of his ships, *Britannic*, lay at anchor in the stream, waiting for a high enough tide to moor at its pier. Another, the smaller *Adriatic*, was fast to the quay while stevedores topped up the freshwater tanks and slung cargo into its forward hold. Ismay lifted a gold pocket watch from his vest and checked the time. *Adriatic* sailed at noon that day and, from the looks of things, on schedule. *Adriatic* and the slightly newer *Britannic* were the most up-to-date combinations of sails and steam engines that had reduced the crossing time between Liverpool and New York to a mere eight days, give or take a few hours.

Bruce lingered quietly by the door for five minutes, then finally hung his coat in its customary place on a bentwood rack he had used as a child and left his father standing at the window. As Bruce approached the office manager's desk to get his assignment for the day, a bell on the wall rang once—a shrill, high note—and one of the men working there jumped up to answer the boss's summons.

Please inform the new office boy, Thomas Ismay said in a stage voice loud enough to carry into the next room, that he is not to leave his overcoat lying about in my office.

Joseph Bruce Ismay, who thought of himself as Bruce even though everyone in his family called him Joseph, coped stoically with his father; the teachers at Elstree School and Harrow; his tutor for a year in France; and all the other men who thought it their duty to stun him into excellence with mean-spirited criticism. Defying them would have been unthinkable, so Bruce retreated into silent fantasies of solo adventures in foreign ports where he knew no one and no one knew him. He armored himself with a practiced reticence that most people interpreted as arrogance. He learned to shut the door on their world and endure the fact that he was the not-quite-capable elder son of one of the world's celebrated shipping geniuses. T. H. Ismay was a shrewd, self-made merchant prince whose road to riches was a matter of Liverpool legend. In 1868, a fleet known as the White Star clippers was doing a brisk business on the sea-lanes to the Australian goldfields when the bonanza down under went bust, taking the company and its bankers with it into bankruptcy. T.H., the son of a boatbuilder, had been scratching out a living with a pair of square riggers. He took the biggest risk of his life when he borrowed £1,000 to buy the White Star name, its flag, and whatever goodwill was left in the wake of the once dependable company. The bankruptcy court put the wooden clipper ships up for auction, but with a flash of insight, Ismay ignored them. Grown knees, forks, timbers, and planks for building ships were already scarce in Europe, and their cost soared when they had to be imported from Canada. The future, T.H. felt certain, was in iron. He refitted his own ships for longer voyages, took over the White Star routes, and carried cargo and passengers attracted by free land and opportunity in Australia and New Zealand. His backhauls still included gold, wool, jugged mutton, and the few passengers who'd gone broke or crazy on the raw frontier and decided to come home to Europe. A year later, Ismay was showing enough profit to be able to peddle four hundred £1,000 shares in his company, keeping fifty shares for himself. When, a little over a decade after buying the White Star name, T.H. put his oldest son to work on Water Street, he owned ten sailing steamers and had four more on order at Harland and Wolff. Not one of his ships carried a mortgage.

Bruce Ismay's apprenticeship in Liverpool ended, mercifully, in 1886. Either because Thomas Ismay figured out that his son despised him or because he despised his son, he assigned him to the White Star office in New York. More than 70 percent of inbound and 60 percent of outbound freight and passengers passed through New York's harbor. The number of emigrants from the Old World to the New approached a million a year, every one of whom arrived by ship. To commemorate that flood of humanity and the optimism it kindled in the underclasses of Europe, France gave the United States a 151-foot-tall statue of the personification of Liberty. Liberty arrived, coincidentally, as Bruce Ismay and his valet moved into a town house on the West Side of lower Manhattan, near the White Star docks.

Mark Twain called it the Gilded Age, and Ismay and his pal Harold Sanderson, who worked for his own family's shipping company, took their places among the tight society of young, rich *bons vivants*. Ismay was not a smooth player among the polished New Yorkers, and many people who encountered the aloof heir to the White Star fortune were left feeling offended by his standoffishness. Sometimes, Ismay's social awkwardness even forced confrontations. On one particular evening, a mutual friend introduced him to the twenty-four-year-old son of a mining tycoon who had just inherited a San Francisco newspaper and was in New York to buy another one. William Randolph Hearst squared his shoulders, lifted his chin, and stuck out his hand to shake. Ismay, startled by the American lack of reserve he had never quite gotten used to, hesitated a moment too long. Hearst turned on his heel and walked away without a word. Who was that again? Ismay asked Sanderson.

Ismay stumbled from stag line to stag line until October 1887, when he abruptly abandoned bachelorhood at a watering hole called the Tuxedo Club by asking Julia Florence Schieffelin to marry him. She was the seventeen-year-old daughter of a member of the Knickerbocracy, the four hundred men who supposedly ruled New York City, and a celebrated beauty who had not been at all impressed when she'd met Bruce Ismay on the circuit a month earlier. After their first encounter, the odd Englishman kept turning up unexpectedly as she stepped from a carriage or a doorway. He would mumble an awkward greeting, tip his black bowler, and go on his way. She was curious about the apparently shy or absurdly arrogant man, but had dreams of her own of far-off lands.

For Ismay, it had been love at first sight. At the Tuxedo Club, his awkward persistence paid off when Julia agreed to brave the elements and walk with him around the grounds of the coastal estate. Half in jest, he made his proposal and was stunned when she accepted. Their engagement ignited a storm of opposition from her father, who buttonholed Ismay and declared that there was no way he was going to let his daughter marry a man who was going to take her away from Manhattan.

Fine, Ismay told George Schieffelin. I promise you that I will live here for the rest of my life. Ismay could think of nothing more wonderful than living in New York and being spared the pains of being a single man in high society.

T. H. Ismay had other plans. A year and a half after the wedding, the young Ismays went to Dawpool for a midsummer visit to show off their new daughter and enjoy the best month of the year in the lush green uplands over the Mersey. The visit went according to form, with picnics, forest walks, trap shooting for the men, and teas for the women. At dinner one night, T.H. stunned his family when he stood up, cleared his throat, and told them he was retiring from day-to-day management of his company but would stay on as chairman. Then, in no uncertain terms, he said that either Bruce would return home to take his place as president or the job would go to James.

After Bruce caught his breath, he told his father he had promised George Schieffelin that he wouldn't take his daughter and grandchildren to live in England. What he didn't say was that he would rather die than work for his brother. There had never been any question that James was the family favorite; for reasons that were never clear to Bruce, his brother delighted his father rather than irritating him. He also didn't mention the fact that running the business with his father looking over his shoulder might simply be more than he could stand. With the decision still up in the air, Bruce and Florence sailed back to New York on the magnificent new *Majestic*, sister to *Teutonic* and, at 10,000 tons, the world's largest steamship. It also held the current record for the Atlantic crossing: five days, eighteen hours, and eight minutes.

Schieffelin was nothing if not a smart businessman. When Bruce told him about T.H.'s ultimatum, he realized that a son-in-law at the helm of one of the world's most profitable shipping empires was better than a son-in-law working as a minion in the White Star agency in New York. He released Bruce from his promise, and the Ismays sailed for Liverpool two months later.

For the next six years, Bruce Ismay rode the tram to James Street every day. He carried his lunch in a satchel, fished, played lawn tennis and bridge on weekends, and kept the White Star Line ships running on time. His father blew into his life from time to time like a squall off the Irish Sea, but

Bruce survived by laying down his own set of rules for the office, his colleagues, and his ships by which he could clearly measure performance and defend himself against criticism. The stories that circulated in the company, particularly among the officers on White Star liners, were anything but complimentary about the tightly wound, mustachioed martinet in the president's chair. According to one of them, Ismay reprimanded the master of *Teutonic* for sailing from Liverpool with some of the windows of his wheelhouse up and some of them down. According to another, memorialized in a letter from a White Star captain, William Marshall, to his wife, "the Big White Chief" spent most of his time during a voyage to New York inspecting details in the galley, staterooms, parlors, and engine room. Thankfully, Marshall also told her, Ismay had enough sense to stay out of the way when it came to the navigation and the actual running of the ship.

———

In Bruce Ismay's office, with the door closed, Pirrie sat in an armchair near the open hearth and talked his partner through Morgan's proposition. It's a two-edged sword, he said. The shareholders of White Star and Harland and Wolff will reap an enormous windfall in cash, but we will also own shares in the combine and eventually have to pay for Morgan's mistake of overpaying us when we have to return dividends on those shares and any other money we borrow to stay in business. On the other hand, if we do not surrender White Star, Morgan will not stop in his attempts to take over our British, German, Belgian, and Dutch competitors. As a part of his combine we will have a chance. As its enemy, both White Star and Harland and Wolff are doomed.

Thomas Ismay would never have let Pirrie steer so momentous a decision about his precious company, but his son had moved into a comfortable orbit around the shipbuilder. Ismay trusted Pirrie completely and was relieved to be doing business with an older man who did not make him feel like an incompetent fool. Ismay was very good at keeping his ships running on time with the windows in the proper position, and he was quite happy to leave the strategizing to Pirrie. On February 4, 1902, the White Star Line ceased to exist as an independent company and became the keystone of Morgan's International Mercantile Marine, known to all simply as IMM.

Pirrie's strategy for saving Harland and Wolff had worked perfectly. The guarantee of all of the combine's construction and repair business in Europe had cost him absolutely nothing. The windfall from his White Star shares would cushion him during the next economic collapse—whenever it came— and allow him to expand his shipyard to build more and bigger ships. Pirrie's prediction about the dismal consequences of Morgan's paying too much for Ismay's company, however, began to come true a year later. White Star staggered under the shared burden of the nearly bankrupt combine and Morgan's inability to corner the market because he failed to gain control of enough other big lines to put together a monopoly. The shipping industry went into an almost fatal price war. In 1903, you could buy a ticket across the Atlantic for £2. Only a boom in travelers saved White Star and IMM. Between 1898 and 1907, fueled by American immigration, the number of passengers increased steadily from 600,000 to 2,400,000 a year. In 1904, with the combine in the depths of its struggle to survive, Pirrie engineered a change of leadership at IMM. He convinced Morgan and the combine boards in America and England to replace its president, Clement Griscom, with the man he had slowly, quietly moved into the embrace of his vision: Bruce Ismay.

The price war didn't send so much as a ripple through the flow of business to Harland and Wolff. Under the terms of his deal with Morgan, the shipyard prospered, with forty orders between 1902 and 1907 from the IMM companies. The Dutch and Germans followed along because Pirrie was the proven builder of big ships, which were far more competitive than smaller ships on the most heavily traveled routes. Pirrie used the cash from the surge in new orders to completely electrify his shipyard, which meant that he could be in production twenty-four hours a day. He also talked the Belfast harbor board into building a dry dock for repairs on liners up to 900 feet long.

Alarms again began going off in Pirrie's mind in April 1904, when it became clear that White Star was losing the battle for dominance over Cunard. Ismay was running his company and the combine with increased confidence and skill, backed by Pirrie's counsel, but Cunard fired a devastating salvo against White Star's premier fleet, known as the Big Four. *Celtic, Cedric, Baltic,* and *Adriatic* were the first great ships of the twentieth century, each of them more than 20,000 tons, *Celtic* and *Cedric* 680 feet long, *Baltic* and *Adriatic* 709 feet long, all capable of cruising at 17 knots with crossing times of under eight days. The success of the Big Four also depended on their reputations for comfortable accommodations in all three classes and the easy passages that only big ships could offer. Only in summer did the North Atlantic promise anything other than rough seas, high winds, and queasy stomachs, so the bigger the ship, the smoother the ride.

That spring, just as Ismay and Pirrie were catching their breath from Morgan's faltering assault on the shipping industry, a shipyard on the Tyne River at Newcastle laid the keel of a true giant for Cunard. RMS *Mauretania* would be 790 feet long and 88 feet wide, weigh 32,000 gross tons, and, most unsettling, cruise at 25 knots with four revolutionary steam turbine engines. It would have a sister, the slightly smaller *Lusitania* being built on the river Clyde in Scotland. The British government's enormous gamble to prop up Cunard with more than £2 million against Morgan's takeover bid looked like it was going to pay off. Together, the Cunard giants would offer unparalleled two-ship express service between Southampton and New York. The White Star Big Four would no longer be the first choice for the crossing.

Nothing like the big Cunarders had been even a figment of a shipbuilder's imagination just a decade earlier, but the formula of building bigger to lower the cost of coal to carry each passenger and each ton of freight across the ocean was impossible to resist. Cunard and its shipbuilders learned, however, that building a big ship might not be as easy as simply scaling up a small ship. *Lusitania* was delivered first, and on its initial speed trial the stern shook terribly; the ship had to return to the yard for weeks of repairs and strengthening, which required tons of steel angle braces and girders.

At about the same time as *Lusitania* was limping back up the Clyde, Lord Pirrie (he'd recently been elevated to the peerage for his service to the city of Belfast) and Lady Margaret Pirrie invited Bruce and Florence Ismay to dinner at Downshire House. The Pirries had married in 1887, just before he moved his base of operations from Belfast to London. They were childless, so they poured their domestic energy into turning their elegant, rambling mansion on Belgrave Street into a showplace. Its drawing room, eighteen bedrooms, and ten bathrooms were open to visiting friends, and Pirrie liked nothing more than offering hospitality to his business associates.

The Ismays had become regulars at Downshire House since White Star had shifted its express service to Southampton, a convenient train ride from the center of London for passengers on their way to New York, South Africa, and Australia. Bruce Ismay was comfortable with Pirrie, who looked a little bit like his father but who was even-tempered, amusing, and tactful with him instead of a dreadful specter of authority. That night in the summer of 1907, dinner was intimate, just the four of them. Afterward, the men lingered in the library for cigars and, as Ismay had come to know from his time with Pirrie, straight talk. Pirrie was always working.

Even in summer, the damp London air welcomed a fire, which Pirrie himself kindled in a fireplace lined with soapstone and fronted with granite. Neither man was a drinker—a bit of champagne now and then—but that night, Pirrie produced a crystal decanter of cognac, which caught and scattered the gas light across his beaming, white-bearded face as he poured two glasses. Ismay wondered what could possibly be on the man's mind that seemed to make him so happy and in the mood to celebrate.

Joseph, Pirrie said after he settled into a creaking cowhide chair (Pirrie was the only person other than Ismay's mother who still used that name), I can build you ships a thousand feet long that will carry three thousand passengers, make twenty-four knots, and be as luxurious as a grand hotel. We'll fill them by making third class more comfortable than any other line. First and second class will be pure profit. Let Cunard burn coal with King Edward's money to break speed records. We will build floating palaces.

I've never doubted you, Ismay said, but you know we'd need two of them to make the service work—better even, three, to have one ship in reserve. And they would cost a fortune before we sold the first ticket. I don't think we have the money.

All you have to do, Joseph, is borrow on the ships you have, Pirrie said. You own them free and clear except for the IMM shares, and Morgan is desperate enough to go along. You'll have one of the ships four years from now, the second nine months later, and a third, if you decide that you want three, nine months after that. If you do it, you can leave Cunard, the Germans, and everybody else in your wake. If you don't do it, and they do, you will lose everything.

ANDREWS

Thomas Andrews knew Titanic *inside and out, her every turn
and art, the power and beauty of her, from keel to truck, knew her
down to her last rivet.*

—Shan Bullock, *A* Titanic *Hero*, 1912

It was not a case of liking Tommy. We all loved him.

—Saxon Payne, secretary to William Pirrie

William Pirrie trusted blood. He married his first
cousin, Margaret Carlisle, who became as essential
to his success as the iron and steel he put into his ships. Margaret had adored Willie since childhood. He was ten years older
than she, and during family summers in Antrim before he left
for the shipyard, she hovered near him, hoping he would muss
her hair. When it occurred to Pirrie that he needed a wife,
he knew she was the woman for the job. Margaret kept his
houses in Belfast and London, a gifted hostess for the stream
of his colleagues, customers, and friends.

At the shipyard, she roamed freely, a gentle counterpoint
to flinty Pirrie, devoting most of her attention to the families
of men with troubles, grievances, and pain. Men died build-

ing the ships at a clip of two or three a month, and they were injured almost as frequently as the tides changed in the Irish Sea. They fell from ships and scaffoldings, were hit by falling wood and steel, and were cut, crushed, and burned. Margaret talked her husband into buying a pair of motor ambulances to rush wounded men across the river Lagan to Victoria Hospital.

Margaret was acutely aware of her role in her husband's rise to the top of his profession. She made a point of letting Irish society know that she was delighted to be by his side. When Pirrie was made a viceroy in 1909, the new Lady Pirrie went to the celebration gala at Dublin Castle in a sea-blue linen gown embroidered with fish and ocean liners in White Star colors. She pinned a small White Star pennant in her powdered hair, and wore a silver comb depicting the bowsprit of a sailing ship, from which hung a veil of lace.

Pirrie's managing director at Harland's was Margaret's brother—and his own cousin—Alexander Montgomery Carlisle, a gold-watch apprentice who hadn't missed a minute of work during his first five years at the shipyard. Carlisle had a long, dour face, but he was a genial man whose passion, apart from building ships, was collecting autographs. He was known for stinginess and an instinct for bringing just the right amount of matériel and manpower to every stage of shipbuilding. Together, he and Pirrie had built more than a hundred ships, beginning with the sailing steamer *Britannic*, completed in 1874 for White Star. Pirrie never deluded himself that his brother-in-law liked him. He knew that his insistence on absolute authority over the shipyard grated on Carlisle, but he admired his brother-in-law's willingness to put the good of the company above his own emotions.

Pirrie's chief designer was his sister's son Thomas Andrews

who had gone to work at Harland's as a fifteen-year-old boy. Thomas loved ships so passionately that his family nickname was Admiral. The first ship he worked on as an apprentice, in 1889, was the 566-foot turbine steamer *Majestic*, designed by Carlisle for the White Star Line. Andrews could not imagine anything more wonderful than helping to build that incredible ship with the exterior lines of a rich man's yacht and the interior of a grand hotel.

Like all apprentices being groomed for management, Andrews made his way from shed to shed to learn plating, punching, riveting, rigging, cabinetry, painting, plumbing, electricity, casting, and engine building, the same way a conductor studied the strings, winds, brass, and percussion in his orchestra. What delighted Pirrie most during Andrews's apprenticeship was that his nephew spent most of his evenings after twelve-hour workdays taking classes in technical drawing, mechanics, engineering, and marine architecture.

If his rigorous routine ever exhausted him, Andrews never showed it. He wasn't playful, frivolous, or outgoing, but people liked him because he never lost his temper, a rarity in the rough-edged society of the shipyard, where barking and quick fists were the rule. As Pirrie told his wife soon after his nephew came to work at Harland's, Tommy Andrews was a good boy with a promising future. A year later, Pirrie knew for certain that the slightly built, earnest young man was a shipbuilder. Usually, a tradesman continued to wear the flat hat called a duncher for several years, but the day Andrews ended his apprenticeship, Pirrie handed him the black bowler of a boss.

———

On an ordinary morning as the summer of 1907 peaked and fell into September, Andrews arrived for work at dawn, as usual. The air had taken on a subtle chill, and the smoke of the banked riveting furnaces, forges, and kilns mingled with the carbon smell of cut, punched, and hammered steel. The mist over Belfast Lough was heavy and corrupted by the presence of industry, but Andrews was invigorated by the scents of the shipyard on such a morning. Just after the opening whistle, Pirrie summoned Andrews, Carlisle, and an assistant engineer named Edward Wilding to the drafting table he kept for himself in the drawing office.

Like everyone else who had ever set foot in the drawing office, Andrews loved the magnificent hall. Under a chalk-white, vaulted ceiling broken between its arches by enormous skylights, the drawing office contained ranks of ten-foot-long, waist-high tables where all Harland and Wolff ships began their lives. Everywhere a window was possible there was a window. The entire end of the room closest to the river was a wall of glass. Beyond it, and slightly to the right, were the dark, hulking shapes of the half-finished 650-foot *Rotterdam IV*, still in frames. Next to it were the remains of the scaffolding of the recently launched, 455-foot oil tanker *Iroquois*. To the west of the drawing office, the clerestory windows overlooked a courtyard the men called Market Square and the timekeeper's gate, through which every man passed at the beginning and end of his shift. In Market Square, too, casual laborers gathered at dawn, ready to slip a boss a matchbox containing a shilling or two for the privilege of a day's work. To the east, toward the lough and the Irish Sea, the view was interrupted by an identical wing off the main building that was the home of the company accountants.

Pirrie pulled a roll of drafting paper from a leather case, smoothed the sheets on the burnished wood of the table, and weighted their corners with shot bags. One glance told Andrews he would remember the moment for the rest of his life. Pirrie had been a gifted draftsman and designer when he'd worked in the drawing office, and the confidence in his freehand drawings had never left him. The hull shape was a variation on the tried-and-true iron sailing ship with a flat bottom, external rudder under an overhanging stern, and a nearly plumb bow, the same cross section as *Oceanic*'s and *Rotterdam*'s.

Andrews studied the dimensions that Pirrie had noted under the profile of the ship: 850 feet long by 92 feet wide by 65 feet deep. Ismay wants two of them, Pirrie said. They would be bigger, but he hadn't been able to talk the harbor commission into building a dry dock in Belfast to handle more than 900 feet. The commission had dragged its feet about doing even that until Pirrie told them he would go to the Clyde or Liverpool to build his big ships if they didn't give him a dry dock to finish them out and repair them. Ismay was tacking two hundred feet onto his piers in Southampton. Morgan convinced New York to add a hundred feet to theirs.

Andrews calculated the implications of what he was looking at. Each ship would displace over 55,000 tons. The hull and machinery, without cargo, coal, and passengers, would weigh 40,000 tons—80 million pounds. Half again bigger than anything else afloat. Bigger, in fact, than any man-made object that had ever moved. A few months earlier, the *Ulster Echo* had quoted Pirrie as saying that his dream was to build ships 1,000 feet long. Andrews hadn't suspected that he would take so big a step so soon.

Pirrie's fluently sketched details of the accommodations were as audacious as the dimensions of the ships. They showed a first-class dining room, its ceiling rising through three decks, capped by a stupendous glass dome; a Turkish bath;

a swimming pool; a gymnasium; a squash court; first-class staterooms bigger than London hotel suites; and second-class staterooms the equal of first-class accommodations on any other liner. In steerage, there were private family cabins and men's and women's dormitories in place of the open decks of beds and hammocks that were common on long-haul steamers. The crew's quarters up forward were also a far cry above the traditional hellholes endured by seamen on British ships for centuries. These ships would be floating palaces carrying 600 passengers in first class, 716 in second class, and an incredible 1,788 in third class, with a crew of 860.

Pirrie, whose fascination with propulsion had known no bounds since his apprenticeship in the engine works, then unrolled his preliminary plans for driving these three-screw behemoths across the ocean. Two triple-expansion steam engines—bigger than any that had ever been built—would power a pair of thirty-foot-diameter, counterrotating propellers on the port and starboard sides. The world's most powerful low-pressure steam turbine, mounted slightly aft of the main engines, would drive a fifteen-foot propeller on the centerline.

Andrews asked Pirrie why, if the ships had only three engines, would they have four funnels, as shown in the profile sketch. The first three will be engine exhaust, Pirrie said. The fourth will be a dummy except for a ventilation fan. Ismay thinks ships with only three funnels might be seen by passengers as somehow less grand than Cunard's new liners, which have four engines and four funnels.

He wants these ships to post decent speeds, Pirrie continued. But they don't have to be record breakers. Twenty-three or 24 knots is enough. Ismay wants to let Cunard, the Germans, and the rest of them fight it out for the Blue Riband for the fastest crossing times between Southampton and New York. White Star will carry more people in more comfort in all three classes than any other line.

Ismay will be here with his pen and his checkbook next summer to look at the plans, Pirrie said. Then we'll have less than three years to put the first one in the river.

Andrews had never seen Pirrie look happier in his life.

———

Before Pirrie left Belfast for London, Carlisle dashed his brother-in-law's good mood. My health is terrible, Carlisle told him. I'm only fifty-three years old but I can't seem to shake the pleurisy. Every day in the yard seems longer and longer to me. It's time I retired to my autograph books, my garden, and my bicycle. I can give you another year, maybe two, but I won't see these new White Star ships in the water.

Pirrie was furious that his managing director would abandon him after he had gotten an order that could make or break the company. There was no question in Pirrie's mind that Andrews would succeed Carlisle, no question that Andrews could do the job. Or was there? His nephew had helped design *Oceanic* and dozens of other ships, but he had never seen one through from keel to delivery as the number one. And he had such a mild disposition. Could he manage fourteen thousand men? Could he handle the engineering? The supply and logistics? What if the pressure broke him? The last thing Pirrie needed just then was even a shred of doubt.

Pirrie went back to London, where he immersed himself in the even more uncertain world of industrial politics and intrigue. Cunard was coming hard at White Star, but there was nothing he could do about that except wait for the new ships to challenge them. The rest of Ismay's fleet was keeping White Star and International Mercantile Marine in business. Just barely. There was no doubt that on the profitable Southampton–to–New York express route, Cunard had the upper hand.

Pirrie was also worried because shipbuilding in general was tailing off into yet another of its cyclical depressions. Just as his men in Belfast were putting pencil to paper for the new ships, Harland and Wolff got hit with a rash of cancellations. Hamburg-America killed its order for *Europa*, sister to the giant *Rotterdam*, two weeks before its keel was to be laid. One of Pirrie's International Mercantile Marine customers, the Red Star Line, scrubbed a ship. And even White Star was forced to back out of an order for a new ship for its Australian route.

In Belfast, Andrews prepared to run the first leg of the race to build the gigantic sisters. By midsummer 1908—less than a year away—he had to present the single set of plans for two identical ships to White Star. Until Ismay approved them down to the last detail, he could not order the millions of pounds of steel and castings needed to build the ships. A single misstep—a late steel shipment, an engineering mistake, a workers' strike, a fire, or any of a dozen other catastrophes—meant that Andrews would not meet his deadline of the summer of 1911 for delivering the first ship, and the spring of 1912 for delivering the second.

Andrews was thrilled to be building ocean liners that would stun the world because it was exactly what he was meant to do. By the time he had apprenticed, he'd understood Archimedes' law, which states that a body immersed in a fluid will experience an upward force equal to the weight of the fluid the body displaces. A ship floated only if it displaced an amount of water equal to or greater than its own weight.

That explained why a steel ship with an enormous volume of air inside floated and a solid steel bar sank. It also explained why, if the hull of a ship were breached, the water flooding into its interior would reduce the amount of water the ship was displacing and it would sink. For Andrews, learning why a ship floated and why a ship sank was like being admitted to a society of sorcerers.

Andrews knew that his responsibility as a marine architect was to make decisions that would strike a balance between a ship that would be built too heavy and a ship that would be built too light. Working from Pirrie's sketches, he began making those decisions, with Edward Wilding helping him calculate the dimensions of the steel for the keel, frames, rivets, and plating.

The keel of a ship is its spine, as crucial to its existence as the cord of bone and nerves that defines a human being. When a ship fractured its keel, it was said to have broken its back. Andrews fabricated this vital beam from solid steel bars 3 inches thick, wide, and deep in lengths of 50 feet. The keel bars would be milled to overlap, and joined by 6-foot-long rivet plates to form a solid piece running 850 feet along the bottom of each ship from bow to stern. The keel bar would form the base of a hollow box 5 feet, 3 inches deep with walls 1½ inches thick. From the top and bottom of that box, steel bars would extend to the port and starboard sides, tied together by eight more solid steel beams running bow to stern. That framework would be covered by steel 1¼ inches thick to form double bottoms for the ship. The massive assembly of the keel box and double bottoms would be pinned together by half a million iron rivets, driven by hydraulic pincers that generated far more force than the men with hammers who would fasten most of the steel in the ship. At a little over a pound each, the rivets in the keel box and double bottom alone would weigh 540,000 pounds.

Andrews then drew the ribs. They would be steel frames rising from the double bottom to crossbeams and plating 60 feet above, tying the port and starboard sides of the ship together at the top. More crossbeams at each of the decks of the hull also tied the frames together, forming a lattice of strength that Andrews reinforced with gussets and brackets at every angle. For most of these frames, Andrews specified 1¼-inch steel placed three feet apart. For some frames in the bow and stern of the ships where the loads would be the greatest, he specified 1½-inch steel. Where the hull curved to the bow and stern, the ribs would be two feet apart instead of three.

To further strengthen the ship's skeleton they would have fifteen steel walls, called bulkheads, dividing the ship's bottom into sixteen watertight compartments. Andrews had to decide how high to make the bulkheads. Watertight bulkheads had been in use for over fifty years. In 1862, the revolutionary iron sailing steamer *Great Eastern* had proved their worth when it sideswiped a rock off the coast of Long Island, opening a gash in its side 83 feet long and 9 feet wide. *Great Eastern* was 692 feet long, five times heavier than any ship that had ever been built, and it could carry 4,000 passengers and 418 crew around the world without refueling. It survived the collision with the rock because it had a double hull from its keel to its waterline, and fifteen watertight bulkheads running up to an iron deck that completely sealed those compartments.

Andrews studied *Great Eastern* and saw that the trade-off for dividing a ship into completely watertight compartments was an inconvenience for passengers moving between those compartments. He compromised by designing the new White Star liners with bulkheads that ran only part of the way to the top deck, allowing much freer passage through the ships. The bulkheads would rise to the fourth deck, 11 feet above the waterline and 45 feet above the keel. Two of the watertight bulkheads in the bow would extend higher, to the fifth deck. The doors in the bulkheads would be controlled either by automatic floating switches or by command from the bridge. Andrews calculated that the ships would stay afloat with as many as four of the watertight compartments flooded.

The skin of a ship had to bind the keel, frames, and beams together to form a single gigantic girder strong enough to resist the force of the worst possible sea conditions. Because the White Star behemoths were so long, Andrews knew that the hull girder would have to be strong enough to span the crests of two or more waves, flex in the middle, flex at the ends, and twist in several directions at the same time—but not break. Smaller ships could ride a single big wave into its trough and then continue up the next wave to its crest, but not these giants.

The British Board of Trade published lists of minimum specifications for building ships. An owner who accepted delivery of a ship that did not meet those standards would never get it insured, so architects submitted their plans to the board for approval as they went along. When Andrews drew up his tables of steel plates and iron rivets, he went beyond the board's standards to err on the side of strength. Nobody—not even the Board of Trade—knew how 80 million pounds of steel would behave at sea. He increased the required 1-inch thickness for the hull plating to 1¼ inches, and increased the diameter of most of the rivets from the required ⅞ inch to 1 inch. The penalty for adding the weight of that extra steel and iron was 4 million pounds, plus the cost of the coal to move it through the water.

To reduce side-to-side rolling and further strengthen his extraordinarily long ships, Andrews also decided to spend precious weight on a pair of beams known as bilge keels. These 1½-inch-thick, 2-foot-wide, 300-foot-long steel plates would be riveted to the outside of the middle of the hull where the side of the ship turned into the bottom. Each bilge keel began 300 feet from the bow, ended 282 feet from the stern, and added more than 400 tons to each ship.

For the top three decks above the main hull—the superstructure—Andrews wanted to use thinner steel—½-inch in some places, ¾-inch in others—to save weight and keep the ships' center of gravity lower. The problem was that the thicker steel of the main hull would withstand the flexing of the ship at sea, but the thinner steel of the superstructure would not.

Andrews came up with an ingenious solution that had been tried but not perfected, simply because no one had ever built a moving steel object so big. Instead of building the top three decks as a single piece of riveted steel, subject to the same flexing forces as the thicker main hull, he would build the superstructure in three sections. These sections would be riveted solidly to the top of the highest deck, but they would be separated from each other by gaps that would vary, as the ship flexed, from as little as 2 inches to as much as 6 inches. Andrews designed the joints to extend into the main hull, where they would end in a V-shaped notch. The gaps in the superstructure would be covered with brass plates and leather sheaths to keep out the weather but allow the joints to move. Carlisle, Wilding, and Pirrie agreed with Andrews that the two expansion joints would not weaken the ship. Above all, they would save weight.

While Andrews and Wilding concentrated on the hull and

the superstructure, Carlisle designed the accommodations and deck gear, including the lifeboats and the davits to lower them into the sea. He, too, used the Board of Trade specification books. Any ship over 10,000 tons sailing under the British flag, they said, had to carry sixteen lifeboats under davits that could launch them quickly. Carlisle also found out that the board had realized that the size of ocean liners had outgrown that twenty-year-old rule, and would probably change it in the near future.

It would be better, Carlisle thought, to specify davits that could handle more than one lifeboat so that White Star wouldn't face expensive refitting when the Board of Trade increased the number of lifeboats required for larger ships. Welin Quadrant, with whom he had done business in the past, had just figured out a system of davits that could be rotated 360 degrees to pick up lifeboats stowed both beneath them and behind them on the deck. Carlisle included the Welin davits in his plans, with 16 lifeboats ready under them and either 16 or 32 more lifeboats stacked on the deck, depending on how many White Star wanted to carry. Bruce Ismay would make the final decisions about spending weight and money that exceeded the specifications of the Board of Trade.

A year later, on July 29, 1908, Pirrie led a White Star entourage on a tour of Harland and Wolff as a prelude to reviewing the plans for the ships upon which they were betting their company. He wanted Ismay to see how radically he had transformed his shipyard to accommodate the White Star order so there could be no doubt that he was committed to building them. The shipping business was still in the doldrums, and

Pirrie knew that a ship owner—even one in whose company Harland and Wolff had a huge stake—might get cold feet about making so enormous a leap into an uncertain future.

Pirrie and Ismay strolled side by side, with Margaret Pirrie on her husband's arm, followed closely by Andrews, Carlisle, and Wilding. Then came an apprentice carrying Pirrie's suit coat on the warm summer day, a service that was a coveted honor among the boys of the shipyard. Pirrie handpicked his coat boy by merit and paid him a £1 bonus, an enormous windfall for a man whose daily wage was a quarter of that. Behind the apprentice, a dozen naval architects from both companies walked in a cluster that shifted its shape as the men jockeyed for position close enough to their bosses to hear what they were saying.

From the back of the drawing office, Pirrie led his procession between the two 900-foot-long slipways where the ships would be built side by side. The concrete foundations of the slipways were four and a half feet thick to support the hulls and the overhead gantry cranes, which were nearly finished. The gantries themselves weighed over 6,000 tons, the largest of their kind in the world. Four scaffoldings rose 75 feet high along the full length of each ship. Tracks ran on the tops of each pair of scaffoldings on which sliding hoists were spaced that could cover every inch of the ships below to lift the frames, plates, and beams to their places.

Pirrie had ordered work on the gantries halted so his voice could be heard. Hundreds of men, many of them just hired for the enormous new project, perched silently in the scaffolding as the inspection party passed below. It took the bosses fifteen minutes to walk leisurely from the top of the slipway, where the bows would be, to the bottom, just a few feet from the river. At the water's edge, Pirrie pointed out another stupendous piece of equipment he had bought specifically for outfitting the big liners: a floating crane that could lift 250 tons. With a crane stationed onshore, workers had to move the ship every time they wanted to lift a boiler, engine casting, or anything else to a new location on the ship; with the floater, they would simply move the crane with a steam tug instead of moving the ship.

Bosses in the shipyard wore black bowlers and were known to the men who worked under them as "hats," a term that usually carried a hint of scorn. As Pirrie steered his entourage back up the sloping concrete ramp of the slipway, Andrews looked up into the scaffoldings around him, smiled broadly, and made the unheard-of gesture of tipping his bowler to the workmen above. First one, then a few, then many, then all of the men hanging in the gantry clapped and banged on the steel frames as the bosses walked below. Pirrie and Ismay glanced up briefly, waved, and continued their conversation. The others, led by Andrews, returned the salute with their hands clasped over their heads and cheers of their own.

For two days, Ismay and his men, along with Pirrie, Andrews, Carlisle, and Wilding, huddled around a cluster of tables in the drawing office as the White Star architects examined the drawings and specifications for the new ships. Two inspectors from the Board of Trade looked over their shoulders to be sure the plans met the minimum specifications for the strength and stability of passenger ships. The inspectors would make hundreds of visits to the shipyard as the new White Star liners were built, checking every detail.

On the afternoon of the second day, Ismay told Pirrie that he liked what he had seen. He had only one major problem: weight. After the initial cost of building a ship, every owner wrote his biggest checks for the coal to fire the boilers, drive the engines, and move thousands of tons of steel, cargo, or passengers across the ocean. The discovery of oil in America fifty years before was promising, and the rush was on to find more. But for the time being, shipping was still a slave to coal. Miners' strikes flared up with alarming regularity, and the cost of coal could double overnight. White Star's gigantic ships would burn 650 tons of coal per day with a full load of passengers and cargo.

Ismay asked Andrews if the ships would be strong enough with the 1-inch plating and ⅞-inch rivets approved by the Board of Trade instead of the thicker plating and rivets in Andrews's specification tables. It would save about 2,500 tons of dead weight, which meant 25 tons of coal every day, year after year.

Andrews hesitated. How could Ismay ask such a question? He had spent months calculating loads, stresses, and the strength of steel and had recommended a thickness of 1¼ inches for the plating, and 1-inch rivets. Andrews knew that if an owner wanted his ship made out of papier-mâché and the Board of Trade approved the specifications, the owner would get a papier-mâché ship. Andrews had no choice but to agree.

Ismay told Pirrie to use the Board of Trade specifications for the steel and for the lifeboats, as well. Sixteen wooden boats under the davits and four collapsible boats with canvas sides would be enough to ferry passengers to a rescue ship. The ships should surely be able to stay afloat long enough for help to arrive on the heavily trafficked North Atlantic route. Why clutter the boat deck promenade with three dozen more boats than the law required?

Late on the afternoon of July 31, 1908, Ismay signed a

letter agreeing to pay three million pounds for the two ships, with the stipulation that Harland and Wolff could bill him for extras as the jobs progressed. Pirrie countersigned the letter. At that moment, the ships the two men had been dreaming about for two years became Harland and Wolff Hull Nos. 400 and 401.

A THOUSAND DAYS

Until Ismay signed the order letter on Friday, July 31, 1908, Hull Nos. 400 and 401 were paper ships. The following Monday the clock began ticking on the thousand days Andrews had to turn the first of them into steel. Pirrie made it clear to him that if 400 was not delivered in time for the beginning of the North Atlantic summer season in May 1911, they would face a defeat from Cunard from which they might not recover.

For a decade, Andrews had been buying steel from David Colville & Sons of the Clyde River valley in Scotland. Harland and Wolff orders accounted for half of Colville's production. Andrews had studied the evolution of iron and steel as diligently as a surgeon learned anatomy. Ancient fire pits with traces of slag revealed that people had been making iron on the Clyde River for a millennium. But steel—an alloy hardened by precisely reducing the amount of carbon and other impurities in raw iron—had been flowing from the furnaces in industrial quantities for only fifty years.

In 1855, Henry Bessemer had invented a way to make steel by blowing air through molten iron in an oval metal container lined with clay. He called it a converter. As the air passed through the molten iron, carbon molecules bonded with oxygen molecules to form carbon monoxide, which burned away at the top of the converter. Silicon, manganese, and other heavy impurities bonded with the oxygen to form slag, most of which settled to the bottom. The amount of air Bessemer blew through his converter regulated the amount of carbon and other impurities, so he could produce steel in varying grades of hardness and flexibility.

Andrews specified the same grade of steel for 400 and 401 that he had been using in big ships for fifteen years. This especially hard alloy was what he'd built *Teutonic* and *Majestic* with. The yard workers called it "battleship steel."

The steel for 400's keel arrived from Liverpool on a blustery day at the end of November. A gang of men under two bosses unloaded the bars and beams from the freighter with steam windlasses, guided them onto single-horse carts with flat, wooden beds, then clucked and whipped the horses back to the slipway over a log road laid over the muck. With direction from the bosses who consulted sheets of plans, they heaved the steel off the cart at approximately the place each would fit into the keel box and bottom, and went back for another load.

On December 16, 1908, Andrews and a half dozen men from the drawing office stood on the spot where the bow of Hull No. 400 would rise, watching a gang align a section of keel bar on the blocks running down the center of the slipway. A four-man rivet squad followed them. Riveters were the princes of the slipways. Piles of raw, rusting metal became ships because a four-man squad could drive 200 rivets per eight-hour shift. Unlike workers on salary or day wages, each rivet squad was paid for the number of rivets it drove, dividing the money according to its own rules.

Every rivet was a test. The heater boy had to bring it to exactly the right temperature. If it was too cold, the riveters could not seat it. If it was too hot, it would sag or crumble. The catch boy had to fit it into the hole quickly, or the rivet would cool. The lead riveter swung a four-pound sledgehammer to a precise cadence. A fourth man with a larger hammer hit the other end of the rivet. If the lead riveter hit the rivet too soon, it would fly from the hole like a red-hot bullet. Most pairs of hammer men who learned how to hit a rivet perfectly time after time stayed together as long as they worked in the same shipyard.

Andrews was glad to have started the work on the two giant sisters, but every day they were on the slipways meant more things that could go wrong. He had fifty bosses making sure the steel was where it was needed at the right time, and another fifty in the sheds keeping the cutting, punching, and fabrication of the plates, beams, and frames moving. So far, there had been no rumblings of a labor strike, but he was alert to the slightest ripple in the mood of his men.

———

Soon after the New Year in 1909, when Andrews was two months away from laying the keel for the second ship, he received a telegram from Bruce Ismay telling him RMS *Republic* had collided with SS *Florida* near Nantucket but was still afloat.

Republic was 570 feet long, had a gross weight of 15,000 tons, and could cruise at 15½ knots. It carried one of the first Marconi wireless stations, advertised in White Star brochures as a convenience to first-class passengers who might want to keep their families and businesses up-to-date on their voyage.

Andrews got the whole story in a dispatch from Pirrie's London office. On the morning of January 23, *Republic* was running at half speed in darkness and heavy fog through the main shipping lane south of Nantucket Island, sounding its foghorn and whistle. At five-thirty A.M., its captain heard an answering whistle close off his port bow. He rang full reverse to the engine room, signaled his emergency order with short blasts on his horn, and threw his helm hard over to port. Before his ship reacted to his commands, the bow of the Italian liner *Florida* slammed into *Republic* at a right angle amidships, tearing open its side from top to bottom. Three sleeping passengers aboard *Republic* and three crewmen in *Florida*'s bow died instantly.

The crash woke up *Republic*'s telegraph operator, Jack Binns. His cabin and the telegraph shack next door were a shambles. The roof was gone, the lights were off, and he could hear nothing over the shrieking steel as the ships disengaged and drifted apart in a swift current. Binns clawed his way to his station in the darkness, hooked up emergency batteries, and tapped out the new Marconi company distress call in Morse code: CQD. *CQ* meant "Calling all stations." *D* meant "Disaster." Binns added *Republic*'s position to his call for help.

The operator on duty at the Marconi station on nearby Nantucket Island picked up the CQD and relayed it to the U.S. Revenue Cutter Service, which sent out the patrol boats *Seneca*, from New York, and *Gresham*, from Boston. Three other ships, including the White Star liner *Baltic*, heard *Republic*'s CQD and sped to the scene of the collision.

Still in heavy fog, *Florida*'s captain nosed his ship back up to *Republic*. The much bigger White Star liner had a huge hole in its side and was obviously taking water. The sea was calm, so he tied up his ship on the other side, and in less than an hour 742 passengers and crew were safe aboard the heavily damaged but stable *Florida*.

Baltic arrived at noon the day after the collision, picked up the passengers from both *Florida* and *Republic*, and headed for New York. *Florida* made it to New York under its own power. Thirty-eight hours after the collision, *Republic* went down in 250 feet of water.

An hour after Andrews read the dispatch, every man in the shipyard knew about *Republic*. It was the biggest ship that had ever sunk.

The sinking of a Harland and Wolff ship was no cause for celebration, but Andrews was quietly pleased. The wireless telegraph—now installed on all White Star ships—had summoned help within minutes of the collision. The ship had been strong enough to last for a day and a half after such catastrophic damage to its hull. Even though mortally wounded, it had been its own lifeboat. Andrews had designed 400 and 401 using the same architectural strategies to ensure strength he'd put into *Republic*. They were going to be strong ships.

On March 31, 1909, as the frames of No. 400 were starting to look like the lines of a ship, Andrews laid the keel of No. 401. The riveting hammers rang around the clock. Andrews put the yard into the warm-weather routine of three eight-hour shifts, hoping to have 400 fully framed and 401 half framed by November, when the winter would slow him down again. Pirrie was having a good year with the order book, and Harland and Wolff had fourteen other ships in the yard. The workforce had swollen to fifteen thousand men.

It took a half hour to move a full shift through the Market Square time stile, tradesmen first, then apprentices, then day laborers. Since Edward Harland's time, the shipyard had kept track of hours and wages with a simple system. The time-keeper gave a new man two varnished chips of wood called "boards" (pronounced "birds"). Each was the size of a large matchbook. On the end of each board, the man's number was die-stamped into the wood.

At the beginning of his shift, a man shouted his number to the timekeeper, who handed him his board, which he kept with him through the workday. If he left his station, even to go to the toilet, he had to get a boss to chalk his initial on the board or risk being fired for moving around the yard without permission. When he returned to his station, the boss erased his mark. At the end of his shift, a man slipped his board into its numbered pigeonhole on his way past the timekeeper. The timekeeper, having logged the numbers of the boards taken by men on their way in to work, compared them with the boards the men pigeonholed on the way out and marked down their hours. The second board was held in reserve in case a man lost one, which cost him half a day's pay. A man kept the same number until he was fired, quit, got hurt too badly to work, or died.

Few men in the shipyard knew each other's real names. As soon as the boss or the other shipwrights in a new man's shed or work gang decided to speak to him, one of the first things they told him was his yard name. A man who stepped on a nail became Nail-in-the-Boot. A man with a raspy voice was Barking Dog. There were Big Harry, Wee Harry, Steelchest, Big Nose, Wing Ears, Dread-the-Winter, Bits and Pieces, Wash Rag, His Nibs, Iodine Willie, Broken Leg, Flat Hat, No Neck, Stumble, Hot Rivet, Cold Rivet, Horse Face, and No Talk. There were thousands of nicknames, and they could change as a man's exploits and failures marked him over and over again.

———

With eight thousand men working on the White Star sisters, Andrews met his November deadline for framing the first ship. They plated it in six months. As spring hinted at an early arrival, No. 400 was beginning to look like an ocean liner. And beside it, No. 401, fully framed and ready for plating, was also on schedule.

At some point—perhaps it was when the walls of steel ran unbroken the length of four city blocks from bow to stern; perhaps when dignitaries and reporters started coming to the shipyard to see the floating palaces rising against the Belfast skyline—Andrews noticed that the men were referring to the ships by name instead of hull number. He asked the carpenters to build signs the size of barn doors, and had them hung on the scaffolding at the bows.

White Star
Royal Mail Steamer
"OLYMPIC"

White Star
Royal Mail Steamer
"TITANIC"

Andrews began plating *Titanic* on April 6, 1910, but the steel had been arriving from the Clyde for weeks. The platers' shed was an around-the-clock hive. Many of the men who worked in it were deaf, some because they had lived with the cacophony of the steel punches for too many years, some because they had been born deaf and had found the perfect place to work. Deaf men came from all over Ireland to work in the platers' sheds at Harland's, living as a colony with their families in a neighborhood of East Belfast.

The platers' shed covered an acre on the west side of the yard and had its own dock along the river. With a forty-foot-high trussed ceiling, it was lit by skylights in the daytime and electric bulbs at night. The noise never stopped. The men used hand signals to communicate, but no shout of alarm was loud enough if a plate or beam got loose on the end of a hoist chain. Of the hundreds of injuries and deaths in the shipyard each year, most came while manhandling steel.

At the end of April 1910, when the first three tiers of plates shaped *Titanic*'s bow, Comet Halley appeared in the night sky over Belfast. Comet hysteria was rampant, since another of the visitors from space, known as the Great Daylight Comet, had put in a sensational appearance in January that same year. The difference with Halley's, the newspapers reported, was that the earth was going to pass through its tail, which they said was made of poisonous cyanide gas. The end of the world was a possibility. At the shipyard, a rumor circulated among the men that somehow the two gigantic ships they were building had something to do with throwing the universe off-kilter, triggering divine retribution.

Andrews did not believe that the world would end. He was not ordinarily a superstitious man, but he felt the comet was a good omen, a fitting cosmic tribute to the ships that were coming along so well.

On an evening in May, Andrews brought his wife, Helen, to the shipyard to enjoy the view of his masterpieces-in-progress with Comet Halley overhead. *Olympic* and *Titanic* had been stealing time from their life together since their courtship, which had begun just after Pirrie announced the White Star order in the drawing office during the summer of 1907.

The couple had married on June 24, 1908, a month before Ismay came to Belfast to approve the plans.

Two years later, Helen was carrying their first child as she stood arm in arm with her husband, watching an uncountable number of men swarm over *Olympic* and *Titanic*. A breeze off Belfast Lough carried the double strikes of the riveting hammers, which sounded like hundreds of badly tuned church bells. The shipyard smelled like coal fires, sulfur, horse manure, and the salt of the nearby sea. Helen had never been so close to her husband's giant ships. They were as otherworldly to her as the diamond-bright comet in the sky.

———

Carlisle retired during the summer of Comet Halley, leaving Andrews to finish the ships on his own. He hit two marks perfectly when he finished plating *Titanic* on October 19, 1910, and, the next day, launched *Olympic* into the river Lagan.

Even the launching of *Oceanic* in 1899—hailed as the most extravagant launching in the history of Harland and Wolff—could not compare with the party Pirrie threw for *Olympic*. An unusually warm autumn was fending off the arrival of winter, and the launch day dawned bright and sunny. A brisk north wind off the lough, which could have been a problem for a gigantic, powerless ship adrift on the river, died down shortly after the sun came up.

Pirrie arrived early, dressed in his customary launch-day tweed suit, topped off with his lucky yachting cap, and squired Lady Pirrie around to greet their guests. A special train from Dublin pulled into the Great Northern Railway terminal, and its passengers joined a steady stream of cars and horse carriages flowing to the shipyard. The turbine steamer *Duke of Cumberland* arrived, bringing Bruce and Florence Ismay, the

White Star executives, their wives, and a hundred English and American reporters. J. P. Morgan was ill, and sent his regrets. Every other member of the board of International Mercantile Marine was in Belfast to celebrate the launching of the ship that might put the combine on its feet for the first time.

Pirrie assembled his personal guests in Market Square just after ten o'clock and led them around his shipyard on special planked walkways. The two hundred lords, ladies, and dignitaries walked two abreast through the platers' shed, past the slipways, and through the machine shop, mast shed, and molding loft. At the end of the tour, near the river at the stern of the ship, Pirrie seated them in a grandstand draped with crimson-and-white banners.

Pirrie had also had grandstands built for Harland and Wolff department heads, their friends, and other invited guests. He sold tickets to all comers for seats in a third set of stands farther away from the ship, against the platers' shed, raising £456, which he donated to his wife's ambulance corps. By midmorning, thousands of people who could not get into the shipyard lined the banks on the Belfast side of the river, hoping to catch a glimpse of the leviathan splashing into the water.

The hulls of White Star ships had been dark gray for fifty years. Pirrie and Ismay thought white would look better in photographs, so they'd had Andrews paint *Olympic* white for the launching. Next to *Titanic*'s unpainted, sooty-black plates, *Olympic* gleamed in the sunlight. The white paint made the ship look even bigger than it was, and the deep red bottom paint gave it a finished appearance, though months of work in the shipyard lay ahead before its maiden voyage.

At ten-fifty, two rockets hissed into the sky and blossomed red over the river to warn ships and boats to steer clear of the

launchway. At eleven o'clock, a third rocket exploded to signal that the launch was imminent. In the crimson-and-white
grandstand, Pirrie shouted, "Now!"

Olympic moved. By the time its entire length was in the
water sixty-two seconds later, the ship was going 12 ½ knots.
In another forty seconds, six anchors connected to the ship
by eight-inch wire hawsers stopped it dead in the water. The
sounds of applause, horns, bells, and the shipyard whistles
went on for five minutes, as five tugboats that looked like toys
beside the giant ship nudged *Olympic* upriver to the outfitting
wharf.

Andrews had just seven months to finish *Olympic,* so his
men returned to work before the crowds had left the shipyard
for an afternoon of celebration in Belfast. Bosses and men tied
up the ship, swung two triple-width gangways into place, and
moved the 250-ton floating crane into position. The next day,
the full force that would swell to four thousand men began
installing *Olympic*'s engines, boilers, and passenger accommodations to transform the bare hull into a warm, safe ship.

———

Seven months and nine days later, *Olympic* was ready for sea
trials. Pirrie had spent most of his time in Belfast during the
last two months of fitting out, and could not have been happier with the way his nephew had handled the job. On April
1—right on time—Andrews dry-docked the ship to put on
its propellers. A gang of two thousand men gave it a fresh
coat of paint, this time black for the hull, with a white superstructure and yellow trim. On May 2, engineers lit the boilers
and started the engines, which ran perfectly for twenty-four
hours. Later that week, Pirrie brought the ship to the dock
and opened it to the public at a cost of five shillings apiece.

More than ten thousand people trooped through the floating palace. Again, the money went to Lady Pirrie's ambulances.

On May 27, a collier delivered three thousand tons of coal, enough for *Olympic*'s two-day sea trials and the run to Liverpool and Southampton. The following morning, a crew of 250 officers, firemen, and able-bodied seamen under the command of White Star's senior captain, Edward John Smith, boarded the ship.

Andrews and Wilding set up shop aboard *Olympic* with two hundred Harland and Wolff designers, carpenters, and engineers, to check and record every detail about the performance of the ship. While Captain Smith ran at half speed on the first day of the sea trials, Andrews roamed around *Olympic* from bow to stern on every deck, feeling the life in the ship he had built. He lingered for the better part of the morning in the stupendous cavern of the engine room, hashing out his misgivings about so large an open space on so large a ship. He was happy to see that the catwalks around the boilers were the right height for the stokers and that the bunkers were convenient for the trimmers, who were in constant motion shuttling coal to the furnaces. He prowled the passageways, opened stateroom doors, and walked each deck, stopping every few paces to make notes in a fiber-bound journal. On the boat deck, he noted that the sixteen lifeboats slung beneath the davits left plenty of space for the first- and second-class promenades. In the wireless room, he sent telegrams to Pirrie and Ismay, telling them that *Olympic* was exceeding even his wildest expectations.

On the second day of sea trials, *Olympic* made a sweeping turn off the Irish coast to head back to Belfast. Andrews asked Captain Smith to bring the ship up to cruising speed and hold it there for at least an hour. Andrews stepped out of the wheelhouse onto the bridge wing to enjoy the wind in his face. He felt the ship shudder as it picked up speed, a distinct shivering in the yellow pine deck beneath his feet that increased as Smith brought *Olympic* to its cruising speed of 24 knots for the first time.

Andrews looked over the railing at the froth of the bow wave in the light chop. His eyes swept down past the white superstructure to the dark sides of the hull. For a long minute, Andrews watched the steel that formed the starboard side of *Olympic* moving in and out. Not much. Maybe two inches, three inches. But it was definitely moving in and out. He turned, walked calmly through the wheelhouse, and continued out to the port rail. Andrews looked down. Same thing. Maybe it was just that he had never before looked at the sides of so big a ship. From the bridge to the stern was a distance of three city blocks. Each side of the hull was covered by an acre and a half of steel. Andrews knew that the whole ship was flexing. He had designed it to flex. But should the sides be panting?

Andrews took out his notebook and wrote: *Sides panting at cruising speed.*

NINE

TITANIC

The increase in the size of ships is not progress. If it were, el-ephantiasis, which causes a man's legs to become as large as tree trunks, would be a sort of progress, whereas it is nothing but a disease, and a very ugly disease at that.

—Joseph Conrad, 1911

O*lympic* finished its sea trials and would sail on time in May 1911. *Titanic* was ready for launching. International Mercantile Marine, however, was in a shambles. J. P. Morgan had become a symbol of everything that could go wrong when too much wealth was in the hands of too few men. The *New York Times* quoted a senator's description of Morgan as "a beefy, red-faced, thick-necked financial bully, drunk with wealth and power, who bawls his orders to stock markets, directors, courts, governments and nations." An editorial cartoon depicted Morgan devouring buildings, ships, and steel mills in one panel, and belching grotesquely in another.

Morgan took it all personally. He suffered from sleeplessness, depression, high blood pressure, rotting teeth, and the other infirmities of a man over seventy years old. His health was not improved by his reading accounts of his greatest blunder—International Mercantile Maritime—in the same newspapers that were celebrating Cunard's brilliant new ships. Morgan juggled cash, bonds, and loans to keep IMM afloat, but the combine was running deeply in the red.

While Morgan, Ismay, International Mercantile Marine, and White Star were enduring the worst of times, Harland and Wolff had never been stronger. Pirrie poured money into the shipyard, replacing the decrepit main office with a three-story brick building—including a new suite for himself—and completed improvements to the sheds and slipways. He fattened his order book by buying control of the Union-Castle Mail Steamship Company, with its forty-four ships. All repair work and new construction for Union-Castle would come to Harland and Wolff. With *Olympic*, *Titanic*, and a dozen other ships in the works, the Belfast yard was already running at capacity. To handle the overflow, Pirrie bought majority shares in two shipyards on the Clyde River. He also bought the White Star maintenance yard in Southampton and was negotiating with Ismay for his repair docks in Liverpool. Yet even as Pirrie was buying ships and shipyards, he started rumors that Harland and Wolff might be interested in selling out, to confuse his competition. He didn't want them to know that he was in the early stages of negotiations for the exclusive British license to build engines that ran on oil instead of coal.

Rudolf Diesel had invented the new engine a decade earlier, and it had been tested successfully on ships. Though supplies of oil were far from reliable, Pirrie intended to be ready. He was convinced that freeing ships from their dependence on coal would be as revolutionary a transformation as the switch from sails to steam.

After *Olympic*'s sea trials, Andrews left the ship at the deep-water dock and went to Pirrie's office. Margaret Pirrie had decorated the chairman's suite like a gentlemen's club, with leather armchairs and a mahogany conference table that Pirrie used as a desk. A fireplace, its mantel supported by four classic marble columns, was shuttered by a filigreed iron screen for the summer. Over it, light flooded into the room through a huge stained glass window of blue, green, and white panes depicting the eastern and western hemispheres above a steamship under way.

With a Board of Trade surveyor standing by to sign the seaworthiness certificates, and Ismay there to formally accept delivery, Andrews told Pirrie that he had seen the hull panting. Pirrie said all ships panted. Pirrie was accompanying the delivery party to Liverpool, so he'd get a firsthand look at the panting for the initial leg of the trip. He wasn't going on to New York, for reasons he didn't care to discuss.

Pirrie ordered Andrews to lead an inspection party to New York and back on *Olympic* and, when the time came, on *Titanic*. Watch the hulls, Pirrie said. Watch everything. If we have to, we can double up steel on the seams over the bottom. We can stiffen the superstructure. We can do the same to *Titanic*. These are big ships, but they are only ships.

Pirrie was not going to let a slight tremor in the ship's hull derail the spectacular party he had orchestrated for launching *Titanic* and sending *Olympic* off on its maiden voyage. The chartered steamer *Duke of Argyll* brought four hundred reporters, White Star executives, and guests, including, this time, J. P. Morgan. All morning, the crowd streamed into the shipyard. Dignitaries toured the yard, then sat in the crimson-

and-white grandstands. On the banks of the river, 150,000 people waited to watch *Titanic* move for the first time, and to wave as *Olympic* sailed for Liverpool, Southampton, and New York in the afternoon.

Olympic towered over Belfast. Against the pewter sky of the spring morning, the ship seemed to glow in its White Star livery of dark gray hull, bright white superstructure, and yellow piping. Its four yellow funnels, striped at the top with gray bands, rose higher into the sky than any other man-made structure in Ireland.

On the gangways, an endless stream of men loaded the ship. Inside, stewards made up the staterooms with linen and filled vases with flowers. Waiters set the tables for the meals they would serve to the company guests in the first-class dining room that evening on the way across the Irish Sea. Porters lugged crates of fresh fruit, vegetables, and meat to the larders. On the bridge, Captain Smith and his skeleton crew of officers and engineers met to plan for a four-thirty P.M. departure from Belfast. The full crew would board the next day in Liverpool.

Under the gantry where it had risen for the past year and a half, *Titanic* rested on wooden platforms coated with twenty-two tons of tallow to ease its passage into the water. At noon, the bosses blew their whistles. More than two hundred shipyard workers, who looked like ants beneath the gigantic hull, scurried to safety. The bosses counted their men and discovered that one of them was missing. After a frantic search, they found a laborer, James Dobbins, pinned beneath one of the wooden timbers that had been removed to free the ship.

Dobbins was the third man to die working on *Titanic*. The first had been a fifteen-year-old rivet catcher, Samuel Scott, who'd fallen from a ladder into the open hull of the ship;

the second, a nineteen-year-old heater boy, John Kelly, had dropped from scaffolding to the floor of the concrete slipway. Six men had died building *Olympic*. In the two and a half years since Andrews had laid the keel for the first of the sisters, two hundred injured men had been loaded into Lady Pirrie's ambulances for the trip to the hospital. Fewer than half of them had recovered fully enough to return to work.

After the ambulance carted Dobbins away, a barrage of red signal flares exploded in the air. The voices of 150,000 people faded, and the clatter of the waterfront fell silent as though all of Belfast had drawn a deep breath. Pirrie stood in the front row of the grandstand, waved his arm in a circle over his head, and shouted his launch command: "Now!"

Two of the bosses released the last of the restraining cables. The launch cradle broke free of the greased slipway, and *Titanic* creaked and groaned until a riot of horns, whistles, and cheering drowned out the sounds of the ship's battle with inertia. In seconds, it was sliding smoothly, picking up speed until it was afloat in the river and stopped dead by straining tugs and anchors. Alongside the glistening *Olympic* just upriver, the raw, unfinished *Titanic* looked like the tough cousin of a dandy.

Pirrie, Ismay, Morgan, their wives, and their titled guests had lunch in the Harland and Wolff dining room. They lifted their glasses to their new ships and then again, to toast Margaret Pirrie; her birthday, May 31, happened to coincide with launch day.

Reporters, company executives, and lesser dignitaries went to the Grand Central Hotel in Belfast to celebrate with a dance band, their own toasts, an extravagant meal, and champagne. They ended the afternoon by sending a telegram across the river to the shipyard, congratulating Lord and Lady Pirrie on the launching, *Olympic*'s impending departure, and Lady Pirrie's birthday.

Afterward, five hundred men and women in the White Star and Harland and Wolff parties boarded *Olympic* as the Belfast City Band played a selection of rags, waltzes, and marches. At four-fifteen, the band struck up "Rule, Britannia!" and the crew stowed the gangways, and longshoremen slipped the lines free of the dock. Tugs on the bow and the outboard side of the ship roared and belched smoke. Almost imperceptibly at first, and then as inexorably as a force of nature, *Olympic* moved toward the mouth of the river Lagan.

Many of the thousands of people who had lined the banks to watch the launching of *Titanic* had picnicked for the afternoon. They were stunned to silence as *Olympic* drew abreast of them, then recovered from their awe and began cheering and clapping. The ship took an eternity to pass by. As *Olympic* cleared the end of Queen's Island, its propellers began to turn faster, sending up a swirl of white water as though a submarine explosion had taken place under the stern. The tugs dropped their lines and joined the flotilla escorting *Olympic* into the Irish Sea in a noisy parade of horns and sirens. In ten minutes, the final notes of Belfast's appreciation for what its shipyard had done went silent. The escorts turned for home. *Olympic* was on its own.

———

Before *Olympic* had faded from view, the bunting was off the grandstands, bosses were barking instead of smiling, and two thousand men were crawling all over *Titanic* at the fitting-out dock. Without its engines and boilers, the ship rode high on its lines, half the red-painted bottom visible above the water. From across the river, an observer could easily measure the progress of fitting out. *Titanic* would sink deeper and deeper into the water until it sailed on its maiden voyage, scheduled for March 20, 1912.

The 250-ton floating crane was busy around the clock lowering machinery into the ship through openings that would eventually be covered by the four funnels. The engines were assembled onshore, tested, dismantled, and put back together on the ship. Rivet squads and carpenters roughed out the rabbit warren of passageways and staterooms on the accommodations decks, turning over sections of the ship to finishers and carpet layers.

Four months into fitting out *Titanic*, Thomas Andrews was savoring the predictable routines of building another on-time ship. With the good weather and a full order book, the Belfast yard was alive around the clock. Every few days, couriers from the Harland and Wolff yards in Scotland and England arrived with progress reports, which Andrews compiled for monthly meetings of the company directors.

Olympic was such a magnificent, profitable ship that Ismay was thinking about ordering a third, to make a trio of perfect sisters. After *Olympic* had completed its first crossing in 5 days, 16 hours, and 42 minutes at an average speed of 21.7 knots, with five boilers unlit, he cabled Pirrie from New York. He told Pirrie that he was thoroughly pleased with *Olympic* and offered his warm and sincere congratulations, signing the telegram, as always, "Yamsi."

Ismay followed up with a letter in which he pointed out a few problems. The mattresses were a bit too soft, accentuating the vibrations from the engines. The first-class reception room needed fifty additional cane chairs and ten tables because it was so popular. A potato peeler should be installed in the crew galley. The first-class bathrooms needed cigar holders. And the first-class suites on B Deck could be enlarged because there was plenty of space for private promenades.

It was the busiest time Andrews had ever known at Harland and Wolff, but he kept pace by working steady shifts from six A.M. to six P.M. On the afternoon of September 21, 1911, he was about to go home to his wife and infant daughter when the courier from Southampton arrived.

Just after noon the day before, the dispatch from Pirrie said, the 360-foot heavy cruiser HMS *Hawke* had slammed into *Olympic*, which was leaving Southampton harbor on its fifth voyage. *Hawke* was a twenty-year-old warship with five-inch-thick steel plating, armed with guns, torpedoes, and an underwater ram made of steel and concrete for sinking enemy ships.

Hawke's bow tore a massive triangular hole in *Olympic*'s flank, just above the starboard propeller where the hull tapered into the overhanging stern. The warship's ram punctured *Olympic* below the waterline. People onshore a mile away heard the collision.

Olympic was never in danger of sinking. The liner was under the control of a pilot when the collision occurred, a maritime custom that put an officer with explicit knowledge of local waters aboard an arriving or departing ship. Though E. J. Smith was *Olympic*'s captain, the pilot was making navigational decisions in the harbor. After the collision, Smith instantly took over and brought his ship into Osborne Bay, on the Isle of Wight. He unloaded the passengers onto tenders that took them back to the mainland, and inspected the damage. Two compartments were flooded, but the watertight doors had worked perfectly. On the next high tide, Smith took *Olympic* back to Southampton, where the Harland and Wolff repair yard went into emergency shifts to close the holes with steel plating below the waterline and wood above. As soon as possible, the courier told Andrews, *Olympic* would come back to Belfast for dry-docking.

The holing of the largest ship in the world was front-page news for weeks as an Admiralty court held an inquiry to assess blame for the collision. HMS *Hawke*'s captain, Commander William Blunt, claimed that the enormous suction of *Olympic*'s giant propellers had drawn his cruiser into the liner. Captain Smith said Blunt was showing off for *Olympic*'s passengers lining the rail as the ship left port and misjudged the clearance on the stern. The Admiralty sued White Star for damages to *Hawke*; White Star sued the Admiralty for damages to *Olympic*. White Star lost but took no action against Smith, who was the company's most senior captain, and the highest-paid sailor on the ocean. Ismay believed Smith more than he believed the Admiralty.

Ismay and Pirrie were annoyed by the interruption in service and the bad publicity surrounding the collision, but it gave them the opportunity to point out that *Olympic* was not only the biggest and most luxurious ship afloat but the strongest. While Captain Smith was ashore testifying at the inquiry, he also gave interviews to the press.

"My ship's frame took the shock well," he said. "There was no panic. Many passengers did not even know there had been a collision, so slight was the shock felt in the dining saloon. The watertight doors held the compartments sealed. Anyhow, *Olympic* is unsinkable, and *Titanic* will be the same when she is put in commission. Either vessel could be cut in halves and each section would remain afloat. I venture to add that even if the engines and boilers were to fall through their bottoms, the vessels would remain afloat."

Smith's conclusions about *Olympic*'s seaworthiness were

reassuring, but the collision left Andrews with an enormous problem. Only one dry dock on earth was big enough to take *Olympic*. At the moment, it was occupied by the ship's half-finished sister. *Titanic* had to come out of the dry dock, which meant it was going to be at least a month late.

———

Pirrie had skipped *Olympic*'s first crossing to New York, in May, because he had been plagued with a pain in his groin and a constant urge to urinate. He'd left the ship in Southampton. A week later, in London, a surgeon said it was only a matter of time before Pirrie was either going to keel over from the pain or agree to have his prostate gland removed. The gland was enlarged and getting bigger. He might have a cancer. He might not. No matter what, the problem wasn't going to disappear by itself.

To Pirrie, surgeons fell into the same hazy category as palm readers. He decided to wait and see what happened. The pain and urination problems were intermittent. As soon as they eased up, he went back to work and waited for the next round. There was simply no other choice, given the fabulous boom he was riding. He definitely didn't want to tell Ismay, Andrews, or anybody else except Margaret that he might have a cancer. When *Hawke* rammed *Olympic*, he was just getting over an agonizing bout with the ailment, but he was feeling pretty good.

Pirrie thought it would inspire confidence if he and Ismay rode their crippled ship from Southampton to Belfast. The wounded *Olympic* steamed back into the river Lagan on the morning of October 5. When the ship was dry-docked, Pirrie and Andrews were shocked at the extent of the gashes in its hull, but they could not banish their pride. The collision with HMS *Hawke* would cost White Star more than

£250,000 in repairs and lost revenue. *Titanic* was behind schedule. But *Olympic* had survived a blow that would have sunk most ships.

What the surveyors found farther forward on the ship a few days later was not such good news. Under the navigation bridge, right where Andrews had watched the hull panting during the sea trials, there were cracks in the steel. Not big cracks—small ones radiating from the windows and rivets. They didn't have much of a pattern except that they were in the front of the ship on both sides. The surveyors also found cracks on both sides of the ship where the plates of the main hull joined the plates of the bottom. The cracks weren't serious, but some steel was moving that shouldn't be moving. There was no time to do anything about the bow of *Olympic*, but Pirrie, Andrews, and Ismay decided to reinforce *Titanic* before sending it to sea.

Any misgivings Ismay had about the strength of *Olympic*'s hull did not prevent him from placing an order for the third ship on October 23. At a ceremony in Pirrie's office, work officially began on Harland and Wolff Hull No. 433 with signatures in the order book. Construction would begin the following month. Ismay said he would name the ship *Britannic*. The first White Star liner to bear that name had made more than three hundred voyages in twenty-nine years of service before retiring in 1903.

Olympic left the dry dock on November 14, 1911, a week before the riveters stitched together the first pieces of *Britannic* under the gantry crane. Andrews decided to keep working on *Titanic* at the outfitting wharf and bring it back into dry dock for propellers and bottom paint in early February. Moving the ship once instead of twice would save three or four days. White Star was still selling tickets for *Titanic*'s first voyage dated March 20, hoping that Harland and Wolff could make up the time lost due to the *Hawke* incident.

Work slowed predictably as December and January brought rain, snow, and dismally short days. The engines, the boilers, and the rest of the machinery were done. The four funnels were on the ship. The bulk of the work was inside now. In January, Andrews pulled riveters and platers from *Britannic* and put them to work enclosing the A Deck promenades on both sides of *Titanic*.

The enclosed promenade allowed for the addition of another café, but most importantly, it strengthened *Titanic* where *Olympic* was cracking. The added steel stiffened the front of the ship from just behind the bridge to the base of the second funnel. Andrews also reinforced the seams in the bow where the double plates of the bottom met the single plates of the main hull. If *Titanic* panted like *Olympic*, the extra steel would reduce the chances that cracks in the hull would develop at that point. He was building *Britannic* from the same set of plans he'd used for the first two ships, so he made notes in red pencil to add the steel in the superstructure and bow seams.

In late February, Andrews put *Titanic* in the dry dock to fit its propellers, give it a final coat of bottom paint, and trim the rudder. Just as the men finished timbering the hull, the bosses shouted at them to stop work and stand by for new orders. *Olympic* was coming back. They had to flood the dock and tow *Titanic* back into the river.

Andrews could hardly believe his bad luck. Two days out of New York, about 750 miles south of Newfoundland, *Olympic* had started shuddering violently; the ship had thrown a propeller blade. It took Smith a week to limp home on two engines.

Replacing a propeller blade was only a five-day job, but *Ti-*

tanic's March 15 delivery date and March 20 maiden voyage were lost. While *Olympic* was in the dry dock, a Board of Trade surveyor inspected the front of the ship. The results stunned Andrews. The fractures on the bridge deck had grown. And there were more loose rivets and plates on the seams above the double bottom.

Andrews wrote to Pirrie, telling him that he had added steel to *Titanic*. They had to do the same thing to *Olympic* as soon as possible.

TEN

MILLIONAIRE'S CAPTAIN

E.J. Smith arrived in Belfast to take command of *Titanic* for its sea trials and maiden voyage on the afternoon of March 31, 1912. The first crossings of the newest White Star liner would be Smith's last, after forty-three years at sea. Smith was more than ready for retirement. All he really wanted to do, he told a reporter in Southampton when he left *Olympic*, was put an oar on his shoulder, walk inland until somebody asked him what it was, and there spend the rest of his life. A sailor's best days at sea, he said, were his first and his last.

When Smith boarded, the ship was swarming with men on last-minute assignments to paint and polish it for departure the following morning at dawn. In his full-dress White Star uniform, he led a porter carrying his valise over the gangway into the first-class reception parlor, and up the staircase to the boat deck. Smith radiated command presence like a scent. Shipyard workers stopped what they were doing and tipped their hats or touched their foreheads as he passed. Some of them gawked. The white-bearded, barrel-chested captain looked enough like Lord Pirrie to give them pause.

Titanic's master's suite was slightly larger than the one he had aboard *Olympic*. It was the most luxurious officer's stateroom afloat, with a parlor the size of three ordinary cabins, a separate bedroom, and a private bath with a copper-plumbed ceramic tub. The rooms were furnished in oak, mahogany, and brass. Nosegays were set out to mask the aromas of fresh paint and carpet glue. Smith was more familiar with the smell of a new ship than any other White Star captain, because he had commanded all of the company's maiden voyages since *Baltic*'s in 1904.

Smith's spacious suite on *Titanic* was a long way from the cabin boy's hammock on a square rigger where he'd begun his life as a mariner when he was thirteen years old. The son of a potter, he'd given up a dull tradesmen's village near Newcastle for the hope of the sea in 1869. The routines of shipboard life soon became second nature to him. A week after his eighteenth birthday, Smith sat for his officer's papers. He sailed as a relief man out of Liverpool for six years, finally landing a permanent berth as fourth officer on White Star's *Celtic* in 1880. Thomas Ismay gave him command of the 565-foot *Majestic* in 1895.

Since then, Smith had developed a following among first-class passengers, some of whom would travel only on liners under his command. He was charming at dinner, inspired confidence during tours of his navigation bridge, and White Star's executives thought enough of him to trust him with their best ships. In 1901, when he brought *Majestic* into New York with a particularly brilliant passenger list of the rich and famous, a newspaper reporter dubbed him "the Millionaire's Captain."

When Southampton replaced Liverpool as the port of choice for transatlantic passenger service, Smith moved his wife, Sarah, and their daughter, Helen, into a twin-gabled, red-brick house a few blocks from the harbor. He went home for a night or two between voyages, tinkered with his collection of naval artifacts, and spent an hour each afternoon sequestered in his study smoking a cigar. Smith loved the aroma of the smoke and kept his door closed so as not to disturb the cloud that formed around his chair. At sea, he smoked with passengers in the salon after dinner.

During Smith's rise to the top of White Star officers' roster, he weathered the consequences of occasional poor judgment. Most recently, the Admiralty had blamed him for *Olympic*'s collision with HMS *Hawke*. Before that, *Olympic*'s rudder had nicked a tugboat in New York Harbor, tearing a hole in its deckhouse. Smith admitted no error, but White Star paid a $10,000 settlement to the tug's owner.

Smith also had a reputation for high-speed, flamboyant arrivals and departures in the tight confines of harbors. He grounded *Coptic* in Rio de Janeiro in 1891, ran *Republic* aground off Sandy Hook in 1899, and put *Adriatic* on a sandbar in Ambrose Channel, near New York, in 1909.

None of those incidents killed anybody or cost the company too much money, so Smith's upward progression within White Star never slowed. For a decade, he had been the subject of newspaper stories celebrating him as the highest-paid sailor in the world. After commanding *Adriatic*'s maiden voyage in 1907, he had given an impromptu speech to reporters on the pier.

"When anyone asks me how I can best describe my experiences in nearly forty years at sea, I merely say, uneventful," Smith told them. "Of course, there have been winter gales, and storms and fog and the like, but in all my experience I have never been in any accident of any sort worth speaking about. I never saw a wreck and have never been wrecked, nor was I ever in any predicament that threatened to end in disaster of any sort. You see, I am not very good material for a story. As for *Adriatic*, I cannot conceive of any vital disaster happening to this vessel. Modern shipbuilding has gone beyond that."

Once Smith took command of a ship, he had absolute authority to make every decision about when it moved or didn't. Everything about *Titanic*—from the conduct of a bedroom steward to navigation through dense fog off an uncertain coast—was his personal responsibility. He had lines of command that reached deep into the recesses of every department on the ship, and his subordinates made decisions about which he would never know. But they were all his decisions.

Smith's first order as master of *Titanic* was to cancel the sea trials scheduled for the next day, April 1. Before he turned in at midnight on March 31st, it was obvious that the wind howling off Belfast Lough was not going to die down anytime that morning. Smith knew the ship was behind schedule, but he was not going to challenge a gale to find out if *Titanic* was seaworthy.

His second bit of business as master was to cable White Star to request the immediate transfer of *Olympic*'s chief officer, Henry Wilde, to *Titanic*. Smith had every confidence in William Murdoch, who had been assigned by the company to be chief officer, but he wanted the only man who had ever served in that position on so large a ship. Smith didn't think he'd made any grave mistakes in the incidents with *Hawke* and the New York tugboat, but he knew there was more to handling a 900-foot-long ship than he completely understood.

When maneuvering in close quarters, he wanted Wilde as his second-in-command.

Ismay replied that Wilde would join *Titanic* in Southampton.

Olympic had performed so well that Pirrie, Ismay, and Andrews scheduled *Titanic* for only a single day of sea trials. On April 2, Belfast Lough was almost flat calm, with the sun on the eastern horizon beginning to banish the light fog that had settled between the headlands. At dawn, Smith gave the command to hoist the gangways and throw off the mooring lines.

Eight hours earlier, the firemen had ignited twenty of the twenty-nine boilers, so *Titanic* had a full head of steam. Smith walked to the wing of the bridge to be sure the tugs were in position to ease the ship away from the pier and keep it in the middle of the river. *Titanic* could not maneuver at slow speed without help from the tugs.

Smith ordered ahead slow on the port and starboard main engines, leaving the center turbine on standby. He stood squared up at the center wheelhouse window with his hands clasped behind his back and gave instructions over his shoulder. His voice was soft and calm, as if he were ordering a meal from a waiter.

Thomas Andrews stood off to the side of the bridge with Board of Trade surveyor Francis Carruthers and White Star's Harold Sanderson. Ismay would make *Titanic*'s maiden voyage, but he would not join the ship until Southampton. Sanderson was representing White Star to formally accept delivery of *Titanic* after the sea trials.

Even at that early hour, crowds had gathered on the riverbanks to send off Harland and Wolff's masterpiece. Against the chill of early spring, some of them had built fires, which sparkled in the last of the night like little salutes to the ship as it sailed into the Irish Sea.

Smith rounded Copeland Island, entering open water, and rang down all ahead half. For an hour, he zigged and zagged, settling on each new heading for several minutes, feeling the motion of the ship to determine if its props, rudder, and hull were enduring the pressures of turning. Like *Olympic*, *Titanic* took plenty of lead time to change course. After Smith threw the helm hard in either direction, at least thirty seconds passed before the bow began to tick through the points of the compass. Once into the turn, the ship was rock solid.

Smith slowed *Titanic* to a dead stop. He shut down the center engine and ran the port engine full ahead and the starboard engine full astern, pivoting the ship clockwise in a complete circle. He performed the same maneuver counterclockwise. Then he rang all ahead half. *Titanic* reached 12 knots running in a straight line. Smith held that for ten minutes. He felt nothing out of the ordinary.

For the first time, Smith rang all ahead full. Ten minutes later, *Titanic* was making 21 knots. The newly enclosed promenade and the extra steel in the bow seemed to have stiffened the ship. *Titanic*'s hull was panting, but well within normal limits.

That afternoon, Smith brought the ship up to 20 knots. Without warning, he rang down all astern full, sounding the emergency-stop alarm in the engine room. Instantly, the engineers vented steam, which shrieked out of vents at the tops of the funnels. The propellers stopped, then growled into full speed in reverse. *Titanic* came to a dead stop 850 yards after Smith had sounded the alarm.

Finally, Smith set *Titanic* on a south-southeast course and rang all ahead full. He ran for an hour toward the Isle of

Man, turned the ship in a wide circle at full cruising speed, and ran for an hour back toward Belfast. At 21 knots for two hours, the ship looked fine.

Andrews went to the Marconi wireless room and sent telegrams to Pirrie aboard his yacht, *Valiant,* and to Ismay in Southampton. *Titanic* was ready to go to work.

At sunset, *Titanic* was back at the dock in Belfast. In the sitting room of the master's suite, Board of Trade inspector Francis Carruthers signed the certificate of seaworthiness, effective for one year from April 2, 1912. Immediately afterward, Thomas Andrews and White Star vice president Harold Sanderson transferred ownership of *Titanic* from Harland and Wolff to the White Star Line.

Andrews went to his first-class stateroom on A Deck and wrote a note to his wife: "Just a line to let you know that we got away this morning in fine style and have had a very satisfactory trial. We are getting more ship-shape every hour, but there is still a great deal to be done." He sealed the note in an envelope embossed with the red-and-white pennant of the White Star Line and gave it to a steward for the last Belfast dispatch pouch. *Titanic* sailed for Southampton an hour later.

———

A new White Star ship always called first at Liverpool for ceremonial inspection by the people of its home port, but Ismay ordered Smith to take *Titanic* straight to Southampton. Coaling, provisioning, and loading would take five days. Easter Sunday, April 7, was a holiday. *Olympic* would sail westbound on April 3, and eastbound on April 11. *Titanic* had to leave Southampton on April 10, synchronized on opposite schedules with its sister to make the most of two-ship express service.

Smith told Ismay that he had a couple of problems that had to be ironed out or *Titanic* might not get out of Southampton at all. Chief Engineer Joseph Bell had just told him that the forward starboard coal bunker was on fire. Smith and Bell had dealt with bunker fires aboard steamships, which were not uncommon. Because wet coal is more combustible than dry coal, water would make the fire worse. The only way to extinguish it was to feed the smoldering coal into the furnaces. When the bunker was empty, the fire would be out. They would then repair the damage to the surrounding steel bulkheads. Smith ordered Bell to keep a gang of men spraying the bulkhead behind the fire twenty-four hours a day to prevent it from warping as much as possible.

The bunker fire didn't worry Smith enough to delay *Titanic*'s departure from Belfast. He had consulted Andrews, who'd told him there was no danger to the safety of the ship as long as they kept the bulkheads around the bunker wet. After the fire was out, Smith should make sure the scorched steel was scrubbed and painted before they reached New York. The American immigration inspectors had to certify the ship as safe for the return voyage, and a burned-out coal bunker wouldn't look good.

Smith's second problem was far more of a threat to delay his departure from Southampton. Ordinarily, coaling a ship was routine, but two months earlier, miners had walked off the job in Wales, Scotland, and England. The White Star storage bins at the harbor were empty. Smith needed 6,500 tons of coal when he got to Southampton or *Titanic* wasn't going anywhere.

Ismay said he was working on it.

At midnight on April 4, tugs eased *Titanic* alongside the White Star docks in Southampton. None of the officers or crew had gotten much sleep, but the ship had performed beautifully on the 570-mile run through a night and a day from Belfast. The Irish Sea remained calm. There was very little vibration or sense of movement. It was like being in a good hotel onshore.

Andrews wrote to Helen from Southampton. "I wired you this morning of our safe arrival after a very satisfactory trip," he told her. "The weather was good and everyone most pleasant. I think the ship will clean up all right before sailing on Wednesday."

On Friday, April 5, Smith left enough officers aboard *Titanic* for round-the-clock watches on the bridge and went home to his wife and daughter for a final few nights ashore. He ordered his ship dressed with all flags flying between its masts in honor of Good Friday, and turned *Titanic* over to the battalions of stevedores and stewards preparing the ship to receive passengers at first light on Wednesday morning.

Southampton is a perfect harbor. The city occupies a promontory formed by the confluence of two rivers, the Test and the Itchen, which empty into the English Channel. The first lucky sailors to find shelter there were Romans, two thousand years earlier, and Southampton has been an active port ever since. Shortly after Ismay and Pirrie had sketched out their dream ships in the summer of 1907, they persuaded the owners of the Southampton wharves to build a dock big enough to hold them. They'd finished in time for *Olympic*'s first voyage in the spring of 1911. The dock was a concrete parallelogram, with one end open to the river and 1,700-foot-long piers on either side, each of which could hold two of the new giants at the same time.

At the head of the dock, White Star had built new warehouses and chandleries for provisioning its ships. Except for the few supplies for feeding crew and workers on the trip from Belfast, *Titanic*'s larders and pantries were empty when it arrived. Gangs of day laborers and stevedores worked around the clock to load one hundred tons of provisions, everything needed to serve three meals a day to 2,200 people on the five-day voyage to New York. The first of the stewards and stewardesses went aboard to make up the passenger staterooms, taking delivery of fifteen thousand sheets, twenty-five thousand towels, and seventy-five hundred blankets.

On the afternoon of Friday, April 5, Ismay told Smith that he had solved the coal problem. He'd canceled the voyages of White Star's *Adriatic* and *Oceanic*, and of the IMM liners *New York*, *Philadelphia*, and *St. Louis*. *Titanic* would get 4,425 tons of coal from those five ships. Added to the 1,400 tons he already had left over from sea trials and the run from Belfast, it would be enough.

With the promise of enough coal for his voyage, Smith gave permission to load *Titanic*'s six cargo holds. Freighters and slower ships handled bulk shipments of ore, grain, dry goods, and the other staples of ocean commerce. The fast liners hauled the more exotic, urgent, refrigerated, and perishable cargo, for which their owners charged double or triple the price for express service.

On its first trip across the North Atlantic, *Titanic* would carry twelve cases of ostrich plumes, three hundred cases of shelled walnuts, twenty-five cases of sardines, four cases of straw hats, three cases of tennis balls, two barrels of mercury, a new Renault automobile, fifteen cases of rabbit hair, one case of Edison gramophones, three cases of hairnets, two cases of shoes, and seventy-six cases of dragon's blood (the sap from a palm tree found in the Canary Islands that was used to color varnish and women's makeup). The cargo manifest listed cases of anchovies, mussels, liquor, wine, linoleum, raw leather, hats, books, soap, cameras, canvas, cheese, hosiery, speedometers, straw hats, candles, rubber, olive oil, lace collars, boots, brushes, sponges, flowers, magazines, cheese, velvet, linen, tea, stationery, silk, pens, butter, potatoes, and seven million pieces of mail.

Titanic had the most powerful Marconi wireless afloat. The sinking of RMS *Republic* had transformed shipboard radio telegraph from a novel convenience for wealthy passengers to an essential part of the safety equipment of a transoceanic ship. Jack Binns, who had stayed at *Republic*'s telegraph key until help arrived, had become a national hero. He'd left the sea and taken a job as a reporter for the *New York American*. Marconi had won a Nobel Prize. *Titanic*'s wireless had a range of 350 miles, depending on atmospheric conditions. On the heavily traveled North Atlantic route, a half dozen or more ships and shore stations should be within range if it sent out a distress call.

Jack Phillips, *Titanic*'s senior wireless officer, was a twenty-five-year-old Englishman who had never wanted to be anything but a telegrapher. As a schoolboy in Surrey, he'd read about Guglielmo Marconi's experiments with invisible waves that traveled through the air carrying messages; he'd later taken a job at the post office to learn telegraphy. Marconi had hired him in 1906, assigning him to White Star's *Teutonic*.

The junior wireless officer, Harold Bride, was twenty-two. Like Phillips, he had been enchanted by the combination of science that bordered on magic and the chance to go to sea. He had idolized Jack Binns and had signed on with Marconi as soon as he'd finished school. Bride had a knack for sending Samuel Morse's code of dots and dashes, with a fast, accurate hand on the telegraph key. On his first assignment in 1911 aboard the IMM liner *Haverford*, Bride had become a rising star because of what other telegraphers called his "fist." The following year, he'd been assigned to the biggest, most luxurious White Star liner.

Titanic's officers spent the last night before sailing on board. First Officer William Murdoch, the son of a sea captain, had gone to sea aboard square riggers sailing between Liverpool and South America. He was so natural a mariner that he'd sat for the second mate's exam after four years instead of five. His last assignment had been as first officer aboard *Olympic*. Murdoch had no hard feelings about Smith replacing him with Wilde. It was only a matter of time before he would become not only chief officer but master of one of White Star's biggest ships.

Second Officer Charles Lightoller's last assignment had been as first officer on *Oceanic*. The son of a mill owner, he'd gone to sea as a teenager, quit after three shipwrecks and a near-fatal bout with malaria, prospected for gold in the Yukon, failed at that, became a cowboy in Alberta, didn't care for that life either, and had returned to the White Star Line twelve years before that night in Southampton. He was a devoted Christian Scientist. Delighted to be rescued from idle days or weeks at the dock waiting for coal, at dinner aboard *Titanic*, he told the other officers that he was a very contented chap to have the chance to sail on so wonderful a ship.

Henry Wilde had also begun his career aboard sailing ships. He'd arrived in Southampton a week earlier as chief officer on *Olympic*, expecting to become the captain on *Oceanic*. When *Oceanic*'s voyage fell victim to the coal strike and Smith asked Ismay to transfer him to *Titanic*, Wilde believed he was making his last trip as chief officer. On his next, he would be a master.

Wilde was pleased to be sailing with his friend E. J. Smith, but he had different feelings about *Titanic* than Lightoller. After dinner, he wrote a farewell note to his sister. "I still don't like this ship," Wilde said in closing. "I have a queer feeling about it."

At sunrise on Wednesday, April 10, Smith returned to *Titanic* to oversee the arrival of the rest of the crew. Eight hundred and sixty-one men signed ship's papers as seamen, firemen, engineers, saloon stewards, bedroom stewards, chefs, and waiters; also signing were a squash professional, a gymnasium instructor, two lifeguards for the swimming pool, and four Turkish bath attendants. Twenty-three women signed on: eighteen stewardesses, two cashiers, a masseuse, a Turkish bath attendant, and a matron to serve as a chaperone for single women traveling in third class.

Stewardess Violet Jessop came over from *Olympic* to add experience to *Titanic*'s female crew. After her childhood in Argentina, she had gone to sea at twenty-one as a stewardess aboard the steamship *Orinoco*. Except for a few brief spells between voyages, she had not lived ashore since. When Jessop sailed on *Olympic*'s first crossing in June 1911, the crew chose her to present Thomas Andrews with a walking stick, to thank him for designing a ship with better accommodations for the men on the crew.

When Andrews was designing the new ships, he had asked crew members what improvements would make their lives at sea better. As a result, *Olympic* was the first White Star ship to have bathrooms for seamen and stewards. On other ships, women crew members took baths behind closed doors but men used deck buckets for washing. Andrews had further improved the crew's quarters on *Titanic*, with more bathrooms, more lavatories, and better mattresses.

The members of the ship's string band were among the first people to come aboard. Band leader Wallace Hartley, three cellists, a pianist, two violinists, and two violists stowed their personal gear in their second-class staterooms, then set up their stands off the reception hall to play for arriving passengers. They were masters of the White Star music book of 352 tunes, including Scott Joplin rags, selections from *Carmen*, the "Emperor Waltz," "Rule, Britannia!" "God Save the King," "Yankee Doodle," "The Star Spangled Banner," and a selection of Episcopal hymns. The band played in two ensembles, one in first class, one in second, coming together for occasional galas.

The newspapers in New York and London touted the maiden voyage of *Titanic* as an even more glamorous high-society event than that of *Olympic* or any of the new Cunarders. William Randolph Hearst's *New York American* reported that *Titanic*'s 329 first-class passengers were worth a total of $500 million. Other papers celebrated the size of the ship. If *Titanic* were stood on its stern, its bow would top the Metropolitan Life Insurance Building in New York, at seven hundred feet the tallest building in the world. Headline writers on both sides of the Atlantic gushed over "The Wonder Ship," "The Last Word in Luxury," "The Unsinkable Ship," and "The Biggest Ship in the World." The *Wall Street Journal* dubbed it "The Millionaire's Special."

The *London Standard* declared White Star the victor over Cunard: "In the fight during the coming season, there will be a scent of battle all the way from New York to the shores of this country—a contest of sea giants in which the *Titanic* will doubtless take highest honors."

There were also detractors. The editors of the *Economist* snarled at shipbuilders attempting to "lick creation with monster ships that involved too great a concentration of life and wealth in a single bottom."

In America, *Engineering News* bashed the trend toward bigger and more luxurious ships, saying, "These latest marine monsters are built primarily to furnish the acme of luxury to passenger travel. Instead of representing an advance in economic transportation, they probably represent an actual increase in cost."

J. P. Morgan followed the news about *Titanic*, but he was going to miss its maiden voyage. The United States had relaxed the import duties on old works of art, and he was preoccupied with shipping his treasures home. In late March 1912, the delicate arrangements with customs and the museums that Morgan had put in place to spirit his collections out of Europe fell apart. One of his key agents abruptly resigned. Morgan, who was in Aix-en-Provence, called a meeting in France for the middle of April; he cabled Ismay with his regrets.

Pirrie, too, was unable to make the trip. In the middle of February, in constant pain and crippled by fever, he'd been ready to try anything. A surgeon had released his bladder in an agonizing procedure using a probe into his urethra, but the blockage had returned within a week. In early March, Pirrie had risked an operation to reduce the size of his swollen prostate, for which the odds were against survival. When *Titanic* was ready to sail from Southampton, Pirrie was recovering from surgery aboard his yacht, *Valiant*, in the Baltic Sea, battling the sepsis that had invaded his guts.

Recuperating on the yacht had been Margaret Pirrie's idea. *Valiant* was 307 feet long, with a crew of fifty, the largest private ship in the world. Pirrie would want for nothing, and his wife knew that he would have loathed the steady stream of well-wishers if he were at home in London or Belfast. On

Valiant, only she, a doctor, four nurses, and the crew would witness the suffering and weakness of a man who had been near death for weeks.

———

At eleven-fifteen, Chief Engineer Bell came to the bridge and told Smith that the bunker fire was still burning but that it should be out by the next day. His men were shoveling the smoldering coal into the furnaces. The steel bulkhead behind the bunker was warping a bit, but not too badly. Bell told Smith there was no reason to delay their departure.

At eleven-thirty, Smith finished the last of a bale of paperwork that had occupied him for most of the morning, the Master's Report to the Company. *I herewith report this ship loaded and ready for sea,* Smith wrote. *The engines and boilers are in good order for the voyage, and all charts and sailing directions are up-to-date. Your obedient servant, Edward J. Smith.*

The Board of Trade surveyor Francis Carruthers completed his last official act before leaving *Titanic,* approving its departure in the Report of Survey of an Emigrant Ship. *I am satisfied that the hull, boilers and machinery are in good condition and fit for the voyage,* Carruthers said. *There is enough coal on board to take the ship to her next coaling port. There is enough water on board, certified to be 206,800 gallons, contained in seven tanks.*

The chief purser reported to Smith that 329 passengers, 5 of them children, had embarked in first class; 285, including 22 children, in second class; and 710, of which 76 were children, in third class. It was not a full load, but the voyage would still be profitable.

At eleven forty-five, Smith sounded the ship's whistle to order visitors ashore. The crew swung the gangways and sealed the boarding hatches. The last boat train back to London left, and the crowd on the dock thinned to stevedores, line handlers, and a few well-wishers who were staying for the day in Southampton. Several hundred locals lined the strand in front of the White Star building. When the whistle blared they broke into cheers and applause.

From the bridge, Smith directed his officers by telephone as they threw the mooring lines to the dock. He had taken hundreds of ships to sea, but the exhilaration of breaking free of land had never left him.

The thumping chorus of the tugboat engines rose several octaves as *Titanic* moved away from the pier and out into the river Test. Over the noise of the tugs, Smith heard what sounded like a volley of rifle shots on the port side. He ran to the bridge wing and saw the 560-foot SS *New York* heading straight for his ship.

It was the HMS *Hawke* accident all over again. *Titanic's* propellers had created a maelstrom of suction, snapping *New York's* mooring lines to set the liner adrift. It was helpless, fifty feet away, and moving fast toward *Titanic's* stern. Black smoke belched from one of the tugboats as it accelerated around *New York's* bow, its crew scrambling to throw a line to men on the deck of the drifting ship.

The passengers lining the rails were oblivious to what was about to happen to *Titanic*. The band was playing a medley from Oscar Straus's *Chocolate Soldier*. Sailors were coiling the mooring lines. On the mooring bridge over the stern, Smith saw Henry Wilde looking on helplessly as *New York* bore down on his ship.

Smith's celebrated career was about to end in ignominy. Clutching at one last straw, he bellowed to the helmsman inside the bridge: Port engine ahead full! He had never heard of a captain fending off another ship with his own propeller wash, but it might work. The engine room took an interminable thirty seconds to respond to his command from the navigation bridge. *New York* was forty feet away. Twenty. At last, a foaming brown hump erupted from *Titanic*'s port propeller. Churning mud from the bottom of the river, the wave surged toward the drifting ship, slammed into its flank, and stopped *New York* four feet from *Titanic*'s stern.

Smith walked back to the center of his navigation bridge. In a voice that betrayed nothing of the dire moment that had just passed, he ordered all ahead slow and set a course across the English Channel for the five-hour run to Cherbourg. After a stop there for passengers and another the following day in Queenstown, on the southern tip of Ireland (now called Cobh), he could settle into the placid routines of the five-day crossing to New York.

Shift change at Harland and Wolff, circa 1910.

Thomas Andrews, chief designer of RMS *Titanic*, died April 15, 1912.

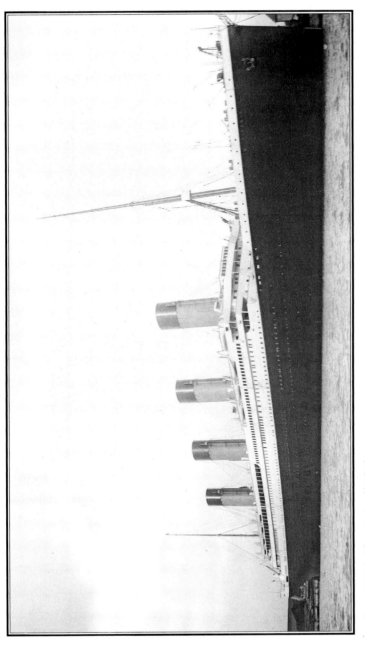

RMS *Titanic*, April 1912. (Photograph © National Museums Northern Ireland, Ulster Folk and Transport Museum.)

CAPTAIN SMITH AND OFFICERS S.S. TITANIC.
Lost on 15th April, 1912, after collision with Iceberg in North Atlantic.

The period caption of this photograph incorrectly identifies the subjects as Captain Smith and the other officers of *Titanic*. In fact, the photograph depicts officers of *Titanic's* sister ship *Olympic*, which Smith commanded until transferring to *Titanic* for its maiden voyage. The correct identities are, *from left, standing*: Chief Purser Herbert McElroy, 3rd Officer Henry Osborne Cater, 2nd Officer Robert Hume, 4th Officer David Alexander, 6th Officer Harold Holehouse; *seated*: 5th Officer Alphonse Tulloch, Chief Officer Joseph Evans, Captain E. J. Smith, and 1st Officer William Murdoch. Of these men, only McElroy, Smith, and Murdoch also served aboard *Titanic*, and none of them survived. Inger Sheil of the Australian National Maritime Museum did the research that resulted in the correct identifications.

(Photograph © National Museums Northern Ireland, Ulster Folk and Transport Museum.)

Senator William Alden Smith,
chairman of the United States inquiry into the *Titanic* disaster.
(Photograph courtesy of the United States Library of Congress.)

Lord and Lady Pirrie embarking aboard S.S. *Arlanza*
two months before his death, which occurred in June 1924.

(Photograph courtesy of Getty Images.)

41° 46' NORTH, 50° 14' WEST

F our nights after leaving Queenstown, Bruce Ismay was drifting off to sleep in the best stateroom on *Titanic*. The parlor suite had two bedrooms, a sitting room, a private promenade, book-matched walnut paneling, and a fireplace. Its tooled mahogany furniture, fluted columns, and rule-straight moldings evoked the ruins of Pompeii that had inspired Louis XVI.

It had taken Ismay a while to wind down. He'd just turned fifty, and sleep had become increasingly elusive, even though he felt better than he had in months. The voyage had been nothing but pleasure so far. *Titanic* was a good-humored ship, with a genial feeling among the passengers and crew wherever he went. Mechanically, it was performing perfectly. Andrews told him that *Britannic* would be even better. With a third *Olympic*-class sister—even a fourth was not out of the question—he would be competing with Cunard on even terms for the first time since his father had died.

White Star was having its best year financially since his

brother, James, had quit after the sale to Morgan. From time to time, Bruce had envied his brother's bucolic life raising show cattle in Dorset, but not that night on *Titanic*. International Mercantile Marine had never made a penny, but as its president Ismay had brought the combine around so at least it wasn't costing White Star or Harland and Wolff any money. The shipyard was more profitable than ever. Pirrie had almost died, but Ismay had heard he would be up and around in July. Before his illness, Pirrie had been obsessed with the notion of ships that ran on oil instead of coal. The recent miners' strike had ended just before *Titanic* left Southampton, but the next one could start anytime. With Pirrie's oil-fired diesel engines, White Star could lead the world into a new age of transatlantic shipping.

Before turning in at eleven o'clock, Ismay had said good night to his valet, Richard Fry, who had his own cabin across the corridor. Fry had been with him for ten years, serving also as his bridge partner and dependable traveling companion. Ismay kept to himself aboard ship, preferring quiet dinners and a card game in his cabin to the soirees with first-class passengers. That evening, he had gone down to the salon alone, run into the ship's surgeon, Dr. William O'Loughlin, and taken a table for two. Ismay greeted passengers who recognized him as he made his way through the enormous dining room, but he didn't stop to chat. Those who knew he was *Titanic*'s owner offered congratulations. Several said that their bonds with the White Star Line were stronger because of the magnificent new ship. Ismay knew that loyalty and word of mouth among them and their friends was priceless publicity. Just the list of their names would make news when *Titanic* arrived in New York.

Isidor Straus, who co-owned Macy's department store, and

his wife, Ida, had been on vacation in Europe. The English journalist and political rascal William T. Stead was on his way to a peace congress organized by President William Howard Taft. Taft's friend and most trusted military adviser, Major Archibald Butt, was aboard, as were London fashion designer Lucy, who was Lady Duff-Gordon, and her husband, Cosmo. Benjamin Guggenheim, the mining tycoon, was on his way back from a business trip that had been shrouded in the mystery that followed the man around like a fog. John Jacob Astor IV, who had shocked New York society by divorcing his wife, marrying eighteen-year-old Madeleine Force, and fleeing with her to Europe, was bringing his new wife home so their first child would be born in the United States.

Ismay had crossed the Atlantic countless times, but this was only his third trip on a maiden voyage of one of his ships. His first had been on *Adriatic*, his second on *Olympic*. Both had been with E. J. Smith in command. Ismay loathed dealing with the press, which was always part of the first voyage of a new ocean liner, especially one that had drawn so much hoopla. He had Sanderson to take care of publicity in England, and Phillip Franklin in America, but there would be no avoiding the reporters when *Titanic* arrived on Wednesday morning. Ismay had endured the press in Southampton, and he supposed he'd have to do the same in New York.

Ismay was finally surrendering to sleep when something changed. His bed shuddered, only for an instant, but enough to fully wake him. Instinct pulled him to his feet, into his slippers, and out to the corridor. He asked a passing steward what had happened. The steward said he had no idea. Ismay stood there, sensing the heartbeats of his ship. Nothing. Probably nothing. No. The engines slowed down. Then they stopped completely. Ismay went back into his sitting room, put on an overcoat, and started for the bridge. Something had definitely happened. Maybe a propeller blade. Damn. It had been going so well. Ismay went forward to the grand staircase in the reception hall, up to the boat deck, and forward to the bridge.

———

After tucking in her first-class passengers, stewardess Violet Jessop had returned to her stateroom on E Deck. She was in her nightgown, reading, happy about her new home and grateful for the electric lights, when, for an instant, she thought she felt something different about the engines. Jessop had learned to be alert to the rhythms of a ship. Every change meant something. She dropped her magazine to the coverlet at her side and listened more carefully. She distinctly heard a low, growling sound. She leaned over the side of her top bunk. Her roommate, Elizabeth Leather, who had been at sea longer than she had, was staring up at her over the side of her berth.

As calmly as if she were commenting on eggs and bacon, Elizabeth said, "It sounds as if something has happened."

Anna Turja, an eighteen-year-old Finnish émigré on her way to a job in Ohio, was in her berth near the stern on the starboard side of D Deck. She was traveling with her brother, Matt, who was in the single men's quarters, far away in the bow. To Anna, *Titanic* was bliss. She was one of twenty-one children, and her cabin was more comfortable than any room in which she had ever slept. She was sharing the cabin with another Finnish woman, Maria Panula, on her way, with five sons, to Coal Center, Pennsylvania, to join her husband, Emil, who had been in America for a year.

As the first tendrils of sleep took hold, Anna heard a rumbling deep in the ship below her. Having been informed that *Titanic* had three propellers as big as Dutch windmills, she assumed that the shuddering had something to do with them. Anna called across the room to Maria Panula, who was sleeping soundly after a day of wrangling her five boys, ages one to sixteen. Maria didn't wake up. The rumbling stopped. The boys didn't stir. Anna climbed out of her lower berth and eased into the passageway. A dozen men and women were leaning out of their doors, clutching their nightclothes to their necks.

In a two-berth cabin in the men's compartment at the bow on F Deck, Olaus Abelseth had been asleep for two hours. He was returning to his homestead farm in South Dakota from a visit to Norway, traveling with two cousins who were in another part of the ship. As a favor to a friend from his town in Norway, he was looking after sixteen-year-old Karen Abelseth. Karen was not a close relative, but Ole had known her all her life. Directly beneath Ole Abelseth, the ship trembled violently. His roommate, Adolph Humblen, woke at the same time. Humblen was also escorting a young woman, Anna Saltkjelsvik, to America.

"What was that?" Humblen said. "I don't know," Abelseth replied. "But we'd better get out of here and find the girls." They dressed, put on their overcoats, and started back to the women's compartments at the stern of the ship.

On every deck, passengers felt the break in the steady, reassuring pulse of the ship. In his stateroom on C Deck, Canadian army major Arthur Peuchen was dressing for bed. He thought the shock was a heavy wave, then remembered how calm the sea had been that night when he'd left the smoking room and taken a turn around the deck. Henry Stengel, a leather manufacturer from New Jersey, was moaning so loudly in his sleep that his wife shook him. Just as he woke, he heard a crash. Then the engines stopped. This is serious, he told her. We have to get up on deck. George Harder and his wife, Dorothy, on their honeymoon, were in bed on the starboard side of E Deck. George heard a rumble and a sharp scraping noise. He jumped up and went to the closed porthole. Through the glass, he saw a mass of white as high as the ship. Then it was gone. His first thought: We have to get out of here.

Thomas Andrews felt his desk move. He paused for a second, then continued doing what he always did in the evening aboard a new ship: making lists in his notebook, and crossing items off old lists. The Harland and Wolff electricians, ship fitters, carpenters, and plumbers were doing a good job of working the wrinkles out of *Titanic*. The doors of some of the third-class cabins and crew dormitories had been tight in their jambs; they'd shaved and rehung them. Some of the windows in the engineers' smoking room on the boat deck had been painted shut; they'd opened them. Only half the burners on one of the stoves in the third-class galley worked.

Andrews had written hundreds of notes, most of them about minor flaws that his men had easily fixed. He had spent part of the day in the engine room, where Chief Engineer Bell had told him that *Titanic*'s power plants were running beautifully. With only twenty-one of twenty-nine boilers lit, the ship loped along at 20 knots, consuming much less coal than expected. That day, the captain had ordered three more boilers lit, and the ship was making a shade over 21 knots.

Bell told Andrews that the port engine had handled the sudden jolt of power when Smith maneuvered to avoid hitting *New York* back in Southampton. No damage at all to the prop, shaft, or bearings. And now that the men knew their way around, they were telling him that working in the enormous engine room was a lot easier than they'd thought it would be.

The only real problem Bell had was the heating system for the second-class staterooms. It worked, then it didn't work, then it did. Bell thought the problem might be in the ducting. He had a crew on it. With the help of the Harland and Wolff men, he would have it solved for the return trip to England.

While Andrews was shaking out *Titanic*, he was also planning the changes he would make for *Britannic*, which was already framed to its double bottom. He would redesign B Deck to make space for two more private promenades, and turn the writing room—which no one ever used on *Olympic* and *Titanic*—into first-class staterooms. The extra steel he had put into the superstructure and the bow seemed to have stiffened *Titanic*. He'd definitely do the same to *Britannic* before launching, and *Olympic* as soon as possible. When he dry-docked *Titanic* in six months, he'd check carefully for the loose rivets above the turn of the bilge that he had found on *Olympic*.

A few seconds after Andrews felt his desk move, the engines stopped. He stood, took his suit coat from its peg near the door, tucked his notebook under his arm, and went to take a look around.

Fred Barrett was in Boiler Room 6, ticking off the minutes until the end of his watch. He was a tall, beefy, twenty-eight-year-old sailor from Liverpool who had gone into the coal pits when he was thirteen, survived five years in the mines, shipped out as a trimmer, and never worked ashore again. He became a fireman, then a leading fireman aboard *New York*. Barrett knew how to rake a good, hot fire, and when he was put in charge of a boiler-room gang, he wasn't afraid to use his fists to keep his men moving.

When Ismay canceled *New York*'s voyage because of the

coal strike, Barrett sprinted to the hiring hall and got himself a berth on the only ship leaving Southampton. He boarded *Titanic* three hours before it sailed.

Barrett was struck stupid the first time he climbed down the ladder into the enormous stokehold. Each boiler room was fifty feet long, spanned the ninety-two-foot beam of the ship, and rose thirty feet up into the hull. He had never in his life been in so large an enclosed space.

Barrett worked four hours on, eight hours off; he took his turn stoking the furnaces and, as leading fireman, kept tabs on the eight men on his watch in Boiler Room 6. For the extra responsibility, he got 10 shillings more per voyage than a fireman's wage of £6.

On Barrett's other ships, firemen stoked their furnaces when they decided the fire needed coal. *Titanic* had a maddening new system that rang bells in each boiler room every few minutes to tell the firemen when to recharge. Since Queenstown, the bells had been coming every ten minutes as the ship cruised at around 20 knots.

Barrett understood that the heat from his fires flowed up through steel tubes and turned freshwater into steam that flowed through more tubes. The steam ran the engines, and the engines turned the propellers. Knowing that he was moving the ship with his fires gave him enough pride to endure the hundred-degree temperature, the bad-tempered men, and the bells that never stopped ringing.

Barrett had been at sea long enough to understand that the maiden voyage on any ship was never easy, but the first three days on *Titanic* had been hell. Nobody knew his way around. The thing was a maze. It took him a half hour to find his messroom and bunk, another half hour to figure out the way to his boiler room through the firemen's tunnel. He had to climb seventy feet up spiral staircases from the engine room to get to the fresh air of the engineers' promenade on the boat deck.

The worst part of the voyage so far had been the bunker fire. It had been burning when he'd come aboard in Southampton, and he'd had the bad luck of being assigned to the boilers right next to it. The chief engineer had ordered extra trimmers to haul the burning coal to the furnaces, putting a lot of extra traffic in front of Barrett's boilers. Barrett had also had to put up with the hose gang spraying the bulkhead to keep the fire from spreading or warping the walls of the bunker. The water turned the air into a soggy mist and made the dust stickier. Everybody in his boiler room had had to work with neckerchiefs over their noses and mouths.

The trimmers had gotten the last of the burning coal out of the starboard forward bunker on the evening of April 13. Barrett wasn't on watch when Thomas Andrews himself had come down with Captain Smith to check the damage. He'd heard they didn't seem too worried about it. The chief engineer had put a gang to work around the clock to wire-brush and oil the steel walls of the bunker, inside and out.

Just before Barrett's watch ended on the night of April 14, the bunker that had been on fire was finally cleaned up. At eleven thirty-five, second engineer James Hesketh came around to inspect it. The aft bulkhead of the bunker looked fine—maybe not good as new, but fit for sea. To check the bunker's forward bulkhead, Hesketh and Barrett went through the watertight door to an empty reserve coal bin in the compartment between Boiler Room 6 and Cargo Hold 2. The steel there looked okay, too. Hesketh bent to look at the seam where the bulkhead met the deck. There was a little bit of warping, but nothing serious. Barrett felt the shudder of the engines changing speed, looked at Hesketh, and held his eyes.

The sound in the boiler rooms was always a deafening cacophony of clanging shovels, slamming furnace doors, and the roar of the fires themselves. Barrett missed the sharp, grinding sound coming from the cargo hold just forward of where he stood with Hesketh. By the time the noise registered, the watertight door alarm was blaring, and he heard the door squealing in its steel tracks. He and Hesketh broke for the closing door. Just before they reached it, a flat stream of green, cold water took their legs out from under them.

━━━

After a dinner party hosted by banker George Widener, Captain Smith was in the chartroom on the starboard side. The bridge was open to the weather, but the chartroom was heated, a much better place to finish his cigar. The temperature had dropped ten degrees since he'd gone down for dinner. Smith took off his coat and started checking his ship's position.

On the bridge, Murdoch was in command of the watch, with two junior officers, a quartermaster on the helm, and two seamen. Lookouts Fredrick Fleet and Reginald Lee were in the crow's nest on the forward mast, connected to the bridge by telephone.

Ordinarily, Smith would have been in his cabin getting ready to turn in, but he had felt the temperature drop after dinner and was worried about ice. A relatively warm winter had littered the shipping lanes off Newfoundland with far more than the usual number of bergs. On spring crossings, Smith and every other captain on the North Atlantic plotted their courses a few degrees to the south to avoid the ice drifting down from Greenland. Earlier in the evening, Smith had ordered a course change to take *Titanic* even farther south of the reported ice, because the Marconi operators had been handing him ice reports from other ships all day.

Just after eight A.M. from *Caronia*:

WESTBOUND STEAMERS REPORT BERGS, GROWLERS, AND FIELD ICE IN 42° N FROM 49° TO 51° W, 12 APRIL. COMPLIMENTS, BARR.

Shortly after noon, from *Baltic*:

HAVE HAD MODERATE, VARIABLE WINDS AND CLEAR, FINE WEATHER SINCE LEAVING. GREEK STEAMER ATHENAI REPORTS PASSING ICEBERGS AND LARGE QUANTITIES OF FIELD ICE TODAY AT LAT. 41° 51' N, LONG. 49° 52' W.

An overheard transmission from *Amerika* right after *Baltic*:

AMERIKA PASSED TWO LARGE ICEBERGS, 41° 27' N, 50° 8' W, ON 14 APRIL.

In the chartroom, Smith felt *Titanic* shiver under his feet. In five strides, he was on the bridge.

What is it, Murdoch? he asked.

"An iceberg, Sir," Murdoch answered. "I hard-a-starboarded and reversed the engines. I was going to hard-a-port round it but she was too close. I could not do any more. I have closed the watertight doors."

———

Five minutes after Ismay's shuddering bed woke him, he walked quickly along the corridor in the officers' quarters, past the Marconi room, and out into the chilly air of the navigation bridge. There were many more men than usual on watch, which alone told him that something was very wrong.

Ismay pulled Smith out of earshot of the others. They stood face-to-face for a few long seconds; then Ismay pivoted and rushed out the open door onto the bridge wing. Ismay was still in his pajamas, slippers, and overcoat, and even with the ship sitting still, the frigid air knifed into him as he ran aft on the boat deck. In a minute, he was in the engineers' smoking hut, then clacking down the metal staircase through six decks. At the bottom, he emerged on the catwalk in the hideously silent cavern of the engine room. Just then, the engines came to life.

After Ismay left the bridge, Smith had ordered all ahead half. Whatever had happened to his ship was not going to sink it, but there was little doubt that he had to make landfall as quickly as possible. He sent a seaman to wake up Wilde and Lightoller, and went to the Marconi room. Smith told Harold Bride to try to get a message through to Cape Race, Newfoundland. Bride said he was barely in range but he would try. Have Cape Race relay a message by transatlantic cable to White Star in London, Smith said. Tell them that *Titanic* is damaged and heading for Halifax. Repairs at Harland and Wolff might be necessary.

The carpenter arrived on the bridge and told Smith that the ship had water in the three forward compartments but he wasn't sure how fast it was coming in. Fourth Officer Joseph Boxhall, who had also been inspecting the damage, told him the mailroom on the starboard side, ten feet above the bottom, was knee-deep in water. Chief Engineer Bell reported that the firemen were working in waist-deep water, damping their furnaces in Boiler Room 6 to prevent a boiler explosion.

Smith ordered all stop. A minute later the engines were still. Two minutes after that, slowed more quickly than usual by the wounds in its bow, *Titanic* was dead in the water. To Smith, the picture of what had happened to his ship was getting murkier instead of clearer. He ordered Wilde to uncover the lifeboats.

Andrews rushed onto the bridge, pulled Smith aside, and the two men left together. Passing the Marconi room, Smith told Jack Phillips to send a distress signal to all ships and stations. He handed him a slip of paper with a rough estimate of *Titanic*'s position and said that Boxhall would get him a more accurate fix on it in a few minutes.

Smith and Andrews used crew passageways and staircases to avoid alarming passengers. On F Deck, three decks up from the bottom, they saw water in the squash court. They saw water in Cargo Holds 1 and 2. That meant that the first three watertight compartments were flooding and the water was already three decks up.

They climbed up to E Deck to skirt the closed watertight doors and went aft until they reached the engineers' staircase. In the engine room, Bell told them that at the last report, the water in Boiler Room 6 was above the six-foot-high stokers' catwalks. He had ordered Fred Barrett and his men to evacuate the compartment by climbing the emergency ladder over the bulkhead.

Smith, Andrews, and Bell went forward to inspect the boiler rooms. Nos. 1 through 4 looked dry. The faces of the firemen and trimmers were smudged masks of bewilderment as the three most important men on their ship rushed past them without a nod. A rumor had spread that the ship had run aground off Newfoundland. Boiler Room 5 had some water in it, but not much. Andrews climbed the ladder and looked over the top of the bulkhead into No. 6. Through a fog of acrid steam, he saw that water had reached the middle of the still-hot boilers. They hissed and crackled as the ocean flowed around them.

———

Ismay was on the bridge when Smith and Andrews got back. He could not remember ever having seen fear in either man, and he recognized it instantly in their dull, wide eyes and the tension in their shoulders. Both of them had always radiated confidence like lanterns giving light; seeing them without it was terrifying.

Smith led Ismay and Andrews into the chartroom. Even the warmth did nothing to ease the grimness in their faces. It's not good, Smith told Ismay. The ship is sinking. If we're lucky, it will last until help gets here. He looked at Andrews. How long do you reckon? Andrews shook his head. The laws of strength and buoyancy that had inspired him for his entire life doomed *Titanic*. Thousands of tons of seawater would quickly outweigh the ability of the ship's hull to support it. Soon, Andrews said. Soon.

Smith bolted from the chartroom. In his dependable, calm voice, he ordered his officers to their emergency stations. Launch the lifeboats, he told them. Now.

Murdoch was in charge of the eight boats on the starboard side; Lightoller, the eight on the port side. Wilde would oversee all of them and lend a hand where he was needed. Nobody mentioned that there was room for fewer than half of the ship's passengers and crew in the lifeboats. Smith had not told them what he, Ismay, and Andrews knew: The ship was sinking fast. Wilde, Murdoch, and Lightoller had no reason to doubt that *Titanic* would stay afloat at least long enough for another ship to reach it.

In the Marconi room, Jack Phillips tapped out the Morse code letters *CQD*—a call for help—followed by *MGY*—*Titanic*'s call sign—and the corrected position Boxhall had given him, 41° 46' north, 50° 14' west. It was precisely for that moment that Phillips had become a telegrapher; he was now fulfilling a heroic vision that had fixed itself in his mind since the seagoing wireless operator on *Republic* had saved hundreds of lives. Without Phillips and his Marconi key, the people on *Titanic* would have had no hope. No rescue ship would come to save them from its flooding decks. Survivors in lifeboats would freeze to death before another ship came upon them by accident.

Phillips's fist was a blur over his sparking key, his plea for help flying through the night to headphones on ships and at the shore station at Cape Race, Newfoundland. During the day, the signals from *Titanic*'s powerful transmitter traveled 350 miles. At night, in the absence of interference from solar radiation, they reached more than 1,000 miles. *Titanic* was not alone on the North Atlantic. The steamships *La Provence* and *Mount Temple* heard *Titanic*'s first CQD, but their replies, from less powerful transmitters, were too faint for Phillips to understand. Hearing the dots and dashes crackling on his headphones was also difficult because the engineers were releasing high-pressure steam from the boilers through pipes on the funnel just outside the Marconi room. The noise was so loud that the men on deck uncovering the lifeboats had to yell to be heard.

Finally, Phillips heard the Cunard liner *Carpathia* loud and clear. *Carpathia*'s telegrapher, Harold Cottam, had picked up *Titanic*'s CQD. He asked if Phillips knew that the Cape Cod shore station was trying to relay a batch of telegrams for *Titanic* passengers. Phillips ignored that message. COME AT ONCE, he tapped. WE HAVE STRUCK A BERG. IT'S A CQD, OLD MAN. POSITION 41.46 N, 50.14 W.

Carpathia replied, SHALL I TELL MY CAPTAIN? DO YOU REQUIRE ASSISTANCE?

Phillips tapped out, YES. COME QUICK.

Carpathia was eastbound out of New York, fifty-eight miles from *Titanic*'s position. Its captain, Arthur Rostron, immediately changed course, sent Cottam back to the Marconi shack to listen for updates on *Titanic*'s position, and ordered his chief engineer to put extra stokers in the boiler room. *Carpathia*'s single engine was built to drive the 541-foot ship at a top speed of 14½ knots. Rostron knew he could stretch that to 17 knots for a sprint and reach the sinking ship in three and a half hours. *Titanic* would easily stay afloat until *Carpathia* arrived.

While Phillips was telling as much of the world as possible that *Titanic* was in distress, the scene a few feet away on the boat deck was more typical of a crowd of after-dinner strollers. No one had told the passengers that their ship was sinking, and few of them were interested in climbing into a creaky wooden boat and being lowered seventy feet down to the freezing Atlantic on a cold, moonless night.

At twelve forty-five A.M., one hour and five minutes after impact, Murdoch sent lifeboat No. 7 into the sea with twenty-nine first-class passengers—eleven women and girls, eighteen men and boys, and the Pomeranian dog belonging to one of the girls—plus three seamen to man the oars. The boat was built to carry sixty-five people, but Murdoch had not been able to convince passengers to leave the warmth and comfort of the ship.

Neither Murdoch nor Lightoller, who was loading his first boat on the port side, was worried about launching nearly empty lifeboats. There would be plenty of time to bring them back to the ship to pick up more passengers, and they could load the boats much more easily through boarding hatches on the lower decks. The lifeboats would be most useful for ferrying people to the rescue ships when they arrived in a few hours.

In the half hour after the first lifeboat was away, Murdoch and Lowe, on the starboard side, and Lightoller and Wilde, on the port side, launched five more boats, all of them carrying only first-class passengers and crew. One third-class passenger, an Italian immigrant with a broken arm named Philip Zenni, managed to get aboard the sixth boat as it went down the side of the ship.

As though cued by some primitive instinct, the mood on the ship changed. A wave of second- and third-class passengers erupted onto the upper decks. Even to a person who had never been aboard a ship, the steadily increasing angle of the deck and the water rushing through companionways in the first four compartments signaled danger.

The passengers and crew who had been in the flooding men's compartments on the lower decks in the bow were in full flight. In the women's and families' compartments in the stern, the danger was not so obvious at first. On the way up from her quarters, Violet Jessop passed crewmen chatting and smoking on the stairs as if nothing was happening. On deck, she reported to Lightoller and tried to give up her seat in boat No. 16. He ordered her aboard. As Jessop squeezed in with Elizabeth Leather at her side, someone handed her a swaddled infant. For the first time, she believed *Titanic* would sink.

Far below the boat deck, most third-class passengers were staying in their staterooms because they did not speak the language of the sea. They did not understand that something terrible had happened to their ship. If they'd woken when *Titanic* hit the iceberg, most of them went right back to sleep. Changes in the sound of the engines meant nothing to them.

By the time the first of them—including Olaus Abelseth,

Adolph Humblen, Karen Abelseth, and Anna Saltkjelsvik—
reached the open air at the stern of B Deck, the calm pace of
loading the first lifeboats had deteriorated into a riot. Abelseth
pulled Karen and Anna up the boat deck stairway where two
seamen were screening out men and allowing only women near
the boats. Just as Karen and Anna went through the barrier,
one of the seamen yelled, "Everybody!" Abelseth and Humblen went up, too. Abelseth lost track of Anna, but he saw an
officer grab Karen and throw her into a lifeboat. Another officer shouted, Are there any sailors here? Are there any sailors
here? Abelseth had fished with his father in Norway from the
time he was ten years old until he'd left for America. He knew
how to handle a small boat as well as any man on *Titanic*. But his
cousins were nowhere to be seen. He couldn't bear the thought
of surviving if they did not. He said nothing to the officer, and
fought his way back into the crowd to look for them.

By one-thirty, almost two hours after impact, a steady
stream of firemen and trimmers were pouring from the engineers' stairwell onto the boat deck near the three remaining lifeboats on the starboard side. Murdoch ordered leading
fireman Fred Barrett to take command of No. 13, already
crammed with sixty-four people.

Anna Turja was on deck in the mob surging around the
last four lifeboats. She wandered for a few minutes, looking for
Maria and her children, until an officer grabbed her arm and
shoved her into a nearly full lifeboat on the port side. Turja
was terrified by the creaking of the ropes and pulleys of the
launching gear as the boat crept seventy feet down the sheer
bluff of *Titanic*'s black hull. It almost landed on top of boat
No. 13, but at the last second veered off and splashed heavily
into the sea. Everyone in Turja's boat got soaking wet.

Red distress rockets exploded over the ship, their light

blotting out the stars for the few minutes it took for them to burn out. All sixteen wooden lifeboats had been launched. At the front of the boat deck, Wilde began preparing the first of the four collapsible lifeboats. They had wooden bottoms with canvas sides and could carry only forty people each.

Bruce Ismay, still in his pajamas and overcoat, ran up to lend a hand with the launching of the collapsible boats. In minutes, they fastened the first one to a davit. Wilde crammed fifty people into it, then turned to Ismay.

There are no more women and children nearby, Wilde said. Get in the boat.

Ismay obeyed, and left *Titanic*.

Wilde and Lightoller wrestled with the last two collapsible boats, trying to move them under the davits. A crowd surged around them. *Titanic* shuddered in an entirely new, much more frightening way. The ship seemed to inhale, then exhale, as though it were taking deep breaths. The noise was deafening, a combination of a high-pitched whine and a deep, groaning note that no one had ever heard before.

In her lifeboat, some two hundred yards from the roaring ship, Violet Jessop held the infant who had materialized in her arms. She didn't know whether it was a boy or girl. Jessop held the baby against her belly, underneath her eiderdown coat, clucking to calm it, and heard the dreadful sounds of the ship's death throes above her. "Surely, this is all a dream," she muttered to no one.

Olaus Abelseth's cousins were lost in the chaos. At the stern of the wildly trembling ship, he cinched on his white kapok life jacket, took a deep breath, and jumped in the direction of a lifeboat below.

Lightoller frantically tried to free the last collapsible lifeboat, which was wedged into its chocks on the roof of the deckhouse with its tie-down ropes snarled. Harold Bride was helping Lightoller. He had stayed at his telegraph key until Smith came to the Marconi room, relieved him of his post, and disappeared into the flooding wheelhouse.

A hump of the sea washed over the deck below the top of the officers' quarters, jarring the last lifeboat free. It tumbled off the ship. Lightoller and Bride fell into the sea alongside it. The lifeboat swamped, then turned over. Underneath it, they flailed in the darkness, swallowing seawater and fighting off the arms of other terrified men. They clawed their way clear and climbed to the top of the overturned lifeboat, where they joined other men clinging to its keel.

Bruce Ismay did not see the end. He was pulling hard on an oar in his lifeboat with his back toward *Titanic*. He turned around once as they rowed away from the side, saw the chaos at the rail, saw Thomas Andrews throwing deck chairs into the sea, saw people jumping, and looked away. Behind him, he heard the strains of "Songe d'Automne." An odd thought popped into his head: No. 114 in the White Star music book.

Ismay rowed some more. The sinister shrieks of tearing steel overwhelmed all other sounds. He heard cables snapping like rifle shots, and risked another look. The forward funnel broke free of the deck, toppled absurdly into the sea, and swamped a lifeboat. For long minutes, Ismay could not force himself to turn around again. The next time he did, *Titanic* was gone. He hadn't felt even a ripple as the ship went down.

The sounds in the endless darkness changed again. Ismay heard the voices of people in the water. He made out a few words: Come back. Help. God. Please. And he heard many words in languages that he did not understand. Ismay fell on his oar. His valet, Richard Fry, and his secretary, William Harrison, had stayed. They were out there. Smith. Andrews. The sailor in charge of the lifeboat hollered at him to row. Ismay rowed. A half hour later the words, screams, and whimpers stopped as though a switch had been thrown.

Carpathia was an hour and ten minutes away.

YAMSI

Ismay knew it was cold because he was shivering. He knew
he could hear because the sailor standing in the back of
the lifeboat was shouting orders: Row. Ship your oars. The
oarlocks clattered. Someone was crying. He heard voices from
the other boats, invisible in the darkness. Ismay knew he could
see. There was an ocean of stars above him. Every few minutes, a rocket sizzled into the sky and exploded, the bright
green light blotting out the heavens. Then the stars returned.
None of it made any sense.

Time passed. Ismay had no idea how much. The stars
faded again, this time replaced by the faint pink tones of
dawn. Then there was a new light. Lower. A shooting star? He
heard a thud that sounded like a cannon. More shooting stars.
Brighter. They were white flares, Ismay realized. Then a ship
materialized against the brightening sliver of the horizon.

Ismay felt sensation returning to his arms and legs. The
sailor barked: Row. When the lifeboat hove to in the lee of the
ship, Ismay helped to fend off from the side. The sailor and
another man grabbed lines that dropped from above. There
was no violence in the sea; it was a calm morning. Ismay sat

until someone grabbed his lapel and pulled him to the Jacob's ladder. The dark side of the ship was a forty-foot bluff. In his bed shoes, Ismay lost his footing on every other rung and clung to the ropes. At the top of the ladder, an officer with wide-eyed terror on his face took Ismay by the arm and helped him to the deck.

"I'm Ismay." He hadn't spoken since he'd gotten into the lifeboat. The words came out in a hoarse whisper. The officer at the rail turned away from him to help the next survivor from the ladder.

Ismay walked four paces to the bulkhead of the deckhouse and settled his back against the cold steel. A man in uniform materialized in front of him.

"I'm Ismay," he said, forcing himself to speak louder.

"Will you not go into the saloon and get some soup or something to drink?"

"No. If you will leave me alone I will be very much happier here," Ismay said. "If you will get me in some room where I can be quiet, I wish you would."

The man put his arm around Ismay's shoulders and coaxed him through a doorway, up some stairs, and into a stateroom, leaving him there in the darkness.

———

At midnight in the newsroom of the *New York Times*, managing editor Carr Van Anda heard the clatter of the dispatch box in its metal chute. When a bulletin arrived at the telegraph room on the eighteenth floor, the operator threw it into a wooden box and lowered it on a rope to the newsroom. Van Anda had just put the first morning edition to bed, with the news that Teddy Roosevelt had beaten William Howard Taft in the Pennsylvania primary election.

The bulletin was from the Associated Press in Cape Race, Newfoundland.

> *Sunday night, April 14 (AP). At 10:25 o'clock tonight the White Star Line steamship Titanic called "CQD" to the Marconi station here, and reported having struck an iceberg. The steamer said that immediate assistance was required.*

Van Anda called the White Star office and got through to the night-duty officer, who knew nothing. Next, he called the *Times* correspondent in Halifax. The reporter told him that a Canadian ship had picked up the distress call and forwarded it to another ship, *Virginian*, en route from Halifax to Liverpool. *Virginian*'s captain had changed course and was racing to 41° 46' north, 50° 14' west. The reporter in Halifax also told Van Anda that *Olympic* and *Baltic* had confirmed that they'd heard the distress call. The last transmission from *Titanic* was sloppy, which was surprising since it had been sent by an experienced telegrapher. It said the ship was sinking by the bow, and ended abruptly at 12:27, New York time. After that, there had been a flurry of messages between a half dozen ships and Cape Race, but nothing more from *Titanic*.

Van Anda decided he didn't have enough facts to replace Taft and Roosevelt with the *Titanic* story in the morning-mail edition. He had a few hours to dig into his story for the next edition that afternoon. For the time being, Van Anda posted the news that the world's biggest ocean liner had sent a distress call on the bulletin board in front of the office in Times Square.

NEW LINER TITANIC HITS AN ICEBERG;
SINKING BY THE BOW AT MIDNIGHT;

WOMEN PUT OFF IN LIFEBOATS;
LAST WIRELESS AT 12:27 BLURRED.

The morning editions of several newspapers carried stories on the calls for help from the North Atlantic but reported that they were unconfirmed. Editors at every paper in town loosed a barrage of assignments to their reporters, with orders to get to the bottom of the puzzling story. At White Star headquarters, Phillip Franklin, general manager of the line's American operations and vice president of International Mercantile Marine, started taking phone calls from the press at seven A.M.

The hearsay that *Titanic* had foundered was preposterous, Franklin told them. The ship's telegraph signal fading abruptly was due to a malfunction in the wireless station or atmospheric interference. White Star and IMM were perfectly satisfied that there was no cause for alarm regarding the safety of the passengers.

At noon, the Associated Press in Montreal relayed a bulletin from Cape Race for which Franklin had been praying all morning: ALL TITANIC PASSENGERS SAFE. THE VIRGINIAN TOWING THE LINER INTO HALIFAX.

Franklin went to work fulfilling White Star's obligations to 1,324 passengers who were expecting to land in New York but were going to find themselves in Halifax, six hundred miles north. The word about the collision and rescue spread among friends and relatives of the passengers, many of whom rushed to the White Star offices to find out what would happen to their loved ones.

At one P.M., Franklin chartered a special express train to pick up the stranded passengers in Halifax. Any friends and relatives who wanted to go north to meet them were welcome to ride along. Franklin commandeered the steamer *Lady Laurier* to sail from Halifax immediately, intercept *Virginian* and *Titanic*, and escort them to port. He dictated a telegram and ordered it sent to every known relative of the first-class passengers: ALL TITANIC'S PASSENGERS SAFE. LINER BEING TOWED TO HALIFAX.

Titanic updates flew among Marconi stations at sea on both sides of the Atlantic. Newspapers posted hourly bulletins on the walls outside their offices. *THE NEW TITANIC STRIKES ICEBERG AND CALLS FOR AID*, said one. *VESSELS RUSH TO HER SIDE.* In London, the *Daily Sketch* ran a story, datelined Montreal, with the headline *CALLS FOR HELP. MANY GREAT LINERS RACE TO THE RESCUE.* Early that afternoon, the banner on the front page of the New York *Sun* proclaimed, *ALL SAVED FROM TITANIC AFTER COLLISION.* The rescue was hailed as another triumph for the Marconi International Marine Communication Company.

On the afternoon of April 15, telegrapher David Sarnoff went to work in downtown Manhattan with the New York *Sun* tucked under his arm. Sarnoff was a Russian immigrant, born in Uzlian, near Minsk, who had been in America for twelve years. He loved his job with the Marconi company and believed he was part of a revolution as powerful as the invention of movable type. His first assignment had been at the Marconi station on Nantucket Island. Sarnoff had been off duty on the morning *Florida* ran into *Republic*, but he'd hurried to work when he'd heard what had happened and had spent the next forty-eight hours helping transmit bulletins on the rescue.

Sarnoff's job in New York didn't involve saving lives, but he was sure New York was a step up from Nantucket. John Wanamaker, the department store tycoon, had installed telegraph stations in his stores to transmit information about sales, inventory, and other company business. At the same time, he offered telegraph service to his customers, giving many of them their first glimpse of the wonderful power of wireless communications. When Wanamaker's was open for business, the Marconi offices were always surrounded by a crowd leaning in to watch the operators tapping their keys and jotting notes on incoming messages.

Telegraphic voyeurism helped Sarnoff pass many long hours at work. He was good at picking the Wanamaker call letters out of the river of electrical chatter flowing into his headphones, but to break the monotony, he listened just as intently for messages from ships at sea. Most of the ships' telegrams he overheard were mundane: HAVING A GREAT TIME. OCEAN AIR WORKING WONDERS FOR ME. PLEASE MEET AT THE 34TH STREET PIER ON WEDNESDAY MORNING. Every once in a while, he heard one that admitted him to the interiors of commerce, which were utterly foreign and fascinating to him: TRANSFER 400,000 FROM NEW YORK ACCOUNT IMMEDIATELY, OR WE'RE FINISHED. Some cables were windows into tragedy: YOUR DAUGHTER ELLEN DIED THIS MORNING, IN TRANSIT FROM MARSEILLE. REQUEST INSTRUCTIONS FOR BURIAL AT SEA.

On April 15, Sarnoff took care of a bit of incoming and outgoing traffic on the company frequency, then switched to the no-man's-land of offshore radio waves. Maybe he could pick up something about *Titanic*. The night before, he had heard faint transmissions between the liner in distress and *Olympic*, which he'd passed on to the press. From the papers that day, it looked like it had turned into an even bigger rescue story than *Republic*'s.

As the sun dropped lower in the sky, there would be less interference. His receiver often picked up signals from ships as far as a thousand miles away. As usual, the air was rattling with amateur chatter, jamming commercial signals. The Marconi company was no longer the only participant in the electronic revolution. Anybody with a little bit of skill and money could build a radio transmitter.

At four thirty-five P.M. Sarnoff heard the unmistakable fist of a professional offshore telegrapher. MCE DE MKC: MCE, this is MKC. From earlier eavesdropping on maritime traffic, Sarnoff knew that MCE was Cape Race, Newfoundland, and MKC was RMS *Olympic*. He tuned his receiver to sharpen the signal. The message was from *Olympic*'s captain, Herbert J. Haddock, for relay by landline to the White Star office in New York.

CARPATHIA REACHED TITANIC POSITION AT DAYBREAK.
FOUND BOATS AND WRECKAGE ONLY. TITANIC FOUNDERED
ABOUT 2.20 AM IN 41.16 N. 50.14 W. ALL HER BOATS
ACCOUNTED FOR. ABOUT 675 SOULS SAVED. LEYLAND LINE
SS CALIFORNIAN REMAINING AND SEARCHING POSITION OF
DISASTER. CARPATHIA RETURNING TO NEW YORK WITH
SURVIVORS. PLEASE INFORM CUNARD. HADDOCK

Sarnoff froze. *Olympic* sent the message again, and again. He took off his headphones, picked up the telephone, and called his boss at the New York office of the Marconi company to get permission to notify the press. An hour later, extra editions of the major newspapers were on the stands. Sarnoff was riveted to his chair, tapping out *Carpathia*'s call sign.

At the White Star office, Phillip Franklin read the telegram from *Olympic* but could not bring himself to believe the death toll was so high. If *Titanic* had sunk—and part of him still did not admit that it had—it would have stayed afloat at least long enough for several nearby ships to arrive. It would have been a simple matter for another ship to pull alongside and transfer every last one of the crew and passengers before *Titanic* went down. Franklin had followed the big new ships through their design, construction, and trials. He knew they were built to take heavy punishment and still survive for hours, if not days. When HMS *Hawke* had slammed into *Olympic*, *Olympic* had not only survived but made it to port under its own power. *Titanic* was as strong, if not stronger.

Franklin went downstairs to make a statement to the swarm of reporters who were milling around in the ticketing hall. Some survivors were aboard *Carpathia*, Franklin told them. Two other ships that were in the vicinity, *Parisian* and *Virginian*, might also have arrived in time to save more passengers and crew. There has probably been a terrible loss of life, he admitted.

By midnight, a crowd of hundreds had gathered in front of the White Star office, all of them desperate to know if their loved ones were among those alive aboard *Carpathia*. In his office, Franklin relinquished the last of his optimism that *Titanic* was still afloat, called back the train to Halifax, and canceled the *Lady Laurier* charter.

In Times Square, another mob shuffled around all night, waiting for handwritten bulletins from the newspapers on the fate of *Titanic*. Most of them knew no one on the unlucky ship. They were there because they sensed a primitive disturbance in the rhythms of life that allowed one day to follow another. The disappearance of a gigantic, unsinkable ocean liner and hundreds of innocent people threatened their belief that the world was essentially an orderly place. They had heard of the Johnstown flood that killed more than two thousand, and countless horrible war stories, but somehow this was worse. In the few short hours since the news broke, *Titanic* had captured the imaginations of millions of people, who were both fascinated and terrified by so outrageous a turn of fate.

In Southampton, dawn washed over a thousand women and children gathered on the cobbles in front of the White Star office. All of them lived in row houses within a few blocks of the waterfront. From time to time, their men came home from the sea to live with them before another ship took them away. During the night, the rumors and conflicting bulletins had flowed into the seafaring neighborhood. *Titanic* had hit an iceberg; another ship was towing it to Halifax. *Titanic* had hit an iceberg and sank, but everyone aboard was safe on two or three ships that arrived in time to rescue them.

In the darkest part of the night, the despicable truth rippled from house to house. More than 1,500 of *Titanic*'s passengers and crew were missing. Fewer than 800 had been taken from lifeboats onto *Carpathia*. The wives of the crewmen stood silently under umbrellas in a soft rain, facing the White Star office, hoping that at any minute someone would emerge to tell them that none of them were widows.

Daylight on April 16 brought no relief in New York City. *Carpathia*'s Marconi had a range of only two hundred miles and could not reach Cape Race. It had cabled the names of a few of the survivors to the nearby *Olympic*, which had relayed them to New York before steaming eastward on its original course. Nine out of ten people who rushed to the White Star office that morning hoping for good news left in tears when the names of their loved ones were not on the first list of survivors sent by *Carpathia*.

In the newspapers, people around the world read that *Titanic* had definitely sunk, along with the sketchy details about survivors. The *New York American*, a Hearst paper, led the way, devoting eight of the twenty-four pages of its early afternoon edition to the disaster.

Jack Binns, the hero telegrapher of the RMS *Republic* who had become a newspaperman, wrote a story on David Sarnoff at his post in the Wanamaker's Marconi station. The rest of the *New York American*'s coverage included stories on the lack of enough lifeboats for everyone on board, icebergs, watertight doors, and *Titanic*'s insurance coverage. A cutaway profile of the ship was spread across the tops of pages 6 and 7. Beneath it, an editorial cartoon depicted the god Neptune sending lightning bolts out of his head to three ships on the horizon, while holding *Titanic* up, speared on the tines of his trident. The caption was *A SACRIFICE TO CARELESSNESS AND GREED.*

The crowd outside the White Star office in New York demanding the names of survivors had grown from hundreds to thousands. It was verging on becoming a riot. The policemen who were already there called for reinforcements. When Franklin or another White Star man appeared at the door, the mob surged toward them, shouting curses and accusations that they had lied to the world about survivors.

Despite the increasingly grim truth that was emerging, hopeful rumors still circulated in New York and Southampton. Some passengers and crew were confirmed to be aboard *Virginian*, *Parisian*, or *Olympic*. Some had saved themselves by climbing from the sinking ship on the iceberg and were waiting there to be rescued.

To ease fears that survivors might still be at the scene awaiting rescue, Franklin told the crowd outside his office that he had wired Halifax and chartered another ship to speed to *Titanic*'s last reported position. He didn't tell them that the cable-laying steamer *Mackay-Bennett* would carry a mortician, a chaplain, a cargo of pine caskets, and forty tons of ice in the hold for preserving bodies.

In Washington, the news reached President Taft, who was

already reeling from his defeat in Pennsylvania at the hands of his once-close friend and mentor, Teddy Roosevelt. Roosevelt had served two terms as president, decided not to run for a third, and handpicked Taft to succeed him. Roosevelt had counted on Taft to stay the progressive course he had set for the Republican Party, but Taft had taken the GOP in the opposite direction. Now Roosevelt had not just beaten Taft in Pennsylvania; he had routed him. For Taft, the additional bad news that his friend Archie Butt might be lost at sea was devastating.

On the morning of April 17, Taft still did not know if Butt was dead or alive. He sent a telegram to Franklin asking for news about his friend and adviser.

Taft waited two hours. Franklin did not reply. Taft was incensed that the man had ignored him. He ordered the fast navy scout cruisers *Chester* and *Salem* to sortie from Norfolk, Virginia, make contact with *Carpathia*, and demand a complete list of survivors.

———

While Taft was sending the navy to run down *Carpathia*, William Alden Smith was across town reading the newspaper coverage of the disaster. Smith was fifty-two years old, had served his first term in one of Michigan's two Senate seats, and was almost certain to be reelected the following year. He was a deceptively ordinary-looking man of average height with a flair for saying just what was on his mind in a way that usually didn't offend anyone unless he intended to offend them. He owned a small railroad and a newspaper in Michigan, and championed small business against big business whenever he saw an opportunity.

Smith had a reputation in Congress as a man who could seize attention by gauging the right psychological moment and then hold it with sheer showmanship. He came by his talents, Smith said, when he was twelve years old. After being turned down for a job as a newsboy because he didn't have the $10 front money for the route, he spent a quarter on un-popped popcorn. He popped the corn, bagged it, and per-suaded a friend who played the banjo to stand with him on a corner in Grand Rapids. While the banjo player strummed "Camptown Races," Smith danced, tossed bags of popcorn to customers, and caught pennies in return. He made $1.25 the first day. Within a year, Will's Popcorn was bringing in a profit of $75 a month, supporting the entire Smith family and the banjo player.

As Smith read about *Titanic*, he was struck by a bizarre coincidence. He reached into his wallet and pulled out a yel-lowed newspaper clipping from 1902. It was a poem about a shipwreck that had strangely moved him ten years earlier. Until that moment he had forgotten that he still had it.

> *Then she, the stricken hull,*
> *The doomed, the beautiful,*
> *Proudly to fate abased*
> *Her brow, Titanic.*

Smith noticed another coincidence, too: There on the front pages of every newspaper on his desk was a photograph of Captain E. J. Smith. Six years earlier, then-congressman Smith and his son had crossed the Atlantic aboard *Baltic*, under the command of E. J. Smith. The captain had invited him and his son to dinner, then took them on a tour of the bridge. Congressman Smith was a student of human behav-ior, and he'd pegged Captain Smith as an extremely level-headed, safety-conscious mariner.

Every newspaper Senator Smith read carried a story about Captain Smith's recklessness in running too fast through a known ice field. One reporter asked naval architect Robert Stocker to look at *Titanic*'s specifications, evaluate the time the ship had stayed afloat, and offer a conclusion. "The *Titanic* must have been making full speed ahead when she collided with the iceberg," he said, "and evidently her compartments must have been sprung from bow to stern."

That was not the E. J. Smith whom Senator Smith knew. The papers painted *Titanic*'s captain as a reckless fool, but that simply could not be true. If it wasn't, Smith wondered, what *had* happened to the ship? What about the ice warnings the papers said Smith had received? Why had the world's largest, finest, and safest passenger ship foundered on its maiden voyage?

Two days after the disaster, while *Carpathia* was still steaming to New York, either out of range or maintaining radio silence, millions of people all over America and Europe were asking the same questions. The newspapers were answering them with accusations and supposition. Smith thought the poem in his wallet was way too much of a coincidence to not mean something. What it meant, he decided, was that he was the man to get the real answers. With a flash of certainty, he knew that his entire life had led him to that moment.

Smith called the White House and reached Taft's secretary, Charles Hilles. What did the president intend to do about the *Titanic* disaster? Smith asked. Most likely, Hilles replied, the president will do nothing.

That morning, Smith drafted a resolution to convene a panel to investigate the wreck of *Titanic* under the auspices of the Committee on Commerce, of which he was a member. At the beginning of the day's Senate session, Smith interrupted the prayer by the chaplain to present his resolution.

James Martine of New Jersey took the floor. "Senators, let us act at once," he said. "True, we cannot help the unfortunate souls who went to their watery graves; but lest another craft shall go to the bottom of the insatiable sea with her human cargo, I urge the passage of this resolution."

The lone objection came from Henry Cabot Lodge of Massachusetts. Lodge insisted that his own Committee on Foreign Relations held the power to deal with any prospective international treaty that might come as a result of the inquiry.

Smith jumped to his feet. "I am perfectly indifferent to what committee it may be referred. But in God's name let us do something!"

By unanimous consent, the Senate gave Smith's committee the authority to conduct an investigation to determine what had happened to RMS *Titanic* on the night of April 14–15, 1912. If the conclusions of the inquiry called for a treaty or other international instrument, Lodge would step in. The Commerce Committee chairman, Senator Knute Nelson, appointed Smith as chairman. The panel of inquisitors would have an equal number of Republicans and Democrats, with a liberal, moderate, and conservative member of each party

The next day, April 18, Smith set his *Titanic* inquiry aside to tend to some business on his upcoming reelection campaign in Michigan. He was dictating a letter to his ally the governor when the telephone rang. Smith answered it himself.

It was a commander at the Department of the Navy, calling at the request of President Taft. The cruisers *Chester* and *Salem* had finally made contact with *Carpathia*. For reasons that were not entirely clear, *Carpathia*'s captain had declined to send a complete list of survivors. The president was furious, and the cruisers were continuing to transmit their demands to *Carpathia*.

Smith was stunned. *Carpathia* had turned down a request by the president of the United States.

There's more, the commander said. The warships had intercepted a telegram from *Carpathia* that might be of interest to the committee getting ready to investigate the disaster.

Read it, Smith said.

TO PAS FRANKLIN WHITE STAR. MOST DESIRABLE TITANIC CREW SHOULD BE RETURNED HOME EARLIEST MOMENT POSSIBLE. SUGGEST YOU HOLD CEDRIC, SAILING HER DAYLIGHT FRIDAY. PROPOSE RETURNING IN HER MYSELF. YAMSI

Who is Yamsi? Smith asked.

We believe it is J. Bruce Ismay, chairman of the White Star Line and president of International Mercantile Marine. He owns *Titanic* and was aboard the ship.

He's alive? Smith asked.

Apparently, sir, the commander said.

Smith slowly hung his telephone earpiece on the hookswitch and sorted through what he had just heard. The man who owned the ship had definitely survived. Why? This Ismay wanted to spirit *Titanic*'s crew out of New York as soon as *Carpathia* arrived. Why? Of course, Smith realized: Once Ismay and the crew were off American soil, he would have no way to subpoena them to testify before his committee.

A minute later, Smith had the solution. If Ismay and his crew would not come to Washington to present themselves to his committee, then Washington would go to them. He called the White House, got Hilles, and arranged a noon meeting with the president.

Minutes before Smith arrived in the Oval Office, the cruisers had intercepted the full list of surviving first-class passengers and transmitted it to the president. Archie Butt was not on it. Smith was shocked to see Taft looking so distraught. His face was bright red, his collar soaked with sweat, his breath coming in gasps. Smith disagreed with Taft on most political issues, but he liked him personally, and he felt sorry for the man.

Smith thanked the president for seeing him at so difficult a time. He said he hoped the president appreciated the importance of the investigation to the nation. Taft responded that he supported Smith's resolution and the formation of the committee. He would do everything in his power to help the inquiry.

Smith asked the president if it was legal to subpoena British citizens and hold them in the United States until they testified. Taft called the attorney general, George Wickersham, who told him that Congress was perfectly justified in holding Ismay and the crew in the country until they satisfied the committee. It was highly unlikely that the British would raise diplomatic objections.

Smith had three more requests. First, he wanted Secretary of Commerce and Labor Charles Nagel, who was in charge of immigration, to go to New York with the committee to make things as easy as possible for the steerage passengers arriving in the country for the first time. Taft agreed. Second, Smith wanted George Uhler, the government's top steamship inspector, to join the panel. Taft agreed. Finally, Smith asked the president to dispatch a U.S. Treasury revenue cutter to rendezvous with *Carpathia* to be sure no one left the ship before it reached the dock. Taft said he would have the cutter under way within the hour.

Smith thanked Taft and told him that he and a few members of his committee were taking an afternoon train to New York. They would arrive just before *Carpathia* docked.

———

In New York, David Sarnoff was still at his post on the roof of Wanamaker's department store. He had been at it for seventy-two hours, catnapping on the floor of the Marconi room and listening to messages from *Carpathia* and the navy cruisers, as well as every other transmission about *Titanic*.

William Randolph Hearst had personally taken charge of the coverage in his *New York American*. As *Carpathia* skirted the coast of New England, a day out of New York, its telegraph transmissions were incomplete or unintelligible. Hearst chartered the seagoing tug *Mary Scully* to get a reporter closer to the ship and make radio contact.

The day before, J. Bruce Ismay's name had appeared on one of the partial lists of survivors intercepted by Sarnoff. Hearst remembered Ismay as the arrogant, unfriendly Englishman he had met at a party twenty-five years earlier and wasted no time in handing the president of the White Star Line to the mob. By Friday, as William Alden Smith went to Union Station to board his train for New York, most papers were leading with the story of the perfect villain in the most sensational tragedy in history.

In the *New York Times*, Admiral Alfred Mahan was quoted as saying, "Ismay could certainly not be held responsible for the collision with the iceberg, but the shortage of lifeboats meant that so long as there was a soul that could be saved, the obligation lay on Mr. Ismay that that one person and not he should have been in the boat."

Hearst's *New York American* ran a full-page cartoon depicting Ismay in a lifeboat watching the *Titanic* sink. The caption read: *This is J. Brute Ismay. We respectfully suggest that the emblem of the White Star Line be changed to that of a yellow liver.*

When the newspapers ran out of facts about *Titanic*, they filled their pages with opinions. The *New York Times* quoted Stanley Bowdle, an engineer. "The loss of life on *Titanic* was a sacrifice to degenerate luxury," he said. "Floating palaces like the White Star liner were degenerate in size, foolish in enjoyment, and criminal in speed."

The *New York Evening Post* published a letter from Admiral F. E. Chadwick. "The *Titanic* was lost by unwise navigation, by running at full speed, though so amply forewarned, into the dangerous situation which might easily have been avoided. This is the fundamental sad, and one important fact. It accounts for everything," he opined. Bad navigation accounted for the disaster. Bad *British* navigation.

In the *Washington Post*, Admiral George Dewey, the naval hero of the Spanish-American War, said, "I think that every passenger who crosses the North Atlantic takes his life in his hands every time. The greed for money-making is so great that it is with the sincerest regret that I observe that human lives are never taken into consideration."

Every section of every paper—News, Arts, Sports, Society, and Business—found something to write about *Titanic*. Money was a topic in many of them. The stock markets had plummeted but were starting to recover. The *New York Times* said there wouldn't be enough capital on two continents to cover the insurance loss. The hull and machinery coverage of the ship itself would be no problem, but the liability exposure was staggering. The diamonds on the ship alone had been insured for $5 million. The *Times* learned that one passenger had taken out a policy worth $600,000 on a string of pearls. An insurance broker told a reporter, "See all those flags at half-mast? Action *must* be taken by the government!"

At three o'clock on the afternoon of April 18, Smith went to Union Station. As he made his way to the train, he was mobbed by reporters. He had hoped to keep his precipitous departure from Washington a secret, but the next best thing to secrecy was telling the truth. Smith held a walking press conference, informing the reporters about the intercepted cable from Ismay and his conversation with President Taft, and naming the members of his committee and its advisers.

Are you going to arrest Bruce Ismay, Senator? a reporter shouted.

We are not going into this matter with a club, Smith replied. The officers of the White Star Line must respond to congressional action frankly and honestly if they are to enjoy the privileges of American ports and retain the confidence of the American people. The hearings will begin tomorrow at the Waldorf-Astoria hotel in New York. Unless Ismay is ill or incapacitated, he will be subpoenaed, and he will testify.

Senator, how can Congress have any jurisdiction over the British? another reporter asked.

We may not have jurisdiction over the individual, Smith explained, but the American Congress is not without jurisdiction over the harbors of the United States. It is for these men who make use of the harbors to meet the public demand for information in regard to the disaster. Good day, boys, Smith said as he disappeared into the train.

In England, April 18 had been a day of national mourning. Memorial services in England, Ireland, Scotland, and Wales had drawn hundreds of thousands of mourners. Alexander M. Carlisle, the retired Harland and Wolff director who had helped design *Titanic*, had fainted in a church in London and been taken to the hospital.

In Aix-en-Provence, France, plans for a grand celebration

of J. P. Morgan's seventy-fifth birthday fell apart when the news about *Titanic* reached him. The next day, his mood plummeted further when he received a cable from his son, Jack, in New York, telling him that the newspapers and Congress seemed to have concluded that Bruce Ismay was to blame for the disaster.

Pirrie remained in seclusion aboard *Valiant* and did not yet know of the tragedy. Franklin had cabled Harland and Wolff as soon as he knew for sure that the ship was gone, then later when he knew that Thomas Andrews had perished with it. At the shipyard, Edward Wilding received the news as he convened the monthly meeting of the company directors on April 16. He excused himself and discreetly sent a cable to Margaret Pirrie, for her eyes only. She decided not to tell her husband.

At 9:07 P.M., the train from Washington chuffed through the tunnel under the Hudson River into Pennsylvania Station, on West Thirty-fourth Street in New York. A delegation from the Port of New York was on the platform. Hurry, they told Smith. *Carpathia* was in sight, escorted by the USS *Manhattan*. The ship was already past the Statue of Liberty, just minutes from docking. They had cabs standing by to take Smith and his party to Cunard's Pier 54.

In the darkness, Smith's convoy of taxis hurtled down Seventh Avenue. Just before heading into the narrower streets of lower Manhattan, the cabs snapped a right onto West Fourteenth Street. At Eighth Avenue, they slowed to a crawl. The cobbled thoroughfare leading to the river was jammed with cars, trucks, horses, and people surging toward the waterfront.

The cabdrivers leaned on their horns, but it took them twenty minutes to cover five blocks, reaching Pier 54 at 9:32.

Policemen held thousands of people behind a rope barrier hung with flickering green gas lanterns. A strong west wind blew off the river, carrying a light mist that threatened to become a chilly rain. *Carpathia* was already tied to the pier. Smith took off on his own, pushed his way through the crowd to the police gate, told the guard who he was, and ran for the canopied gangway. Passengers were leaving the ship. Murmuring Excuse me, he moved past the descending men, women, and children. None of them said a word as they stood aside. None looked Smith in the eye. All of them seemed timid. Damaged.

At the top of the gangway, Smith caught his breath and squared up in front of one of the two officers helping passengers from the ship. I am Senator William Alden Smith, and I am here to see Mr. J. Bruce Ismay, he said. One of the officers shrugged at the other, then nodded to Smith.

Follow me, he said. The officer escorted Smith into the ship, up a stairway, and along a corridor that smelled of sweat, stale kitchen aromas, and cigarette smoke. He stopped in front of a door on which was a hand-lettered sign:

PLEASE DO NOT KNOCK.

INVESTIGATION

Smith had seen a newspaper photograph of Bruce Ismay, who was rabbitlike, with a thin face and small eyes. The man who answered the stateroom door aboard *Carpathia* was beefy and florid. He introduced himself as Phillip Franklin and told Smith that Ismay was far too ill to receive a guest.

Smith shouldered his way past Franklin, who put up no resistance. The stateroom smelled worse than the corridor, a combination of must, vomit, and cologne. Ismay was slouched in a chair, his hair matted. It was obvious that he had not washed in several days. He was shaking visibly and did not make eye contact with Smith.

Smith recited the command he had practiced on the train: "I am empowered by the Congress of the United States to demand that you refrain from leaving my country until my committee has the opportunity to question you about the events surrounding the sinking of *Titanic*. If necessary, I will issue a subpoena to detain you."

In a voice that was weak but surprisingly clear, considering his disheveled condition, Ismay told Smith that a subpoena would not be necessary. He would cooperate in any way he could.

Smith asked about the surviving crew members, still afraid that Ismay would spirit them out of the country before he could interview them.

Most of the crew died, Ismay said. The ones who did not die were at the Institute of the Seamen's Friend. He told Smith to let Franklin know whom he wanted to interview, and Franklin would make it happen. Ismay said he had considered taking his crew to England immediately only because he wanted to reunite them with their families as soon as possible.

Smith had relaxed after Ismay agreed to cooperate with him, and his obviously genuine concern for his crew softened Smith even further. He offered his hand. Ismay remained seated, reached up, and stiffly shook it once.

Smith told him that the hearings would begin at ten the following morning at the Waldorf-Astoria hotel. Ismay would be the first witness.

"And after that?" Franklin asked.

"That will be determined by tomorrow's developments," Smith said.

Smith left the stateroom for the boat deck and some fresh air. He stood at the rail, watching *Titanic* survivors and *Carpathia*'s passengers flow from the gangplank into the crowd. Each arrival triggered a surge of sobbing or laughing, a mingling of joy and sorrow that chilled Smith like nothing he had ever expected to hear in his life.

———

The following morning, the chairman of the White Star Line looked better but not good when he walked into the East Room of the Waldorf-Astoria. Ismay was carefully groomed, wearing a dark blue suit, starched white shirt, and black tie. His eyes moved around constantly, like those of a prey animal.

The formal reception hall, with brocade drapes, floral-print wallpaper, and sparkling glass chandeliers, had been arranged so that the only furniture was a large conference table in its center and straight-backed chairs against the walls. The room had been opened to reporters and onlookers at nine A.M. and had filled up in minutes. An hour later, it was a fog of cigarette smoke. The tone inside verged on that of a mob rather than a hearing of the United States Senate.

As Ismay walked in, trays of photoflash powder added the stench of burning magnesium to the air. Smith, who was sitting at the conference table, yelled, "Get those cameras out of here."

"Mr. Ismay," Smith began, with no preliminary remarks, "will you kindly tell the committee the circumstances surrounding your voyage and, as succinctly as possible . . . your place on the ship on the voyage, together with any circumstances you feel would be helpful to us in the inquiry?"

Ismay shut his eyes, opened them, and spoke. His tone was firm, his accent so crisp that it sounded like a theatrical parody of the way an upper-class Englishman spoke.

"In the first place, I would like to express my sincere grief at this deplorable catastrophe. I understand that you gentlemen have been appointed as a committee of the Senate to inquire into the circumstances. So far as we are concerned, we welcome it. We have nothing to conceal, nothing to hide. The ship was built in Belfast. She was the latest thing in the art of shipbuilding; absolutely no money was spared in her construction."

Smith let Ismay talk for ten minutes without interruption. He described *Titanic*'s sea trials and the departure from Southampton, leaving out the incident with SS *New York*. Without notes, Ismay recited the speed of the ship and number of propeller revolutions at which the engines were turning for each day of the voyage. It was immediately obvious to Smith that he was responding to criticism about the speed of the ship that had surfaced in the newspapers. Ismay bluntly stated that a full-speed test of the ship had been tentatively scheduled for the day after the disaster, but that *Titanic* had never in its life reached its top speed. He had in no way encouraged Captain Smith to increase speed to reach New York ahead of schedule.

Senator Smith had mentally sketched his agenda for the investigation on the train north from Washington, and through the night at the hotel in New York. Stories help people make sense of the world. Smith wanted to write the story of *Titanic* in his report to the nation so it would not seem like random death, which was far too difficult to understand. He was sure that the iceberg alone did not account for the magnitude of the tragedy.

The facts had to be right. Smith wanted to know what had happened: Why did an unsinkable ship go down so quickly? Why were there not enough lifeboats for all the passengers? Why were more people not saved? Who was to blame?

Titanic sailed under the British flag, but it was owned by J. P. Morgan. Smith had been an enemy of Morgan's and an opponent of trusts and monopolies. Whatever conclusions his committee reached, they had to emerge from a scrupulously transparent and unbiased process. Smith knew that the British would conduct their own inquiry, but on their home soil, where the invisible forces of their internal politics were much more likely to govern their conclusions.

Smith recognized that it was also his duty to give Ismay a

chance to respond to the accusations by the press and others who had vilified him. Most of what had been written about Ismay centered on the simple fact that he had left the sinking ship while 1,504 men, women, and children who held tickets on his magnificent ocean liner died horribly in the freezing water. Smith had allowed Ismay to turn his opening testimony into a defense against accusations that *Titanic* was running at full speed through the ice field. Now it was time to find out why he got into the lifeboat.

"Will you describe what you did after the collision?" Smith asked.

Ismay recalled the terrible night. The impact woke him up. Captain Smith told him the ship had hit an iceberg. He never mentioned sinking. Ismay went to the engine room. Chief Engineer Joseph Bell said he, too, thought the ship had suffered major damage, but he was confident that it would stay afloat.

One of Smith's aides brought in a profile of *Titanic* on an easel. Smith asked questions about speed, the extent of the damage to the ship, and the scene on the boat deck, and arrived at the ultimate moment. Ismay used the profile to show where he was at various times after *Titanic* hit the iceberg.

"What were the circumstances of your departure from the ship?" Smith asked.

"The lifeboat was there. The officer called out asking if there were any more women, and there was no response. There were no passengers left on deck."

"There were no passengers on deck?" Smith repeated, unable to stifle an incredulous note in his voice that sent a wave of murmuring through the crowd.

"No, sir," Ismay said. "As the boat was being lowered away, I got into it."

Smith led Ismay through *Titanic*'s final moments. Ismay

said he was facing away from the ship when it went down, that he was grateful that he had not seen it sink, that *Titanic* was in one piece the last time he looked at it. Ismay shut his eyes in mid-sentence and stopped talking. Smith changed the subject.

"Do you know whether the ship was equipped with its full complement of lifeboats?"

"If she had not been," Ismay said, sounding exasperated with Smith's interrogation tactics, "she could not have sailed."

Smith excused Ismay, telling him to remain available in the United States for recall. The reporters broke for the exits to launch extra editions of their papers with the excuses of the man who'd fled his sinking ship, leaving hundreds of innocents to die.

———

After lunch, Smith called *Carpathia*'s captain, Arthur Rostron, to the witness chair, knowing that the testimony of the disaster's most obvious hero would be a dramatic counterpoint to that of its villain. After rising to greet Rostron as he entered, Smith let the captain roam at will through his account of racing to *Titanic* to pick up the survivors in lifeboats.

"The whole thing was absolutely providential," Rostron said. "I will tell you this, that the wireless operator was in his cabin at the time, not on official business at all, but just simply listening as he was undressing. He was unlacing his boots. He had his listening apparatus on his ear, and the message came. That was the whole thing. In ten minutes he would have been in bed, and we would not have heard the message."

A few in the audience were so moved by Rostron's tale of his lucky Marconi operator that they applauded. Then the mood changed from one of relief at that bit of good luck to one in which the stark reality of what Rostron saw dragged the crowd into a place so dark it dismantled the pretensions of order they trusted the hearing to maintain.

"By the time we had the first boat's people, it was breaking day. I could see the remaining boats within an area of about four miles. I saw icebergs all around me. I maneuvered the ship and we gradually got all the boats together. There was hardly any wreckage, only small pieces of broken-up stuff." Rostron paused. "By eight-thirty, all the people were on board. I asked for the purser, and told him that I wanted . . ." Rostron stopped, stifled a sob, and began to weep. "I wanted a short prayer of thankfulness for those rescued, and a burial service for those who were lost."

The hearing was transformed from an inquisition into a funeral service. Many wept openly, including Smith, who leaned across the table and grasped Rostron's forearm.

Rostron went on: "I then got an Episcopal clergyman, one of our passengers, and asked if he would do this for me, which he did willingly. While they were holding the service, I was on the bridge, of course, and I maneuvered around the scene of the wreckage. We saw nothing except one body."

"Floating?" Smith said hoarsely.

"Floating."

The room was absolutely quiet for a long minute. Smith broke the silence with a line of questioning about the authority of *Titanic*'s captain. Rostron said he knew Captain Smith, and knew without a doubt that he would never have taken orders to increase speed or anything else from Ismay or any official of the company who happened to be aboard.

"At sea, immediately I leave port until I arrive at port, the captain is in absolute control and takes orders from no one," he said. "And neither would E. J. Smith."

Ismay, who was sitting inconspicuously against the wall, slumped with relief. Rostron had effectively refuted the charge for which Ismay had been tried and convicted by Hearst and the rest of the American press. He had not ordered Captain Smith to fire all boilers to break a speed record, because after thirty years in the shipping business, he would know that Smith would never have obeyed such an order.

"One more question," Senator Smith said. "Some complaint has been made because the message of the president of the United States which was sent to the *Carpathia* was not answered. Do you know anything about that?"

"I heard last night that there was a message about a Major Butt," Rostron said. "I asked my purser about it. He said, Yes, *Olympic* sent a message asking if Major Butt was on board. It was answered, 'Not on board.' That is the only thing I know about it."

Smith thanked Rostron, shook his hand, and called a break.

———

Charles Lightoller, the highest-ranking member of *Titanic*'s surviving crew, appeared in the hearing room wearing the blue working uniform in which he had left the ship. Ismay and Rostron had been dramatic, but one of them was not a mariner, and the other had not been aboard *Titanic*. Smith hoped Lightoller would be a willing and expert eyewitness. Lightoller's first few answers to Smith's questions revealed him to be terse and guarded.

"When did you board *Titanic*?" "In Belfast." "When?" "March 19 or 20." "Did you make the so-called trials?" "Yes, sir." "Of what did they consist?" "Turning circles and adjusting compasses."

If Lightoller wanted to play criminal defendant with Smith, then Smith would happily oblige him with a grilling he would never forget. For two hours without a break, Smith peppered Lightoller with questions. Lightoller parried with vague and evasive answers.

"I wish you would describe a life belt," Smith said, after two questions on the same topic that Lightoller slipped like a boxer ducking punches.

"It consists of a series of pieces of cork. A hole is cut in there," he said, pointing to an illustration on an easel, "for the head to go through and this falls over front and back, and there are tapes from the back then tied around the front. It is a new idea and very effective, because no one can make a mistake in putting it on—"

Smith interrupted. "Have you ever been into the sea with one of them?"

"Yes, sir."

"Where?"

"From the *Titanic*."

"How long were you in the sea with a life belt on?"

"Between half an hour and an hour."

"What time did you leave the ship?"

"I didn't leave it."

"Did the ship leave you?"

"Yes, sir."

"I wish you would tell us whether the suction incidental to the sinking of this vessel was a great deterrent in making progress away from the boat."

"It was hardly noticeable."

Smith left Lightoller at the moment he was swept into the sea to ask him whether third-class passengers were allowed on the boat deck. Of course, Lightoller told him. There was no restraint at all. Everyone was calm. And orderly. Lightoller said neither he nor any of the passengers believed *Titanic* was in danger of sinking, even after they started launching lifeboats. He had heard and felt the impact of the iceberg from his cabin but thought it was nothing serious.

When Lightoller described the events that followed the impact, he closed his eyes, as though visualizing himself walking to the bridge, learning that the ship had struck something, and receiving Captain Smith's order to launch the lifeboats. His brows pinched in a clearly sorrowful expression.

He had shown no emotion until then. Smith set off on a long line of questioning about the process for measuring the temperature of the sea, Marconi messages warning of ice in the vicinity, the speed of the ship, the changing of the watch shortly before impact, and Captain Smith's order to launch the lifeboats. Smith's interrogation of Lightoller was making those of Ismay and Rostron seem like parlor chats.

After a break, Lightoller's responses were still terse and evasive but colored by impatience. Smith detected weakness, and brought him back to the moment when he'd abandoned ship.

"Where did you last see the captain?"

"On the boat deck, sir."

"Was the vessel broken in two or intact?"

"Absolutely intact."

"On the decks?"

"Intact, sir."

Smith asked Lightoller why he launched his first lifeboats half empty. Lightoller shocked Smith by replying that he believed the situation was not serious enough to risk lowering inexperienced passengers seventy feet down into the water in fully loaded boats.

Silence filled the East Room as everyone thought the same thing: How could the fourth-highest-ranking officer on the ship not have known that the situation was urgent?

Smith finally spoke: "Supposing you had known it was urgent, what would you have done?"

"I would have acted to the best of my judgment then."

"Tell me what you would have thought wise," Smith shot back at him.

"I would have taken more risks."

Smith pounded away on the loading of the lifeboats for fifteen more minutes, but Lightoller seemed to have hit his weakest moment and gained renewed strength. It took Smith a half hour to extract a second-by-second description of *Titanic* sinking, the absence of crying and lamentation among the dying crew and passengers, the explosion Lightoller felt when he was in the water under the overturned lifeboat.

Smith gauged the mood of the crowd. It was generally unsympathetic to Lightoller's diffidence, but he didn't want to risk pushing it any further. If Smith continued, it might look like he was badgering the poor officer who had his ship leave him. He excused Lightoller but told him he would definitely be recalled.

Smith was exhausted. After a ten-minute recess, he was not in a mood to engage in another battle of wits. He called *Carpathia*'s Marconi operator, Harold Cottam, who spent a congenial thirty minutes describing *Titanic*'s distress call and the exchanges of messages with other ships and shore stations over the next seventy-two hours.

Smith ended the session with first-class steward Alfred Crawford, who brought the room to tears for the second time that day.

"Did you know Mr. and Mrs. Straus?" Smith asked.

"I stood at the boat where they refused to get in," Crawford replied. He had the calm, mannered voice of an English butler.

"Did Mrs. Straus get into the boat?"

"She attempted to get into the boat first and she got back out again. Her maid got into the boat."

"What do you mean by 'she attempted' to get in?"

"She went to get over from the deck to the boat, but then went back to her husband."

"What followed?"

"She said, 'We have been living together for many years. Where you go I go.'"

———

The first session was over, but the long day was not. While Smith and his committee were taking testimony at the Waldorf-Astoria, hundreds of newspapers were interviewing their own witnesses and printing whatever they said. There was no such thing as a bad *Titanic* story, or one that was not taken for the truth.

Ismay told Smith the ship never went over 75 revolutions and 21.5 knots. The evening edition of the *New York Times*, and dozens of its corresponding papers around the world, ran an interview with *Titanic* fireman John Thompson. He said, "From the time we left Queenstown until the moment of the shock it never went below 74. During that whole Sunday we had been keeping up to 77. Surely she was going full speed then."

Smith announced that he was not reading newspapers, and that the only legally binding conclusions would come from the inquiry. Courts in the United States would consider only sworn testimony in deciding whether or not White Star and International Mercantile Marine were concealing negligence aboard *Titanic*. If they were, they would be liable for damages under American shipping laws because the ship was owned by a trust chartered in the United States. The critical question was, Was Ismay, as president of IMM and chairman of White Star, aware of any negligence in the building of the ship or its operation? If the answer to that question was yes, then hundreds of American citizens could sue Morgan's trust. In all likelihood, they would win.

Late Friday evening, Smith and his committee agreed that Lightoller was concealing something, but they weren't sure what. The main thing they derived from his testimony was that *Titanic*'s surviving crew members would probably say as little as possible to avoid negligence charges.

After the hearing, Ismay had pleaded with Smith to let him return with the crew on the steamer *Lapland*, scheduled to leave the following morning. Smith had refused. While he believed Ismay to be innocent of the worst suspicions bandied about in the press, he did not think it would be fair to citizens of the United States to let him and his crew return to England, where American law could not reach them.

Minutes after Smith told Ismay he could not leave the country, an IMM lawyer repeated the plea. The company simply could not be responsible for the bed and board of more than two hundred British citizens in New York for the duration of the hearings. Fine, Smith told him. I want Ismay, the four surviving officers, and a dozen or two crewmen. Which crewmen? the lawyer asked. Smith said he'd get a list to him first thing in the morning.

At midnight, an old friend of Smith's from Michigan, Sheriff Joe Bayliss, arrived. Bayliss had taken a night train to New York and spent the day at the Institute of the Seamen's Friend eavesdropping on members of *Titanic*'s crew. He handed Smith a list of twenty-nine crewmen who had either been in charge of a lifeboat or who were freely telling horror stories about the ship's navigation and management. Smith asked Bayliss to come back at first light, saying he would give him subpoenas for all of them. Then Smith and one of his Senate aides stayed up for another two hours preparing the documents.

The following morning, Bayliss served the subpoenas while Smith grappled with the implications of a report that had reached him at breakfast. The British consul in New York was at that moment on a train to Washington to protest the Senate's treatment of the crew of *Titanic* and White Star officials. The IMM lawyers had spent the better part of the night on the phone with senators and congressmen friendly to J. P. Morgan, arguing that a federal committee could not legally subpoena foreigners in the sovereign state of New York. Smith sized it up as a states rights versus the federal government debate that would go nowhere. Still, he wasn't going to take any chances. He had already heard enough to know that White Star was going to lean heavily on the men on its payroll to keep any hint of negligence out of the committee record. He hoped he was a good enough interrogator to penetrate the wall of half-truths they would erect, but he couldn't do it if they left the country.

Smith didn't want to risk letting Morgan swing enough weight to quash his subpoenas in New York, so he decided to go back to Washington and continue his hearings on federal territory. He would hear testimony from one more witness in New York, a man who was too ill to travel, then leave town immediately.

Marconi operator Harold Bride appeared in the East

Room of the Waldorf in a wheelchair, looking like a sick, frightened teenage boy. He testified for a little over an hour, his voice weakening by the minute as he described sending the distress calls, *Carpathia*'s response, and the confusion in the radiosphere over the Atlantic until Captain Smith relieved him. Bride's voice was almost a whisper when he told how he was swept into the water and clambered atop the overturned boat. Bride said he was the last man invited on board. Everyone on the overturned boat was a member of the crew.

Smith asked Bride what he saw in the water around the overturned lifeboat.

Dozens and dozens of men, women, and children, Bride said. Struggling to get on.

To Smith, it was obvious that Bride was telling the truth. Lightoller, who had said the people in the water were some distance away, was a liar. Was Lightoller also lying about the ship being intact until it sank? About the loading of the lifeboats? Who else from *Titanic*'s crew was going to lie to him?

Smith called a recess until three in the afternoon.

Before he left the room, Joe Bayliss took him aside. *Lapland* had sailed that morning with five of the men Smith had subpoenaed aboard. The others had agreed to testify. Smith pulled Bayliss into the lobby, went to a phone, and called the Brooklyn Navy Yard. Send a cable to *Lapland*, now leaving New York Harbor, he told the duty officer who answered the call. Order *Lapland* to await a federal boarding party. Two hours later, Bayliss arrived off Sandy Hook on the navy tug *Barrett*, boarded the idling *Lapland*, and took the final five men on the witness list into custody.

At three o'clock, Smith read a statement canceling the next hearing. The committee would resume taking testimony on Monday in Washington to hear from the rest of the crew who had been subpoenaed, and also from many of the passengers.

On his way out of the hotel, surrounded by a clutch of reporters, Smith said, "The surface has barely been scratched. The real investigation is yet to come."

———

On the day Senator Smith was fleeing New York, Margaret Pirrie prepared to tell her husband that *Titanic* was gone and Thomas Andrews was dead. Edward Wilding's cable about the disaster had reached her two days earlier, when *Valiant* was inbound for the Thames with the Danish coast well behind. They would be in London the next day. Pirrie had been taking a few painful steps on the deck every morning and evening, but he still spent most of his time in bed.

On Friday, April 20, Margaret knew she had to tell him. Once they were in London, every paper in the country would be filled front to back with stories on the lost ship. It would be impossible to keep the secret. Better that he hear it from her than from strangers. It was not a moment for mincing words. *Titanic* had sunk, Margaret said from the chair next to his berth where she had spent countless hours. It hit an iceberg and was gone in just over two hours. Tommy Andrews died a hero helping others to survive. All nine Harland and Wolff men who were with him were lost. She gave him what other details she had: Hundreds were dead; the Americans were holding Ismay and the crew to interrogate them.

Pirrie bucked against his pillows as though he had been shot. He lay without speaking in his dimly lit stateroom for what seemed like an hour, finally asking Margaret for his lap desk.

To his sister, Thomas Andrews's mother, Pirrie wrote in

longhand on a piece of plain, deckled stationery, telling her, "A finer fellow than Tommy never lived." Pirrie told her that Andrews had been brave and unselfish to the end.

Pirrie told Margaret to be sure his note went to Belfast by special courier as soon as *Valiant* reached London, then asked her for a telegraph pad. Sick, sore, and saddened beyond anything he'd ever thought he would have to endure, Pirrie went to work. *Valiant* had a low-voltage wireless transmitter, but it was powerful enough to reach the Ramsgate shore station, at the mouth of the Thames.

His first cable went to Edward Wilding at Harland and Wolff.

FIND OUT WHAT HAPPENED TO THAT SHIP   PIRRIE

SECRETS

ROGER WRONG, ROGER RIGHT

Ninety-three years later, Roger Long stared at a television monitor in his office in Cape Elizabeth, Maine, trying to make sense of the newly found pieces of *Titanic*. They were definitely part of the bottom of a ship. The bilge keels and red antifouling paint were unmistakable. But he had no idea where they fit into the hull. Unless he could orient them correctly, the patterns of bending and tearing left in the edges of the steel would tell him nothing.

For a month after he'd gotten home from the expedition, Long had made up for lost sailing days and put out fires in his business that had started while he was away. He ran a one-man shop from a single room in his house, doing as much work there as he had when he'd employed two other engineers. Long had bought his first computer in the mid-1980s, and instantly understood the power of the new machine for calculations and record keeping. Fast graphics cards soon opened the floodgates for design software to analyze buoyancy, stability, and the other critical variables in building a ship. One man could do the work of three. Long missed the camaraderie of a drawing office, but he loved the freedom.

Long's proudest memory as a naval architect had come from solving the mystery of a ship that failed. On June 3, 1984, the 120-foot bark *Marques*, en route from Bermuda to Halifax, rolled over and sank in less than a minute. Nineteen of its crew of twenty-nine died. The ship was owned by one of Queen Elizabeth's cousins, who had somehow secured exemptions from periodic inspections required by the nation that invented shipping regulation. The British government convened a Wreck Commission, hiring Long as a friend of the court to develop an independent analysis of the ship's stability.

The government was anxious to show that even if it had insisted on the inspections, the vessel would have been found to be safe. Long analyzed the same plans, records of modifications, and rigging notes as the other experts who had concluded that the ship was sufficiently stable. He proved, however, that after haphazard refits over the years, *Marques* had had far too much sail area for the ballast it was carrying. A slight increase in wind speed under full sail had capsized the ship. A lawyer representing the family of one of the dead crewmen demanded that the commission find the owner guilty of murder.

The Wreck Commission agreed that the ship was unstable but maintained that nobody had known it until Long told them. The owner, therefore, was not negligent. The Wreck Commission's clever twist offended Long's sense of justice, reinforcing his belief that whitewashing a tragedy was always an exercise in power. With *Titanic*, he might be able to challenge the official conclusions about the most notorious shipwreck in history.

After Long's first pass through the video footage of the pieces of *Titanic*'s bottom, his hopes for another shipwreck coup dimmed. He had to know two things. First, where did the pieces come from? They were obviously part of the middle section of the ship, because that's where the bilge keels were and he could clearly see parts of the bilge keels. But exactly where did they fit in the puzzle of tortured steel? Second, he had to figure out what the hull had done as it came apart. Bend up? Bend down? Twist? The narrow views from the video cameras made it impossible to answer those questions.

Long asked Chatterton and Kohler to hire *Titanic* artist Ken Marschall to look at the video, then draw three-dimensional images of the pieces of the bottom and their places on the ship. Marschall's paintings, drawings, and books inform every modern visualization of *Titanic*, including those of James Cameron, who relied heavily on them in his movie. Marschall had viewed hundreds of hours of video footage and photographs to construct his supremely detailed images. He might be able to create realistic-looking pictures of the pieces so Long could see them in their entirety instead of through the tunnel of the video camera lens.

Three weeks later, Marschall's archeological-quality drawings arrived at Long's office. They showed the pieces interlocking to fill a huge gap in the bottom directly under the third funnel, where Long believed *Titanic* had broken in two. Marschall also sent detailed representations of each piece, showing them from the top, ends, and sides, where the bilge keels were visible.

Using Marschall's drawings to orient him, Long went back to his video monitor. He focused on the condition of the steel at the edges of the new bottom pieces, comparing it with the edges of the bow and stern sections of the main wreckage.

He saw evidence of both compression and tension failure of the ship's outer and inner bottoms. At some point, *Titanic* had bent down, like a shallow V, then up, like an inverted V. It would take a much more complex process than the high-angle break to explain what the steel from the ship's bottom was telling him.

My God, Long thought when it hit him. The ship didn't break up as it was sinking. It broke at a low angle on the surface and then sank. As Long went over the events of the breakup and sinking with that new assumption, he realized that the end would have been less dramatic than the high-angle-break scenario, but it would have been far more terrible in terms of what the doomed passengers and crew experienced.

In the high-angle-break scenario, everyone on board knew the ship was starting its final plunge. There was no doubt that they would soon be in the water. If *Titanic* broke at a low angle, however, it would have happened during a period of apparent calm. *Titanic* would have been settling slowly as water flooded into the ship. Hundreds of people still inside the warm interior without intercoms to tell them otherwise would have believed they were awaiting rescue aboard a ship that would float for several more hours. For those still on *Titanic*, stranded after the departure of the lifeboats, the dreadful message that they were about to die would have come in the form of loud cracks and shivering under their feet when the hull broke. Less than five minutes later, the entire ship was underwater.

Long was sure that the low-angle break took place well before *Titanic* pitched forward into its final plunge. That meant the timing of the sinking was determined by the structural failure and not the flooding. The ship would have remained afloat for some time longer if the hull had not broken. If *Titanic* had lasted only a few minutes more, it could have meant life for people who would have had time to cobble together a life raft of deck chairs. If it had lasted another hour, the half-empty lifeboats could have returned to pick up hundreds more. If it had lasted an hour and forty minutes longer, *Carpathia* would have arrived. Long could not be sure exactly how long the ship would have stayed afloat if it had not broken, but he knew that the *Titanic* story had just blown wide open.

———

The following week Long brought his theory to Chatterton and Kohler. He used a plan of the ship to show them the stages of flooding of the bow and center compartment, and Marschall's drawings of the bottom plates to illustrate how the plates broke and fell away as the ship bent under the third funnel.

"It's heretical on two counts," Long said. "First, the high-angle break has been accepted for so long there is going to be a storm of opposition when we trot out my scenario. It's the biggest scene in the movie, for crying out loud."

The conventional wisdom said that the ship was strong enough to lift its own stern that far out of the water before it broke. A paper by the architect who worked for the last American company to design a large ocean liner and a professor of naval architecture at one of the top schools in the country was full of analysis of the ship at forty-five degrees. *Titanic*'s hull should have been strong enough to go to forty-five degrees, but it broke at around eleven degrees. It had to be deeply flawed in some way that its designers and builders did not anticipate. Long said that was a big hole in his theory. The principles of hull strength were well understood when *Titanic* was built. The ship simply could not have been so weak.

Long's conclusions took the investigation in an entirely new and unexpected direction. Chatterton and Kohler had come to his office prepared to hear a version of the grounding theory. If there was even the slightest possibility that Long was right about the low-angle breakup, they had to keep going.

Why not present their new theory to people who knew much more than they did about the wreck? Long called Bill Lange, who agreed to host a conference of some of the most respected *Titanic* theorists at Woods Hole. He invited David G. Brown, Ken Marschall, Simon Mills, and Parks Stephenson, all of whom had been advisers on the expedition that discovered the missing pieces. For decades, they had studied the construction of the ship, accounts of the sinking by survivors, and the behavior of the passengers and crew. They would be able to quickly punch more holes in Long's theory. Or fill in the one he already had.

Long's low-angle-breakup theory, with or without the hole, was sensational news. During *Titanic*'s last moments as Long described them, death came for fifteen hundred people in a much more terrible way than everyone thought it had. The sudden breakup eliminated the hope that all or part of the ship might stay afloat and save them. Chatterton and Kohler gave the story to the Associated Press, which had broken their discovery of *U-869*, and invited a reporter to the Woods Hole meeting.

At nine-thirty on the morning of December 5, a dozen people milled around Billy Lange's laboratory, drinking coffee and eating pastries. They all knew one another, at least from Internet forums or e-mails, and had often disagreed bitterly on crucial points about the ship. In person they went out of their way to be gracious. The conference in Lange's lab was a rare opportunity to participate in something other than endless discussions that went nowhere because there was never any new evidence from the wreck.

Simon Mills arrived with a sheaf of plans for the *Olympic*-class ships from the British National Archives. He took Long aside and asked if he had ever seen a drawing of one of *Olympic*'s expansion joints, the gaps in the superstructure designed by Thomas Andrews to allow it to flex.

Long had lain awake the night before knowing that he had no answer for the big question that was sure to come: How could Harland and Wolff have built a ship so weak that the hull would fail the way he thought it had? *Olympic* and *Titanic* had been built from the same set of plans. Now, there on the drawing in front of him were the details of an expansion joint so primitive and crude that it could easily explain the difference in strength between a ship that should have been strong enough to lift its stern to a forty-five-degree angle and one that had failed at eleven degrees.

Long was familiar with the technology of the expansion joint. He also knew that this design feature had fallen out of favor long ago because, even after decades of development since the *Titanic* design, it was still structurally suspect. He turned from the table and burst into the group where Chatterton, Kohler, and Wolfinger were talking.

"You have to see this," he said, motioning them over to the drawing of the expansion joint. "The root of the joint has a small radius that would create an enormous concentration of stress in the hull right where it began to break under the third funnel."

Long, a calm, precise analyst, was as excited as a man seeing his lottery numbers tick onto the television screen.

"The stress in the area just below where these two plates are riveted to the main hull would have been off the charts," he said. "Once a small crack started there, it would have run quickly through the most highly stressed part of the hull. This could explain everything."

Long rarely expressed an opinion off the top of his head, especially about something as potentially important as an explanation for how a great shipbuilder could have built a weak ship. He decided not to incorporate the implications of a crude and dangerous expansion joint into his presentation that morning, but when he stood up to speak, he felt a lot better about the hole in his low-angle-break theory.

"The weight of the water in the bow was not only lifting the stern out of the water," Long began. "It was bending the ship. When a structure like a steel hull or a girder bends, the top of it stretches while the bottom of it is pushed together. Tension at top, compression at bottom." He used a pencil to demonstrate the hull bending, pointing out that the top of the ship would have been affected differently than the bottom.

"The edges of the top decks where the ship came apart are mangled and crushed. The edges of the bottom where the ship came apart, which should have been compressed, they appear to have been cleanly broken off. If the ship had broken at the high angle, everything up above should be quite clean, and the chaos, the jumbling, should be down at the bottom."

As Long talked, he referred to a series of drawings of the ship as it flexed, first in one direction, then the other. They showed the bow flooding, the bottom plates falling away, the middle compartments flooding fast, the bow breaking away, and finally the stern disappearing beneath the surface. He described the breakup beginning at as little as eleven degrees and happening in two stages. The bottom broke separately from the rest of the ship. As those bottom plates ruptured, the middle compartments flooded catastrophically. After that happened, the ship sank suddenly.

"The breakup was not just something that happened during the final plunge," Long said. "The breakup caused the final plunge. It determined whether a lot of people lived or died. One thing is certain: The steel doesn't lie. It does not have false memories. It does not protect reputations. It never forgets."

The others in the room had been speculating for years about what precisely had happened during *Titanic*'s last moments. Earlier proponents of the low-angle break had come and gone, defeated by the sensational imagery of the stern rising at a high angle against the star-washed night sky. Roger Long's interpretation of *Titanic*'s last moments, with the evidence from the steel, made more sense than anything else they had ever heard.

"What you have just said was backed up by personal testimony of the survivors," Parks Stephenson said. "The launching of the lifeboats was very orderly. The crew appeared to think they had longer to get people off the ship."

"Crew members actually stated that they did not think the ship was going to sink," David Brown said. "They thought it would settle to a certain point, and then it would stop sinking. I think everybody thought *Titanic* would float as its own lifeboat until *Carpathia* got there."

Billy Lange called for a break. Over the buzz of the conversations that erupted around the room, the sound of the door opening and shutting marked the departure of the Associated Press reporter. The story he must have dictated on the telephone made the afternoon editions of the East Coast papers and, the next day, papers around the world. It quoted Stephenson as saying that Long's low-angle theory depicted the breakup more accurately than ever before, and it pointed out that the end would have been even more horrible than previously believed. The reporter recapped the discovery of the wreck in 1985 and quoted Robert Ballard, who balanced Stephenson's enthusiasm by playing down the importance of the discovery.

"They found a fragment, big deal," Ballard was quoted as saying. "Am I surprised? No. When you go down there, there's stuff all over the place. It hit an iceberg and it sank. Get over it."

Ballard's remark ignited storms of protest among Titaniacs and the mainstream press. Three days later, the *New York Times* editorialized about the new evidence and what it meant about the last moments in the lives of fifteen hundred doomed passengers and crew. The *Times* wagged a critical finger at Ballard's reaction. "There is really no getting over *Titanic*," the paper insisted, "at least not where the human imagination is concerned."

For six months after the Woods Hole meeting, the high-angle versus low-angle controversy dominated the Titaniac forums and e-mail debates. Long's supporters cited testimony by survivors that the ship had barely disturbed the surface when it disappeared. His detractors cited testimony by other survivors that the final plunge had been accompanied by explosions and a wave that swamped lifeboats. James Cameron said the new evidence was interesting but nowhere near conclusive enough to change his mind about the high-angle break. Roger Long, he said, was Roger Wrong. Despite the pieces of the ship found by Chatterton and Kohler, and Long's deductions after analyzing the patterns in the steel, the debate was a stalemate.

In early spring 2006, an e-mail to Roger Long from a man named Tom McCluskie changed everything. McCluskie said he had read about Long's version of *Titanic*'s last moments in the newspaper and thought it was the most exciting development since the wreck was discovered.

"The true story of *Titanic* has never been told," McCluskie wrote. "I know things nobody else knows. Let's talk."

Since embarking on their investigation, Chatterton, Kohler, and Long had wasted plenty of time on dead-end leads and crackpot theorists. When they checked McCluskie's background, it looked like he might be the real thing. He had worked at Harland and Wolff from 1965 to 1997, ended his career as the company archivist, and was the author of four books on *Olympic*-class ships. His access to shipyard records made him the world's most direct living link to the people who had built *Titanic*.

Long put together a package of video footage, Marschall's drawings, and his own sketches and sent it to McCluskie in Belfast.

FIFTEEN

WEE MAN

Tom McCluskie was the son of the son of the son of a shipbuilder, with a lineage reaching back to the switch from sails to steam in the shipyards on Belfast Lough. His great-grandfather worked for Edward Harland. His grandfather began as a teenage apprentice under Pirrie and worked in the shipyard until the day he was killed by a taxicab as he trudged home from the yard a year shy of his sixtieth birthday. McCluskie's father, whose yard name was Sand Dancer, started out as a driller, became a hole cutter, then a boss.

McCluskie remembered his father's stories about the viciousness in the shipyard, his muttering accounts of the maiming and death of his friends on the job. He remembered his mother, Charlotte, packing his father's piece—his lunch box—every morning. She washed his work clothes every weekend, the water in the tub turning black with rust and soot as the navy blue of the overalls returned. To a child growing up in the afterglow of World War II in Northern Ireland, none of that was brutal tedium. It was the fair price his father paid for the privilege of building the heart-stopping ships that rose over the river Lagan in the middle of the twentieth century. To McCluskie, the names of the passenger ships, tankers, and freighters were resonant notes in a song of pride and accomplishment. *Southern Cross. Iberia. British Honour. British Power. Amazon. Aragon. Arlanza.* Above all, the magnificent 818-foot, 45,270-ton *Canberra*, Harland and Wolff's last great ocean liner. His father had been on one of the gangs that laid the steel for *Canberra*'s keel, a luminous event in dinner-table recollections of family history. Harland and Wolff was too much to resist for a Belfast boy who hated school, came from shipbuilding people, and wanted to please his grouchy father in the sincerest possible way by following in his footsteps.

In the summer of 1965, when Tom was fifteen years old, Sand Dancer and his son left the house together with their pieces tucked under their arms. They walked through the rows of two-up houses in the north end to the ferry for the five-minute trip from Belfast to Queen's Island, across the Lagan. On the open deck, Tom stood in a crowd of men who looked tired and lifeless on a bright morning, staring silently at the smokestacks, cranes, and scaffolds of Harland and Wolff rising to meet them. Even with the bass thump of the ferry's diesel, Tom heard the sounds of the shipyard, the snaps and crackles of hundreds of arc welders, the bells of moving cranes, the howls of saws tearing through steel plates.

"You've suddenly gone quiet," his father said. "I bloody well hope you aren't having second thoughts about starting here, because it's too late now."

McCluskie's father had called in favors to get his son an easy starting job as a messenger boy. Later, if Tom didn't foul up, he could join an apprentice class at the training school.

"No. No second thoughts," Tom replied. "I'm just a bit surprised by how miserable everybody looks."

At the Market Square gate, Tom's father handed him off

to the timekeeper. Tom McCluskie's board number, which he would have until he was fired, got hurt too badly to work, or died, was 155314.

The timekeeper explained that the company granted every man a total of seven minutes in the bathroom each day. Every time he went into one of the drafty buildings where the toilets were cement latrines, he would hand his board to a man at the door, who would mark down his number and the time he went in. After seven minutes, his pay would be docked, and he would be crapping on his own time.

Before the end of his first day, McCluskie got something else that would remain with him for the rest of his life at Harland and Wolff: his name. The product of generations of compact Ulstermen marrying even smaller Ulsterwomen, McCluskie stood five feet, two inches and weighed 140 pounds. The timekeeper passed him on to the clerk in the mail office, who took one look at his new messenger and said, "You're a Wee Man, you are."

For a year, Wee Man ran around the yard delivering letters, tubes of drafting sheets, and messages between bosses. The day after his sixteenth birthday, he became an apprentice engineer. It was a step up for only as long as it took him to realize that as a small man at the bottom of a vicious pecking order, he was going to be miserable for a long time. The cruelty of the masters under whom he worked was exceeded only by the brutality of hazing among the apprentices.

McCluskie lasted three months as an apprentice. In early October, he was standing at a workbench putting together a valve when he felt a tap on his shoulder. He thought it was the instructor, turned around, and got hit in the face with a paintbrush loaded with red lead antifouling paint.

McCluskie was sure he was blinded for life. The apprentice master rushed him to the shipyard nurse, who washed out his eyes. You'll be fine in a few days, the nurse told him. Who did this to you?

Cruelty endured at Harland and Wolff because the men rarely broke the code of silence, keeping revenge to themselves. Failing to obey the silence meant far worse punishment. McCluskie told the nurse he had accidentally splashed the paint on himself when he'd opened the can.

That day, Wee Man walked away from Harland and Wolff on sick leave. A week later, his eyes still burning, he found a new job at the parts counter of R. E. Hamilton's Ford dealership in Belfast. Not long after, he fell in love with a tiny, pretty girl named Sylvia who had come to the garage to pick up a muffler for an Anglia sedan. Soberly facing the realities of a man about to be married amid rumors that Hamilton's was going out of business, Wee Man went back to Harland and Wolff. His number was still 155314.

Wee Man was again an engineering apprentice. He graduated to the drawing office, married Sylvia, and bought a house outside town with a small down payment and a big mortgage. Among his chores was responding to requests from shipowners for plans, manuals, and other documents, most of which he filled as quickly as possible with the approval of the chief technical manager. There were also letters asking for information about *Titanic*, many of them poignantly written by relatives of the victims of the disaster. To these, McCluskie replied with a form letter that said, "The company is unable to assist you in obtaining the information you have requested."

At the end of one day in an endless succession of days at the shipyard, McCluskie asked his boss if he could devote some of his time to researching questions about *Titanic* and writing answers to all those letters. His boss told him that Harland and Wolff would just as soon forget that *Titanic* had ever existed, but if McCluskie wanted to spend a few hours a week on the letter it was okay with him.

McCluskie opened storeroom doors that had been shut for decades. He found stacks and boxes of files, ledgers, and correspondence, none of it organized by topic, chronology, or hull number. There were at least a million individual drawings and plans for hundreds of ships, and thousands of photographs. He had always done his work at the shipyard as well as he possibly could, advancing upward through the ranks. But that was a job. Organizing the archive and answering letters about *Titanic* became a vocation. After Ballard and Michel found the wreck in 1985, the trickle of letters asking for information about *Titanic* increased to a torrent.

From 1968, when McCluskie returned to the shipyard, until 1986, when he submerged himself in the archive, Harland and Wolff had built only forty ships. The episodic downturns the company had weathered for a century had become a death spiral. Shipyards in Asia were building the same ships for half the price. Harland and Wolff hadn't turned a profit in decades. It was no longer a privately held company but a heavily subsidized public corporation propped up with massive loans. The British government wanted nothing more than to unload it and, in 1989, finally succeeded, selling it for pennies on the dollar to Norwegian shipping magnate Fred Olsen, who changed the name to Harland and Wolff Holdings.

As Harland and Wolff staggered into the last decade of the twentieth century, maintaining the archive became a low priority. Hoping to justify its existence, McCluskie turned his office into a small business, selling copies of the plans, memorabilia, and photographs. He launched a collaboration with local manufacturers to produce a line of merchandise evoking the golden age of ships and shipbuilding. The Harland and Wolff Maritime Collection featured bone china, crystal glasses, linens, and silverware in the patterns of the White Star Line.

In 1994, McCluskie got a call from Los Angeles.

"We want to rebuild *Titanic* for a movie," the speaker said. His name was Peter Lamont, and he was a production designer working for producer-director James Cameron. "We want you to help us."

By then, McCluskie had gotten used to calls asking for advice and help with fantastic schemes. He was skeptical, but something in Lamont's voice signaled a higher grade of confidence than the crackpots and wannabes. McCluskie agreed to meet him in Belfast.

"Would tomorrow be convenient?" Lamont asked. "I can be on the first flight this morning."

The next day, Lamont made a deal with Harland and Wolff to borrow McCluskie as a technical adviser. The moviemakers would pay his salary and expenses; the company would give him a leave of absence. Because of the eight-hour time difference between Belfast and the West Coast of the United States, McCluskie worked at night from home, checking e-mailed scenes and photographs of sets for accuracy. Near the end of his work on the film, Lamont sent him a scene in which two men in the engine room were brewing tea using steam from one of the boilers. Lamont called it a thumbprint. He and Cameron had remembered McCluskie telling them how the engineers made tea, and left the scene in the movie as a private thank-you for his contribution to their work.

McCluskie was celebrated by historical societies, moviemakers, and shipping buffs, but his life inside Harland and

Wolff deteriorated into a bitter conflict with its chief executive. For a while, McCluskie's resurrection of the archive did not rise high enough in the bureaucracy to attract attention from the top. Fred Olsen, the new owner, had installed a seasoned industrial pro, Per Nielsen, to preside over the winding down of the shipyard and the emergence of Harland and Wolff Holdings as a real estate development company. Nielsen was infuriated by McCluskie. Reminding people that Harland and Wolff had built the notorious ship that killed hundreds of innocent men, women, and children was corporate suicide, not a point of pride. McCluskie's Maritime Collection was a bad idea, too, making a heavy industrial corporation look like an amateur museum.

Once Nielsen figured out what McCluskie was doing, Wee Man knew it was only a matter of time before Harland and Wolff would pitch him out the door. He began negotiating with the Ulster Folk and Transport Museum and the Public Record Office of Northern Ireland to find a permanent home for the archive's treasures.

In the spring of 1997, McCluskie was promoting a gala to celebrate the Belfast screening of Cameron's *Titanic*. He wanted to set up tents and hold the afterparty on the site of the slipway where the ship had been built, and invite people to come in period costumes to mingle with movie stars. Nielsen killed the party. "It wouldn't make us any money," he told a newspaper reporter. "It was a side issue to the main job of building ships and keeping the company going."

Later that year, McCluskie and Nielsen got into a screaming fight. McCluskie had retrieved the *Canberra*'s builder's plate from the breakers' yard, a priceless artifact that McCluskie wanted to install in the shipyard as a monument. Nielsen ordered him to put it in storage.

Two days later, Wee Man's war with Nielsen ended. After working late, McCluskie left his office, drove home, stretched out on the sofa with a bad headache, and had a stroke that left him paralyzed and blind in one eye. It took him three years to relearn how to speak, move his arms, and walk. For six months, Harland and Wolff paid him half his salary. After that, he got nothing. In 2000, at the age of fifty, he asked for his job back. Not a chance, Nielsen told him. Take your pension. You're done.

———

When McCluskie emerged from the international arrivals hall at Boston's Logan Airport, Roger Long's heart sank. The jockey-sized old man carrying a satchel was balding, with a comb-over and thick, arched, dark eyebrows, and he walked with the hesitant gait of exhaustion. His skin tone was only a shade away from the white of his sport coat. Long was afraid that the man he was hoping would fill the hole in his theory was going to keel over before he ever had a chance to talk to him.

A half hour later, after checking into their hotel near the airport, Long took McCluskie to dinner. The Italian restaurant was dark, aromatic, and packed with families and couples on dates. Long ordered a beer and chicken cacciatore. McCluskie ordered water and spaghetti.

McCluskie would do an interview the next day in front of a camera, but Long couldn't wait.

Tom, I want to hear what you have come to tell me, he said. You know what we think happened to the ship from our e-mails and the stuff I sent you. What we can't figure out is how it could have been so weak.

Long's blunt question transformed McCluskie. The exhausted, timid man from the airport was replaced by a pedant who confidently explained himself.

It's the stroke, he said. When I'm tired, people tell me I look like I'm drunk or very sick. But I get little bursts of energy.

To begin with, McCluskie said in answer to Long's question, Thomas Andrews saw *Olympic*'s hull panting during sea trials.

Long knew exactly what that meant. The hull of a steel ship is in constant motion, flexing, bending, and even doing what Andrews had called panting, with the sides of the hull moving in and out. The motion is rarely visible to the unaided eye. It was a question of degree.

How do you know? Long asked.

I read Andrews's engineering notebooks for *Olympic*, McCluskie said.

McCluskie had read everything. He talked about Andrews's adding steel to *Titanic*'s superstructure, the cracks in the hulls of both ships, the dismal condition of the bow plates and rivets after *Hawke* collided with *Olympic*. Pirrie, Andrews, Ismay, Wilding, and everybody else at Harland and Wolff had had no idea whether *Olympic* and *Titanic* were strong enough to hold together at sea.

They were cultural egomaniacs, McCluskie said, as if he were personally offended by all of them. They thought they could do anything they wanted to do, build anything as big as they wanted it to be.

As McCluskie had gotten to know *Titanic*, its builders, and its owners, he'd found himself unable to ignore the monumental hubris of the age. Inventors and builders had entered the nineteenth century using only their own and animal power, with a little help from wind and water—the same things they had used for millennia. They had entered the twentieth century with capacities for transportation, production, and manufacturing multiplied a thousandfold by the power of machines. It was regrettable, but completely understandable, if shipbuilders thought they could make ships as big as they wanted them to be.

Pirrie, Andrews, and Wilding had simply scaled up the hull of *Oceanic* and much smaller ships, doing their strength calculations with pencils. Long knew that engineering a hull was never a matter of merely putting more steel into it; the trick was to use just enough. It was easy to be wrong. In fact, it was a miracle if one was right. *Titanic* was nowhere near as strong a ship as it would have had to be for the high-angle-break theory to be true.

Why are you talking to me about this now, Tom? Long asked.

I'm tired of carrying it around in me, McCluskie said. After the stroke, every day might be my last.

———

The next morning, Roger Long and a video crew were set up in Bill Lange's conference room at Woods Hole. McCluskie looked rested and relaxed. John Chatterton was due sometime that morning; Richie Kohler was at home with his children.

"Okay, Tom," Long began. "Let's start with what you said Thomas Andrews observed during *Olympic*'s sea trials. What you told me at dinner last night."

"You don't design two sister ships, you design one," Mc-Cluskie said. "Then you use the same set of plans to build both of them. On the *Titanic* drawings, over which I have spent many hours, you can see lots of changes made by Thomas Andrews after he discovered design flaws during *Olympic*'s sea trials, things that could have been done better or been done differently."

McCluskie went into far more detail than he had over dinner the night before. After Andrews noticed that the hull was panting during *Olympic*'s sea trials, he worried that the hull wasn't stiff enough. White Star had scheduled *Olympic* to sail on its first crossing immediately, so Andrews couldn't change anything right then. But he could, and did, add steel bracing to *Titanic*, particularly in the bow and the superstructure of the front of the ship. The most dramatic change he made to *Titanic* was enclosing the promenade deck with steel. White Star said it was to turn the promenade into a small restaurant, but that wasn't true. It was to stiffen the ship. There was a tremendous amount of vibration in that part of *Olympic*, so Andrews tried to stop it on *Titanic*. He also added reinforcing steel to *Titanic* at the bottom where the double bottom met the main hull.

Roger Long managed to stay in his chair, but he felt like doing cartwheels around the room. If *Olympic* had been panting and cracking in calm seas, it must have been right on the edge of coming apart.

"What about the possibility that the ship broke up on the surface, and that it would have stayed afloat a lot longer if it had not?" Long asked.

"At the inquiry, Harland and Wolff did not offer any opinion about the ship breaking up on the surface," McCluskie said, his voice stronger and more assertive than ever. "They avoided the question. However, from private documentation within the company which I saw many times, they determined that it was very likely that the ship had broken in half. It was never made public."

After Harland and Wolff's confidential investigation determined that *Titanic* had probably broken up on the surface, McCluskie said, they had come to a horrible conclusion. Using estimates of the amount of water flooding into the ship through its damaged bow, they calculated that if *Titanic* had not broken, it would have remained afloat for three to three and a half hours. Plenty of time for half-empty lifeboats to return, or for *Carpathia* to arrive.

John Chatterton, who had come in a few minutes earlier, tapped Long on the shoulder and whispered, "Am I hearing what I think I'm hearing?"

McCluskie glanced at Chatterton, paused, and went on.

"No one at the inquiry asked the right questions," he said. "Edward Wilding, who testified on behalf of Harland and Wolff, had been instructed to volunteer nothing."

One of the first disturbing pieces of evidence McCluskie had found in his exploration of the Harland and Wolff archive was in the design notes. Andrews had specified 1¼-inch plate for the *Olympic*-class hulls, but Ismay had told Andrews that the ship had to be built lighter than his original design. He had calculated that the hull needed to be 1¼-inch steel to have an acceptable degree of strength. White Star had insisted that all they really needed under the Board of Trade rules was 1-inch steel. Harland and Wolff managers would have known that the lesser thickness of steel would have weakened the hull, but they did what the customer wanted them to do. If Andrews had built the ship he'd wanted to build, things probably would have turned out a lot differently.

"Roger, I have to ask you now, on the record with the cameras rolling," McCluskie said, sounding like an interrogator instead of an interview subject. "Have you seen the internal memos and design notes which describe how Harland and Wolff thought *Titanic* broke up?"

"Absolutely not," Long answered, obviously taken aback by the question out of the blue.

"Well, when I saw your analysis, I was sure that you had seen these memos. I was charged for years with keeping them secret, and that would have meant that I had failed. As far as I know, they have never been seen outside of Harland and Wolff. The scenario you reverse engineered was very, very, very close to what Harland and Wolff already knew in 1912."

After Harland and Wolff's internal investigation, Pirrie and Ismay had decided on their own to retrofit *Olympic* with a double hull, build *Britannic* with a double hull, and redesign the expansion joints and other weak points in the ships. There was no law that required them to do that. *Titanic* had perfectly conformed to the regulations of the British Board of Trade.

"What about the Board of Trade inquiry?" Long asked.

"It was a whitewash to reassure the world that British ships were safe," McCluskie said. "Harland and Wolff didn't want people to think their ships were substandard, which they certainly weren't, according to the law. But it would be easy for people to think that they were if Harland and Wolff had revealed everything they knew."

━━━━━

After McCluskie's confirmation of Long's theory about the sinking, and his allegation that Harland and Wolff had covered up the probability that *Titanic* was a weak ship, Chatterton and Kohler could think about little else but returning to the wreck. A week after the Woods Hole revelations, their hopes were dashed when the Russian government recalled *Keldysh* and the *Mir*s, canceling all *Titanic* charters for the foreseeable future.

Chatterton and Kohler had lost their return to *Titanic*,

but they could still get to *Britannic*, which lay off the coast of Greece in 400 feet of water and was reachable by scuba. If Pirrie and Ismay had pushed the envelope of strength too far when they'd built *Olympic* and *Titanic*, the changes they'd made to *Britannic* would reveal what they thought was wrong with the first two sisters.

BRITANNIC

The night *Titanic* sank, the first of *Britannic*'s frames was rising from its keel on the slipway at Harland and Wolff. After two months of mourning and indecision, Pirrie and Ismay agreed to complete the hull but to wait to outfit the ship until there was a chance that passengers would have forgotten enough about *Titanic* to buy tickets on its sister. *Britannic* went into the river Lagan with no fanfare in February 1914, after which it lay derelict at the dock for more than a year. When the war began, Pirrie finished it with money from the Admiralty. His Majesty's Hospital Ship *Britannic* left Belfast painted bright white with three giant red crosses on each side.

At dawn on November 21, 1916, *Britannic* was steaming south of Athens on its way to pick up British wounded in Turkey when it struck a mine that had been laid across its path by a German submarine. The explosion blew a hole in the starboard side a hundred feet from the bow. *Britannic*'s captain steered at full speed toward the island of Kéa, six miles away, reckoning that his best chance was beaching the ship. The decision to beach a crippled ship is instinctive to a seasoned mariner in sight of land, but it was a mistake. *Britannic* flooded much more quickly as it plowed ahead than it would have had it stopped dead immediately. Thirty minutes after the mine exploded, the foredeck was underwater. Kéa was still two and a half miles away.

The captain ordered the lifeboats launched to evacuate the 1,067 crew members and medical staff. Where *Britannic* stopped, the channel was only 400 feet deep, so the bow of the 882-foot liner hit the bottom while more than half of the ship was above the surface. *Britannic*'s three gigantic propellers were still revolving, creating a vortex that sucked in the fleeing lifeboats as soon as they were lowered to the sea. The deadly situation was immediately obvious to the experienced sailors in command of the boats, who ordered the doctors, nurses, and orderlies to jump for their lives. Most obeyed and were able to paddle away from the crackling, thundering mass of the sinking ship. Thirty men and women died under the propellers when their boats were smashed to matchsticks. The Aegean in November is warm. Greek fishermen and passing warships rescued 1,037 men and women who had survived the ordeal of abandoning ship into the lifeboats, and then abandoning their lifeboats for the open sea.

Among the survivors was Violet Jessop, who had also survived the sinking of *Titanic*. Aboard the rescue ship *Carpathia*, she had complained about forgetting her toothbrush when she left the doomed ocean liner.

"Oh, yes," another survivor had said sarcastically, "never undertake a disaster without making sure of your toothbrush."

When Jessop went into one of *Britannic*'s forty-four lifeboats, and then into the sea with parts of bodies mangled by the propellers floating around her, she had her toothbrush in the pocket of her smock.

After the lifeboats were away, the weight of the water flooding *Britannic* drove its bow into the seafloor while half of its length remained above the surface. The ship corkscrewed to the right and the hole in its starboard side opened wider. Less than an hour after it struck the mine, *Britannic* was on the bottom. Except for the crumpled bow, it looked like a ship that had lain down to sleep on the floor of the sea.

———

Chatterton had already been to *Britannic*. In 1998, the wreck had almost killed him when his rebreather quit inside the hull at 400 feet. The rebreather gave a diver more bottom time than ordinary scuba, but it depended on a computer and sensors to maintain the proper balance of oxygen in the air supply. Chatterton was in the firemen's tunnel leading to the boiler rooms, hoping to see if the watertight doors were open, which might have explained why *Britannic* sank so quickly. He shined his light on the LED that was supposed to tell him exactly what he was breathing; it was blank. Chatterton risked a couple more breaths, not knowing if too much oxygen or too much carbon dioxide would cripple him in an instant. He swam back to his emergency air tanks and survived, but he hated having gotten so close to the watertight doors and failed.

Before Chatterton and Kohler left for Greece, Roger Long told them that what they found out about *Britannic* could confirm that Pirrie and Ismay had feared that *Titanic* was a weak ship. The two joints Andrews designed for *Olympic* and *Titanic* were disasters waiting to happen, he said. Pirrie had put three expansion joints into *Britannic*, but no one knew whether they were different from those on *Titanic*. If the expansion joints were different, it meant that not only had Pirrie and the other

Harland and Wolff engineers suspected that *Titanic*'s hull plating was too light but that they'd also been worried that *Titanic* had broken on the surface because the expansion joint under the third funnel was a critically weak point in the ship. Long wanted to see videotape of at least one of *Britannic*'s expansion joints.

———

Britannic had lain undisturbed until Jacques Cousteau found it. Cousteau was using new side-scan sonar to map the seafloor off the Attica Peninsula, in southern Greece, when he came across the wreck on December 3, 1975. It was unmistakable, an enormous steel mass in 400 feet of water eight miles from where the British Admiralty chart said it was.

Cousteau's discovery set off a squall of controversy, resurrecting German allegations that the hospital ship *Britannic* had been carrying fresh troops and munitions to the Turkish front, which was why German naval forces had mined the Kéa Channel. The British, according to the darkest suspicions, had intentionally marked the incorrect location of the wreck on the chart so no one would find it and prove the German accusations were right.

For Cousteau, the controversy was a gift. In the twenty years since he and Louis Malle had shot *Le Monde du Silence* (*The Silent World*), winning a medal at Cannes and forever changing the mass-audience appeal of documentary films, he had produced a steady stream of television shows, which had made him famous. His success also drove him and the crew of *Calypso* to come up with dozens of new and interesting stories from beneath the sea every year. The wreck of *Britannic* was perfect. No one knew why the double-hulled ship had gone down so quickly. The Germans had accused the British of lying to the world. Best of all, *Britannic* was *Titanic*'s sister ship.

Cousteau ran ads in British newspapers to recruit *Britannic* survivors for his film. He got only one response. Sheila Macbeth Mitchell, an eighty-six-year-old woman from Scotland, had been a volunteer nurse aboard the ship. She had leaped out of a lifeboat to save herself from the deadly propellers and had been rescued by a fisherman. For Cousteau's cameras, she recalled her duties aboard *Britannic* as an attendant in an officers' ward in the enclosed promenade on B Deck, port side. She denied that the hospital ship had been anything but what the British Admiralty had said it was. She had seen no signs of troops or guns. Mitchell asked Cousteau if he would return the favor of her interview by retrieving her alarm clock from her cabin on D Deck. Cousteau said he would try.

Cousteau and his divers descended in teams of three, breathing helium and oxygen mixed in oversized tanks that gave them fifteen minutes of bottom time. They ascended in stages to 130 feet, where they entered a submersible decompression chamber; the chamber was then hoisted aboard *Calypso* for the remaining decompression time.

After inspecting *Britannic*'s holds and accommodation spaces, Cousteau declared that it had carried no troops or munitions. It had been only what the British had said it was: a hospital ship on its way to pick up wounded from the Battle of Gallipoli. Cousteau said, the catastrophic damage to its bow was not the result of the detonation of hidden munitions, as the Germans had alleged. It had probably come from coal dust explosions. None of Cousteau's divers had penetrated far enough into the hull to retrieve Sheila Mitchell's alarm clock.

Expeditions continued over the next thirty years, using

submersibles, remotely operated vehicles, and scuba gear, but none explored or photographed the interior of the hull to see whether the watertight doors were open or closed. Nobody had given any thought at all to the expansion joints.

———

Chatterton and Kohler had never organized anything on the scale of the expedition to Greece. Their trip to *Titanic* had been more expensive, but exploring *Britannic* would be infinitely more complex and dangerous. Very few people in the world are capable of diving to 400 feet, spending enough time on the bottom for meaningful investigation of a shipwreck, and enduring five hours of decompression on the ascent. They put together a team of fifteen, all of them friends and every one of them in the top tier of any ranking of technical shipwreck divers.

They also hired two men who knew the corridors and compartments of *Britannic* as well as the streets and alleys of their own neighborhoods. Englishman Simon Mills actually owned the wreck; he'd bought its salvage rights a decade earlier. Mills had written the definitive book on *Britannic* and had been on the *Titanic* expedition with Chatterton and Kohler. Parks Stephenson, a systems engineer from California and a lifelong student of the *Olympic*-class ships, had created an interactive computer simulation of *Britannic*'s bow section.

Chatterton and Kohler had three veteran divers to tend the decompression station and provide shallow support. Bill Lange and his assistant, Maryanne Moran Keith, brought their cameras. Kirk Wolfinger was there with his cameras. Petar Denoble, from the Divers Alert Network, was the expedition doctor. *Titanic* veteran Bob Blumberg, from the State Department, came along to help with diplomatic problems, of

Apollon, a fishing long liner converted into a dive boat for the *Britannic* expedition.

(Photograph by Joe Porter/*Wreck Diving Magazine*.)

Bill Lange conducting a class for the divers on the use of his underwater video cameras. (Photograph by Joe Porter/*Wreck Diving Magazine.*)

Preparing for the dive into the firemen's tunnel on *Britannic*,
from left: Parks Stephenson, Kirk Wolfinger, Richie Kohler, John Chatterton.
(Photograph by Joe Porter/*Wreck Diving Magazine*.)

John Chatterton (*left*) and Richie Kohler, before the firemen's tunnel dive.
(Photograph by Joe Porter/*Wreck Diving Magazine*.)

Richie Kohler. (Photograph by Joe Porter/*Wreck Diving Magazine*.)

John Chatterton. (Photograph by Joe Porter/*Wreck Diving Magazine*.)

Preparing to search for the expansion joint on the promenade deck,
from left: Parks Stephenson, Richie Kohler, Mike Pizzio, Mark Bullon,
Leigh Bishop, Simon Mills, Mike Barnette, Evan Kovacs, Frank Pelligrino.
(Photograph by Joe Porter/*Wreck Diving Magazine.*)

Richie Kohler finding the forward expansion joint on *Britannic*.

(Photograph by Mike Barnette.)

Greek police boarding *Apollon* to seize videotapes of the dives to *Britannic*.
(Photograph by Joe Porter/*Wreck Diving Magazine*.)

Britannic 2006 expedition photo,
from left, squatting: Joe Porter, Maryanne Moran Keith, Tina Tavridou,
Jonathan Wickam, Mark Bullon, Frank Pelligrino, Joe Brunette, Roz Lunn,
Eduardo Pavia, Carrie Kohler; *standing*: John Chatterton, Richie Kohler,
Carl Spencer, Mike Barnette, Tom Eichler, Mike Pizzio, Mike Etheridge,
George (the boat driver), Heeth Grantham, Evan Kovacs, Parks Stephenson,
Mike Fowler, Petar Denoble, Martin Parker, Leigh Bishop.

(Photograph by Joe Porter/*Wreck Diving Magazine.*)

which there were likely to be a few. Although Mills owned *Britannic*, both the British and the Greek governments had final say over who could dive to the wreck and what they could do when they got there. Every expedition after Cousteau's had been mired in bureaucratic muck.

Chatterton and Kohler decided to use their first dive to find out whether *Britannic*'s watertight doors were open or closed. This would be as difficult as going into the wreck to search for an expansion joint, but there was one advantage to making it their first dive: Chatterton had already been in the firemen's tunnel.

They previewed their dive using Stephenson's computer model of *Britannic*'s interior and Mills's drawings of the ship. Their plan was to descend to the wreck on the shot line, enter the hull, swim about seventy feet through the firemen's tunnel, go around the boilers in Boiler Room 6, see the watertight doors, and take the pictures.

Both Chatterton and Kohler had been to 400 feet before, but not many times, and they had never stayed at that depth as long as they would on *Britannic*. *Andrea Doria*, long the standard of qualification for an elite wreck diver, was at 250 feet. *U-869* was at 230. Going to 400, and staying there for forty minutes, would be the most difficult dive Chatterton and Kohler had ever attempted together. Venturing inside the hull on their first descent was very close to foolhardy. Usually, a first dive on a deep wreck is extremely conservative, a chance to get used to the depth and the darkness and find one's bearings on the wreck. Without the detailed briefings on the inside of the ship Stephenson and Mills had given them, and the fact that Chatterton had already been to the wreck, they would not have risked penetration on their first dive.

They used rebreathers for the return to *Britannic*. After a decade of evolution, these devices were far more reliable than the one that almost killed Chatterton, offering enormous advantages over ordinary scuba. With mixed gas in a conventional tank, bottom time at 400 feet was ten or twelve minutes. With a rebreather, divers could spend forty minutes on the wreck, and decompress for five hours without any support from the surface unless there was an emergency.

Suiting up for the dive took them almost an hour. Dehydration during a deep technical dive was among the culprits that would make them susceptible to the bends. For two days, Chatterton and Kohler had been drinking water constantly. The first pieces of gear they put on were condom catheters to get rid of the water through a one-way valve in their dry suits.

The alternative to a catheter was a diaper, usually used by women but occasionally by men. As they dressed for the dive to the firemen's tunnel on the deck of the converted fishing boat *Apollon*, Kohler reminded Chatterton of how ridiculous he'd looked the time he tried a diaper.

The sight of you parading around in that diaper scarred me for life, J.C., Kohler said.

Scar this, Red, Chatterton said, pointing to his crotch. Kohler always dove in a red dry suit. Chatterton called him Red. Kohler reciprocated by calling him J.C. It was as close to affection as they got.

Forty-five minutes to splash. The banter between J.C. and Red was as much a part of their preparation for a dive as the methodical order in which they put on their equipment. In the water, they seemed to be able to read each other's minds; above sea level, they were usually pissed off at each other, like squabbling brothers—especially when things went wrong, as they had on Kéa. The Greek diving supervisor had delivered defective equipment, then left the island without paying *Apollon*'s captain, who was threatening to quit if he didn't get cash. People were getting sick, probably from the drinking water. One guy had gotten mugged by a taxi driver in Athens.

Chatterton and Kohler slipped into thin polypropylene diving underwear, which was enough insulation for a dive into the relatively warm Aegean Sea. Cotton was no good. They sweated while they were on the surface, and cotton wouldn't wick away the moisture. In the water, the drying sweat would chill them, which was another way to get the bends. Over the underwear, Chatterton and Kohler put on their dry suits.

In five minutes, they were sweating as if they'd run a mile on a hot day. They strapped on two razor-sharp sheath knives, one on each thigh, within easy reach. Into the pockets of their dry suits they put two marker buoys and reels of line for sending emergency signals to the surface. The sea was calm, so the footing on *Apollon*'s deck was good when they bent over to put on their fins. Finally, they backed up to a bench to slip into their rebreathers, and rested for a few minutes.

Chatterton poured a bucket of seawater over Kohler's head to cool him down. Kohler returned the favor. They switched on their rebreathers.

Kohler didn't get throw-up scared anymore. When he was twenty years younger, and other divers were dying on the *Doria*, he would get so sick he felt like he was going to vomit into his mouthpiece. By the time he'd prepared himself for descending to *Britannic*, the fear was different. He never believed he was going to die. It was more like the fear he got on an amusement park roller coaster.

Chatterton had polished his fear into a little nut that he tucked away like a piece of gear in the pocket of his dry suit. When something went wrong, he knew there was a certain pucker factor, but he had made a lot of dives where everything didn't go the way it was supposed to go. He knew that if he had made dives only when nothing had gone wrong, he would know how to dive only if nothing went wrong. Chatterton had been on dives when he'd lost his air, dives when a guy he was with had died, dives when his computer or his rebreather had quit. He knew how to fix problems. The key was to not overreact. To Chatterton, fear was a healthy emotion, but panic didn't do him any good at all.

Since he had failed in his attempt to reach the watertight doors in 1998, Chatterton had been thinking about the firemen's tunnel. Sitting on the bench on *Apollon*, he thought of Carl Spencer, one of the other divers who had been to the tunnel but had not made it to the doors either. While Spencer was briefing Chatterton, he had thrown his animated English lad's face into a mask of horror. There are monsters down there, John, he'd said. Then his face had snapped back into a normal expression, as he said, I'm not kidding.

The eight-foot drop from *Apollon*'s rail into the sublimely cool water ended the sweltering torment on the surface and relieved them of the staggering weight of a hundred pounds of equipment. Chatterton splashed first. Bill Lange's crew handed him the video camera. Then Kohler was in the water with him. They made eye contact, checked for obvious leaks in their rebreather loops and air bottles, swam to the shot line, and descended into the embrace of the Aegean Sea.

At 160 feet, they passed a school of hundreds of fish, three to four feet long, thirty or forty pounds each. They were there for a moment, silver against the blue background, then gone in a blink.

At 200 feet, the wreck began to emerge in the dim blue glare below them, a gigantic dark mass that extended into invisibility. A minute later, they were at 300 feet, at the end of the shot line chained to a davit on *Britannic*'s deck. Visibility was about 100 feet.

Chatterton and Kohler spent a minute of their precious bottom time orienting themselves. They were on the rail of the ship's port side and could clearly see the bottom 90 feet below. *Britannic* lay on its starboard side, its hull draped with snagged fishing nets, covered with sponges, oysters, barnacles, and a brownish algae. In the fishing net closest to them, they could see a half dozen eight- or ten-pound lobsters tangled in the web. The entrance to the firemen's tunnel was a four-by-eight-foot rectangle at the centerline of the ship, 45 feet below them.

They descended, reached the entrance, and saw that it was covered by a fishing net. Kohler ducked underneath the net, finding plenty of room between it and the hull. As soon as one of them kicked into the tight space, visibility behind him would drop to zero. Chatterton and the camera went first, with Kohler swimming blindly behind him.

Instantly, the diffuse blue light from above was gone. They adjusted their buoyancy to be slightly negative so they could hold themselves up from the wall of the tunnel below them and finger-walk in. There was a metal grate on their right. The steel wall above them dripped with the hard spikes of rusticles and tangled wires, which scraped the plastic shells of their rebreathers as they moved.

After 70 feet of crawling in the tunnel, they broke out into the boiler room, a cavern 45 feet up and 45 feet down, with the four boilers, each 15 feet in diameter, straight ahead of them. It looked exactly like the pictures they had seen of the same boiler room on *Titanic*. Every wreck dive produces a single indelible moment, and on *Britannic*, that was it. Neither of them had ever been in so large an enclosed space underwater.

They had to get past the boilers to see the room's watertight door. Kohler stayed put while Chatterton descended 30 feet and disappeared into the space between the bottom two boilers. Kohler hung strobe lights at the opening into the firemen's tunnel to mark the way out, ascended to the gap between the third and fourth boilers 30 feet above, and shined his flashlight beam between the boilers. The light coming out on the other side would guide Chatterton to his exit point. By entering low and coming out high, Chatterton wouldn't have to swim through the sediment he kicked up on his way in, and he would have a well-lit course to follow in case he got disoriented.

Holding the camera in front of him, Chatterton was scraping his belly and the top of his rebreather on the boilers. Twenty feet in, the beam of his light flattened against something dead ahead of him. A piece of metal. It was a wheelbarrow wedged between the boilers. Chatterton swam to it, surrounded by a cloud of silt that had caught up with him when he'd stopped. With one hand, he held the camera to the side; with the other he pushed on the wheelbarrow. It was wedged tight. The silt around it was like concrete.

I got a problem here, Richie. Over.

Go. Over.

Obstruction. Viz going to shit. Over, Chatterton said, his voice coming in staccato bursts. Kohler recognized the danger signal.

That's three problems, Kohler thought. He's blocked from going ahead. He can't see anything. He's huffing and puffing. One problem, maybe we keep trying. Three, no way.

Abort. Abort. Abort, Kohler barked.

Roger. Abort, Chatterton said.

———

Back on the surface, things had turned as sour as they had in the boiler room on *Britannic*. The bureaucrat from the Greek

Department of Antiquities assigned to the expedition as an observer was furious. During the dive to the boiler room, Bill Lange had lowered a remote-controlled camera to *Britannic*. As *Apollon* drifted away from the wreck, the camera panned over the bottom for a few hundred feet before Lange pulled it up. The guy from Antiquities claimed Lange had lowered the camera to search for other wrecks and debris, a violation of their permit, which limited exploration to only *Britannic*. He said they were also violating their permit by going inside the wreck.

Chatterton and Kohler knew that they had specifically asked for permission to enter *Britannic*'s hull, been told that the permit was in order, and figured somebody was trying to shake them down for more money. They would ignore the bureaucrat and dive to find the expansion joint the next day.

An hour after making their decision, Chatterton was retching into the sink in his hotel room. He had a fever burning behind his eyeballs and couldn't stop shaking. He managed to drag himself out of the bathroom long enough to call Kohler, who arrived five minutes later with the expedition doctor. Chatterton probably had food poisoning, or maybe a bug from the water. With rest and hydration, he would be better in forty-eight hours, but he was unfit to dive the next day.

I'll go alone, Kohler said.

I know you can do it, Richie, Chatterton said. But you've got to have somebody running the camera. Roger Long has to see what you see.

A 100-foot penetration of a shipwreck was dicey under the best of circumstances. This one would be the most difficult dive Kohler had ever made. It was one thing for him to do it; it was another thing to ask one of the other divers to go with him. Every one of them would say yes, but Chatterton and Kohler didn't want to put the obligation on any of them.

What about Barney? Chatterton asked. You guys have spent a lot of time on wrecks together.

Mike Barnette—Barney—was a marine biologist with the National Oceanic and Atmospheric Administration in St. Petersburg, Florida. Kohler compared Chatterton to a partner he danced with in serious competitions, and Barney to a partner with whom he danced for fun. Barney knew all the moves, and he knew Kohler's moves, too. They had been on wrecks at 300 feet, never had a problem, always seemed wordlessly in sync underwater. Kohler knew that Barney had been to 400 feet enough times to feel comfortable at that depth. He was a master rebreather diver.

Probably the man, Kohler said. It sucks that we won't do this together, John.

No choice, Richie. Unless I'm completely misreading this shit with the Greeks, they're going to shut us down. One more dive is probably all we're going to get. It frosts my ass that we won't get another shot at the boiler room, but the expansion joint is what we came for.

The next morning, two policemen in an SUV were parked on the dock watching the divers load gear, water, food, and cameras. When *Apollon* backed into the channel, it felt like a jail break.

Barnette had a different style in the water than Chatterton. He moved a little slower, more deliberately. On the descent, he filmed Kohler from above, until at 250 feet, Barnette swam down to the wreck and filmed him from below. All business. Kohler felt confident when he splashed with Barnette, and even better after they tuned in to each other's rhythms on the drop to the wreck. Behind them, Mike Fowler and Mike Pizzio descended to inspect the outside of the hull for evidence of the expansion joint, while Kohler and Barnette were inside.

When Kohler got to what he thought was B Deck, something was very wrong. Stephenson and Mills had said if he saw a door at the entrance to the promenade he was on the wrong deck. Kohler was sure he was where he was supposed to be. He had counted the decks during his descent, and the promenade looked exactly like the one in the plans of the ship he had studied for weeks. It had been used as an officers' ward, a comfortable, well-ventilated corridor that must have been the best place on the ship on a hot day. There were windows where there were supposed to be windows. Only the door shouldn't have been where it was. Kohler decided to bet that Stephenson, Mills, and the plans were wrong. At some point between drawing the ship and building it, a doorway had been added to the promenade on B Deck.

Kohler kicked and entered the wreck. The light was pretty good inside. The windows above him that weren't broken were covered with algae and anemones, transforming the blue of the abyss into a stained glass effect. Church light, Kohler thought. Below him, through doorways and windows in the interior wall, he peered into staterooms. The wooden walls had rotted away, revealing plumbing and the bright white ceramics of sinks and bathtubs. He saw piles of wooden wheelchairs half-eaten by worms, the metal frames and springs of hospital beds, open cabinets glimmering with bottles and glasses. If Kohler hadn't had a job to do, he would not have been able to resist going farther into the middle of the ship.

Kohler counted windows, moving from the bow to the stern. One window equaled ten feet. The expansion joint was supposed to be one hundred feet in. Kohler swam carefully, alert to the possibility that wreckage beyond the beam of his lights could block the way at any point. At seven windows, his clock showed eighteen minutes elapsed. Something's got to happen pretty quick, he thought.

The expansion joint was supposed to be covered by a brass plate on the floor of the promenade, which was to Kohler's right. Nineteen minutes. Kohler thought he saw something bright wink at him. He reached out and drew his hand through the coating of fine silt and algae. Nothing. He was right at the ninth window. Maybe they were wrong about that, too. He glanced over his shoulder, careful to not look directly at the camera lights. There was Barnette. Calm. Perfectly neutral, hovering slightly above him.

The tenth window. Nothing. Kohler and Barnette reversed course. Kohler pushed his face to within six inches of the deck. Nothing. Back to the ninth window. Kohler was turning to shake his head at Barnette when he saw it. A definite gap in the steel covered by a plate of a different kind of metal. Shinier. It wasn't in the floor of B Deck. It was in the ceiling and walls. But no doubt about it. The expansion joint. About fourteen inches wide. Like a door threshold.

Kohler backed away to make room for the camera. Barnette shot the joint along its full length from every possible angle. He videotaped the place where the joint was supposed to be but wasn't.

They were twenty-five minutes into the dive. It was going to take eight minutes to swim out of the ship. That left five minutes for sightseeing. The likelihood that either of them was ever going to dive on *Britannic* again was remote. Before they splashed, they had agreed that if they had any time on the clock after getting the job done, they would reward themselves with a swim through the navigation bridge.

When they came out of the promenade, the wing of the

bridge the officers used for docking was directly over their heads and to the right. Kohler looked at Barnette and made the hand signal for a steering wheel. Barnette nodded.

The bridge of *Britannic* was identical to *Titanic*'s. Kohler saw the engine-room telegraph, its commands clearly visible: FULL AHEAD. STOP. ASTERN. When Kohler reached out and touched it, his imagination put him not on an ill-fated hospital ship but on the bridge of *Titanic*. It was the sweetest moment in his life as a wreck diver. He imagined Captain Smith, Murdoch, Lightoller, and Andrews on the bridge. The reprehensible Ismay. He saw the patient sailor on the helm responding to commands by echoing the commands for course changes. He looked to his left, toward the bow, shined his light through shards of broken glass, and saw the surface of the open ocean stretching out ahead of him, blue and endless.

———

Kohler's delight at correcting the experts about the layout of the promenade, finding the cover of the expansion joint, and hearing Fowler and Pizzio's report that the joint ended in a thermometer-like bulb was short-lived. At the entrance to Kéa's harbor, a police boat, its blue lights flashing, burbled up to *Apollon* to escort it to the dock.

Chatterton had recovered enough to meet them there with the news that the cops wanted all of the videotapes. The Department of Antiquities guy had accused them of breaking the law by going inside the wreck. Chatterton informed the two policemen squared off in front of him that he wasn't surrendering the tapes unless they told him in writing when he was going to get them back. As Kohler joined Chatterton on the dock, the policemen flipped open their holsters.

You will now come with us to the police station.

They sat on a bench in a sweaty little office while one of the policemen stood guard. Chatterton held up his cell phone. The guard nodded okay. Chatterton called one of the camera techs aboard *Apollon* and told him to start making copies of everything. An hour passed. Chatterton called Bob Blumberg, who said he was making inquiries but wasn't optimistic. He said he'd never run into such a nonresponsive group of people in an international situation. Nobody was taking his phone calls.

Chatterton's phone rang. The camera tech had gotten everything duped. The police had just boarded *Apollon* with their guns drawn and taken the originals.

Ten minutes later, two cops marched into the office with a plastic bag and vanished into a back room. One of the cops came back with a piece of paper in his hand.

We have ten tapes. You write us a receipt for those tapes, and you can leave.

I didn't give you those tapes, Chatterton said. I'm not signing something that says I did. I have no idea what's on those tapes. I don't know where you got them. I don't even know if they're ours.

If we sign your paper, it's as good as a confession, Kohler said. No fucking way. Let's get out of here.

I forbid you to leave, the policeman said.

I'll tell you what, Chatterton said. We're going to stand up and walk out the door. If you want to shoot us in the back, shoot us in the back.

———

It was one in the morning in Maine. The phone call from Chatterton and Kohler woke Roger Long from deep sleep, but it was the best middle-of-the-night call he had ever gotten. They were talking on speakerphone, finishing each other's sentences like an old married couple. Kohler had seen one of the expansion joints on *Britannic*. It was wider, with a metal cover, and a round bulb rather than a V notch where it met the hull. Definitely different than *Olympic* and *Titanic*'s. The cops had taken the originals of the video, but they were pretty sure they had dupes. They were going to try to get out of Greece the next day.

Proof that the expansion joints on *Britannic* were different than those on *Titanic* meant that Pirrie and Ismay had suspected that they were weak points. A lot of things can cause a hull to fail, Long said. They'd obviously thought *Titanic*'s hull plating was too light because they'd added thousands of tons of steel to *Olympic* and *Britannic* by doubling their hulls. The quality of the rivets and steel when *Titanic* was built was nowhere near what it is today. Every porthole was a weak point from which cracks could propagate.

Every flaw in *Titanic*'s hull had stolen minutes from the lives of 1,504 people. Pirrie and Ismay must have been terrified when they'd figured that out. A public discussion of the weaknesses in their Ship of Dreams would have ruined them. They'd had no choice but to keep them secret.

EPILOGUE

COVER-UP

The wound in Pirrie's groin no longer smelled foul, but he was still emaciated and able to stand for only a few minutes each day. Over the strenuous objections of his wife, he willed himself to work. Pirrie was heartsore over the loss of Thomas Andrews and the ship he had lived his entire life to build, but he would not allow his emotions or his health to divert his attention from his life's most perilous moment.

Pirrie instinctively knew that something had been dreadfully wrong with *Titanic*. *Republic* had stayed afloat for a day and a half after being opened up amidships from the rail to below the waterline. The damage was not much different from that sustained by *Titanic*, but everyone on *Republic* who hadn't been killed in the collision had been saved. *Olympic* had taken a blow from HMS *Hawke* that would have sunk most ships, but it had made it back to Southampton on its own power.

From London, Pirrie ordered work on *Britannic* stopped immediately. He told Edward Wilding to mathematically re-create every possible flooding scenario in which the ship sinks two hours and twenty minutes after its hull is breached. Wilding, who was in line to replace Andrews as Harland and

Wolff's chief designer, would use his conclusions to represent the company at the British Wreck Commission hearings in London.

An Admiralty judge and old friend of Pirrie's, John Charles Bigham, Baron Mersey of Toxteth, was appointed to preside over the commission. Mersey would be assisted by one of the nation's leading naval architects, a distinguished engineer, two navy officers, and a veteran solicitor general. They would take testimony from *Titanic*'s builder, owner, and survivors, to answer twenty-six questions drawn up by the British Board of Trade. The questions addressed the seaworthiness of the ship, the voyage, the extent of the damage, and the conduct of the crew and passengers. The British inquiry would begin on May 2, but Mersey gave Harland and Wolff more time to prepare its testimony. Wilding would not testify until the end of the month.

After receiving Pirrie's instructions, Wilding scrambled to calculate the amount of damage that could explain why *Titanic* sank so fast. Ismay had sent reports from America saying that the ship had struck the iceberg below the waterline at the bow. Wilding asked himself how much water it would have taken to sink the ship in just two hours and twenty minutes, then worked backward to figure out the size of the opening in the hull that could have admitted that much water. He calculated the weight of the water and the angle at which the ship would have begun to come apart. There was a good chance that *Titanic* had broken up on the surface.

When Pirrie learned about Wilding's conclusion that *Titanic* might very well have broken up on the surface, he told the engineer that his first responsibility was to protect the reputation of the company. Pirrie and Harland and Wolff's own lawyers told Wilding that he was to answer questions narrowly, volunteering nothing. Pirrie knew that Mersey and his inquiry wanted the same outcome he did, and would not press for answers they did not want to hear; there must be no doubt that Harland and Wolff ships were strong, and that *Titanic* had simply been the victim of a tragic accident. It was just good business for all concerned to preserve the reputation of the British Empire's greatest shipyard.

Pirrie began planning for strengthening the hulls of *Olympic* and *Britannic* immediately. *Olympic* would be fitted with a double hull by fastening steel plates to its interior. To do that, they would have to sacrifice space inside the ship, which would require changes in the accommodations and reconfiguration of the machinery compartments. If construction began again on *Britannic*, they would widen the entire ship by eighteen inches, rather than sacrificing space on the inside. The watertight bulkheads, which did not extend to the top of the hull on *Titanic*, would go all the way up on *Britannic*. *Olympic* would be examined for cracking, especially around the expansion joints, and redesigned or reinforced to stop it.

Two days before Wilding testified in London, Senator William Alden Smith released the conclusions of the American inquiry. It was good news for Harland and Wolff. The committee had heard from eighty-two witnesses, produced 1,100 pages of testimony, and blamed only Captain E. J. Smith, for running at nearly full speed through a known ice field. The Americans exonerated Bruce Ismay, the White Star Line, all other officers and crew of *Titanic*, and Harland and Wolff. The committee concluded that the ship had sunk in one piece, and had met or exceeded all standards governing the construction, equipment, and operation of a British passenger liner. Negligence by its owners or builders, therefore, was not an issue in American insurance claims.

Lord Mersey and the five members of the Wreck Commission sat at desks on a dais at the front of the Drill Hall of the Scottish Regiment, near Buckingham Palace. To the commissioners' right were a forty-foot-long drawing of *Titanic*, a twenty-foot-long half model of the ship, and a fifteen-by-fifteen-foot chart of the North Atlantic showing *Titanic*'s course. The ceiling of the cavernous hall was fifty feet high. The acoustics were terrible.

The Board of Trade's chief counsel, Sir Rufus Isaacs, read the order for formal investigation. He summarized the twenty-six questions the board wanted the Wreck Commission to answer. Questions 1 through 8 related to what happened before the accident and before there was any suggestion that the ship was sailing into an ice field. Questions 9 through 14 asked about what happened after the captain was warned about the ice. Question 15, by far the broadest, concerned the accident itself. Questions 16 through 24 inquired as to the steps taken after the accident to save lives and save the ship. Question 25 related to the construction and equipment of *Titanic*. Question 26 asked the commission to evaluate current shipping regulations and suggest changes.

The next day, the solicitor general asked the first of what would become 25,621 carefully numbered questions of witnesses.

"Is your name Archie Jewell?"

Jewell, a lookout who had gotten off his watch in the crow's nest an hour and forty minutes before *Titanic* hit the iceberg, said that was his name. He answered 329 more questions about the routines of sailors aboard *Titanic*, using the huge chart of the ship to show his duty station and his quarters.

Following Archie Jewell, ninety-six witnesses told their stories. Lightoller calmly answered 1,600 questions, fencing with his inquisitors as he had with Senator Smith in America. None of *Titanic*'s officers, he said, did anything in the navigation and evacuation of the ship that could be subject to criticism.

Fireman George Beauchamp said he was in Boiler Room 6 at impact and that he continued working for at least fifteen minutes before being ordered to evacuate. This conflicted with Fireman Fred Barrett's testimony that Boiler Room 6 was so catastrophically damaged on impact that the water immediately drove him to flee from Boiler Room 6. Barrett also said that Boiler Room 5 was taking water when he arrived. The inconsistency meant that the ship might not have been damaged as far back as Boiler Room 5 and that Barrett was either lying or mistaken about his location when he saw water burst through the hull. Mersey did not examine the inconsistency.

Every utterance of a witness or inquisitor made news around the world, but none was more sensational than the testimony of Sir Cosmo and Lady Duff-Gordon. They had fled the ship in one of the first lifeboats, with only ten other passengers. There was no question that Lady Duff-Gordon had a right to be in the boat. Cosmo Duff-Gordon, who was a regular item in the endless stream of gossip that rolled around Europe, convinced the Wreck Commission that his leaving *Titanic* while there were still women and children aboard was perfectly legitimate; no one else wanted to go.

Ismay answered 849 questions. He denied any involvement in the navigation of the ship. He denied getting into the lifeboat while there were any other passengers—men, women, or children—nearby. He denied any participation in drawing up the specifications for the ship, including the number of lifeboats it would carry.

Harold Sanderson followed Ismay, testifying for the better part of two days. The thrust of his testimony, guided by several inquisitors, was that the White Star Line equaled or exceeded the rules of the Board of Trade relating to construction of their ships and lifeboat capacity.

Alexander Montgomery Carlisle, Pirrie's brother-in-law and a former Harland and Wolff director, showed up looking dazed and exhausted. He testified that he had argued for more lifeboats. His original specifications for *Titanic* had called for forty-eight. He knew that the rules required only sixteen lifeboats on all ships over 10,000 tons. But *Titanic* was five times bigger. His original specifications for lifeboats, with which Thomas Andrews concurred, had been overruled by Ismay.

Isaacs tried to discredit Carlisle by pointing out that Carlisle had been a member of the board's committee that made the rules for lifeboats. Carlisle had signed the committee's recommendations in 1911, which required not more but fewer lifeboats. The Board of Trade and everyone else in the world believed that ocean liners had become virtually unsinkable.

Carlisle, gray-bearded and haggard, shook visibly as he stood at the witness lectern. "I regret having signed a report with which I did not concur," he said, sounding as though he were about to begin sobbing. "I must have been soft."

Edward Wilding answered 1,113 questions on three consecutive days, from eight different commissioners and lawyers. In painstaking detail, referring to the builder's model and the profile of the ship, Wilding spoke for hours about the construction of *Titanic*, the dimensions of its steel, watertight compartments, deck gear, rigging, engines, and lifeboats. He told the commission that he had calculated that the iceberg had made holes in the ship totaling twelve square feet, between the bow and Boiler Room 5, possibly as far aft as Boiler Room 4. *Titanic* had remained afloat for a long time, considering that catastrophic amount of damage. Wilding said he was sure the ship had gone down in one piece.

A week later, at the request of a lawyer representing a seamen's union, Wilding was recalled to the witness podium. The lawyer asked how Wilding had calculated the strength of the ship to ensure that it could survive the worst sea conditions it might encounter on the North Atlantic. A big ship, the lawyer reasoned, had to span more waves than a small ship, which would place far greater loads on the hull. He read a letter from the Board of Trade, written in November 1910, asking Wilding to submit detailed calculations of the strength of the ship. Wilding had replied that reproducing those calculations would take three months and asked the board not to press for that information.

"And, in fact, they did not press for it?" the union's lawyer asked.

"They did not," Wilding replied.

One of White Star's lawyers jumped to his feet and asked permission to address the witness.

"Is there any foundation at all for saying that you defied the Board of Trade?"

"I really know of none," Wilding said.

"Or that the ship was allowed to be built by the officials of the Board of Trade in violation of their rules?" the White Star lawyer asked.

"We have to comply with all their rules, and we make some sacrifices to do so," Wilding replied.

The day after Wilding finished testifying, he wrote to Pirrie to say that he was going back to Belfast himself the next day unless Pirrie ordered him to stay in London. The last paragraph of Wilding's one-page letter was an account of his fending off the barrage of questions about strength calculations from the seamen's union lawyer, after which Mersey had not pursued the subject. Their secrets were safe.

Pirrie knew about Wilding's testimony before he received the letter. He had stayed away from the Drill Hall but received daily reports as the hearings ground on into July. Pirrie had decided that Wilding was finished at Harland and Wolff. He had avoided the big questions, but he had talked way too much.

Ultimately, the British Wreck Commission agreed with the Americans. *Titanic* sank because its captain chose to speed through a field of ice about which he had been warned. The iceberg *Titanic* struck ripped a three-hundred-foot-long gash in the starboard side, flooding five watertight compartments. The ship did not break in two. As the bow sank, its stern rose out of the water to a fifty- or sixty-degree angle before making its final plunge. Mersey's report specifically stated that *Titanic* had been constructed by Harland and Wolff in accordance with Board of Trade rules.

The biggest ship Pirrie had ever built had taken 1,504 people to their deaths. His shipyard was still alive.

ENDINGS

When Bruce Ismay arrived in Liverpool aboard *Adriatic* at the end of April 1912, a small crowd on the dock broke into applause as he descended the gangway. Six months later, Morgan and his directors forced Ismay out as president of International Mercantile Marine. At the same time, he resigned as chairman of the White Star Line. Ismay remained as a director of both IMM and White Star until 1916, when he severed all connections with the combine and his family company. He continued to work as an adviser to British insurance companies and was active in maritime charities. He donated money to build the cadet training ship *Mersey* and gave £11,000 to a fund for widows of lost seamen. Ismay divided his time between London and Ireland, where he had a fishing lodge and was known among his guides as a good companion. He died after suffering a stroke on October 17, 1937, leaving an estate worth £693,305, approximately the equivalent of $52 million today.

The White Star Line settled $16 million in claims arising from the *Titanic* disaster for $664,000. The next year was the most profitable in its history. In 1913, 2.5 million passengers crossed the Atlantic between Europe and the United States, setting a record that has never been broken. White Star carried 200,000 of them, Cunard about the same number. In 1927, White Star was bought by the Royal Mail Group, which soon defaulted on its Admiralty loans, leaving Great Britain as its majority stockholder. In 1934, the government merged White Star and Cunard in return for financing the 80,000-ton, 965-foot *Queen Mary*. *Britannic III*, the last ship to carry the crimson-and-white burgee of the White Star Line, was taken out of service in 1960.

RMS *Olympic*, refitted with a double hull, became known as "Old Reliable." On the night of May 15, 1934, it rammed and sank the *Nantucket* lightship off Cape Cod, killing seven of its eleven crewmen. After picking up survivors, *Olympic* steamed into New York under its own power. A year later, it was sold for scrap.

In March 1913, J. P. Morgan died in the royal suite of the Grand Hotel in Rome. At the end, he was suffering from hypertension, dementia, and the pain of having had all his teeth pulled and replaced by dentures. After a decade of bank panics and stock market crashes, Americans had realized that giant private trusts were not the way to manage the wealth of the nation. Morgan had been living in Cairo and Rome because lawyers, congressional committees, and the press made life at home miserable for him. His body was shipped back to New York City aboard the S.S. *France* and taken by train to Hartford, Connecticut, where he had been born, for burial.

Even after *Titanic*, Morgan believed that International Mercantile Marine would prosper. He was certain America's future depended upon its presence in international markets. A year after his death, IMM defaulted on its bonds and went into bankruptcy. The *Wall Street Journal* concluded, "The ocean was too big for the old man." The shipping boom during World War I saved IMM, after which it sold off its European holdings and reorganized as the United States Lines. It went bankrupt again in 1937, reorganized as a holding company, and disappeared for good in 1986.

William Pirrie built two hundred ships after finishing *Britannic*, the largest of them only two-thirds the size of the *Olympic* sisters. He recovered fully from his prostate surgery to lead Harland and Wolff through the wartime boom; the company set records for profits every year in the following decade. He continued to expand, enlarging the Belfast shipyard and buying three others in Scotland and England. He invested heavily in oil exploration and production and built a new factory to manufacture diesel engines.

Pirrie died of pneumonia aboard a ship he had built, RMS *Ebro*, in the Panama Canal on June 7, 1924. Twelve days later, his body was put aboard *Olympic* in New York for the voyage home to Belfast, where he was buried with a state funeral. The inscription on his coffin read: "William James, First Viscount Pirrie, K.P., Born Quebec 31st May, 1847. Died at sea. 'Deeds not words.'"

After Pirrie's death, the Harland and Wolff board of directors appointed Margaret Pirrie as president of the company. She erected a monument over her husband's grave; on it were two bronze panels, one depicting *Venetian*, the first steamship he built, the other *Olympic*. Margaret Pirrie died at home in London on June 19, 1935. She was buried next to Pirrie under his monument in Belfast City Cemetery.

John Chatterton and Richie Kohler had begun their investigation into *Titanic* hoping to discover evidence that might explain how the iceberg had damaged the ship so badly that it could not survive. Like millions of other people, they believed that *Titanic* had been a heroic ship, a testament to the power of the industrial age that had been undone by bad luck.

Roger Long's low-angle breakup, Tom McCluskie's revelation of the cover-up by Harland and Wolff, and what Chatterton and Kohler found on *Britannic* proved that *Titanic* had not been a heroic ship. It had been a deeply flawed testament to hubris and greed that killed 1,504 people. Chatterton and Kohler were infuriated because there was no way to punish the men who had sent a ship to sea not knowing if it was strong enough to survive.

Until they decided to tell the world what really happened to *Titanic*.

ACKNOWLEDGMENTS

In Memoriam
Robert C. Blumberg

John Chatterton, Richie Kohler, and I worked together on Titanic*'s Last Secrets* every step of the way. They were tireless, inquisitive, and always available. They brought key insights to difficult parts of the narrative, plunged wholeheartedly into the research, and carefully edited the book for accuracy. Their investigation into the wreck of *Titanic* illuminates a new understanding of what transpired on a terrible night almost a century ago, and honors the memory of the 1,504 people who died in the disaster. I am forever indebted for the pleasure and privilege of sharing this work with them.

Heather Schroder at International Creative Management saw the potential in our story, and held back nothing as its champion. More than anyone else, she is responsible for bringing the truth about *Titanic* to light.

Together, we thank the members of the joint American-French team that discovered the wreck in 1985, and all the explorers who followed them. They worked under dangerous and difficult conditions to add to our understanding of *Titanic*, without which our own exploration would never have been possible.

Thanks to Dr. Anatoly Sagalevich and the crew of the R/V *Akademik Mstislav Keldysh,* who made our discoveries possible, especially the courageous *Mir* pilots who routinely risk their lives with incredible grace.

Thanks to Jacques-Yves Cousteau and the crew of *Calypso*, who found and explored HMHS *Britannic* in 1975, making our exploration of the wreck possible thirty-one years later.

Thanks to Carla Chatterton and Carrie Kohler for their inspiration and patience.

━━━

Many other people gave generously of their time, insights, and secrets.

I am grateful to Tony of FonaCab in Belfast, who took me in his taxi to the remains of Harland and Wolff and introduced me to his city. In Belfast, I also met Una Reilly; Tom and Sylvia McCluskie; and Ian Montgomery, Ian Farr, and the rest of the staff at the Public Record Office of Northern Ireland. To all of them I offer thanks.

Paul Louden-Brown told me about the White Star Line with charm and wit, drawing me into the history of that fascinating company. Paul's terrific book *The White Star Line* is indispensable for anyone trying to understand the golden age of ships on the North Atlantic.

Many dedicated people work to document and preserve what is known about the building, voyage, and loss of *Titanic*. I am grateful to all of them, especially David G. Brown, Simon Mills, and Parks Stephenson. Their willingness to share their knowledge in interviews, e-mails, and phone calls was essential to writing this book. Ken Marschall's superb drawings and his knowledge of the ship contributed immensely to my understanding of the new evidence we found on the bottom. Thanks, too, to Edward and Karen Kamuda at the Titanic Historical Society.

I'm grateful to Grainger Lanneau, M.D., for his account of his dive to *Titanic* in 2000; to Harry W. Herr, M.D., for his paper on the treatment of prostate diseases a hundred years ago and an e-mail correspondence on that topic; and to Clifford Ismay, who shared his family history.

David Concannon granted me many hours of interviews and shared his notes and articles on his own exploration of *Titanic*.

Bill Lange provided fabulous images, a great moment during the expedition in 2005, and the details of his life and work. Cinematographer Ralph White was a great guide and inspiration on the *Titanic* dives.

During the exploration of the wreck of HMHS *Britannic* off the island of Kéa, Greece, expedition members were generous and patient in their explanations of the intricacies of technical diving. Thank you, Mike Barnette, Leigh Bishop, Mark Bullon, Petar Denoble, Mike Etheridge, Mike Fowler, Evan Kovacs, Martin Parker, Frankie Pellegrino, Mike Pizzio, and Carl Spencer. Thanks also to Joe Brunette, Jonathan Wickham, Tom Eichler, Roz Lunn, and Tina Tavridou.

Bob Blumberg brought his gigantic spirit with him on the expeditions to *Titanic* and *Britannic*. None of us who spent time with him will ever forget the air of kindness he lent to every day. His work on the *Titanic* treaty is a lasting legacy. Bob died on August 25, 2007.

Joe Porter, the editor of *Wreck Diving Magazine*, was the topside photographer during both the *Titanic* and the *Britannic* expeditions. He took many of the pictures in this book and went out of his way to make sure I had them when I needed them.

Heeth Grantham, diver and logistical ringmaster at Lone Wolf Documentary Group, was a steady, reliable presence during the expeditions. Later, he helped find historical photographs and secure permission to reproduce them. Thanks also to his many colleagues at Lone Wolf who shared material from their library.

Roger Long created the theoretical core of this book with his open-minded interpretation of the new evidence from the wreck of *Titanic*. He spent many hours explaining the different scenarios of the sinking and reviewed the manuscript for accuracy. Roger was a tireless, good-humored, brilliant collaborator whose contribution cannot be overstated.

Without Kirk Wolfinger and Rush DeNooyer at Lone Wolf, this book would not have happened. They never stopped contributing to its success, solving problems in the narrative, and reviewing the manuscript. They were also wonderful company.

Thank you, Jonathan Karp, for bringing Titanic's *Last Secrets* to Twelve, and for nourishing this book with your superb understanding of storytelling. Working with an editor as gifted as you is the dream of a lifetime for a writer. I am also indebted to Nate Gray, the brilliant copy editor Bonnie Thompson, production editor Dorothea Halliday, and the rest of the bookmakers at Twelve for tending to the many details along the way.

To Richard Abate, my agent at Endeavor, I can only say: *I like the two guys in the ball.* Your support of my work is matched by no other. I'm grateful for you every day.

The MacDowell Colony and Theodore W. Kheel's Nurture Nature Foundation provided me with crucial support and affirmation, for which I am deeply grateful.

In Seattle, Kay Wilson and Kurt Esveldt have given me a sweet, safe refuge for the past fifteen years. Thank you for all of it.

At home, Laara, Jonas, Milo, Diane, Eva, and Nyta made sure I was never really alone during the months of solitude required for a job like this one. Without you, my family, I simply could not have done it.

Brad Matsen
Vashon Island, Washington
January 2008

NOTES

The contemporary and historical characters, action, and situations in this book are re-created as accurately as possible from research conducted over two and a half years. I drew on facts from reliable sources, checked them thoroughly, and here share them with you. Conversations and dialogue that were not recorded or transcribed verbatim but were reconstructed from reports of meetings, public records, diaries, biographies, interviews, and correspondence are presented as plain text. Verbatim conversations are denoted by quotation marks. Correspondence, contracts, logs, and other records are denoted by italics.

CHAPTER ONE. HISTORY

The phone conversation in which David Concannon proposes an expedition to *Titanic* to find the ribbons of steel is built on recollections by him and John Chatterton, from interviews in the fall of 2006 and the winter of 2007.

David Concannon's description of his descent to the wreck of *Titanic* in 2000 is based on interviews on March 7 and March 20, 2007.

The navigational coordinates of the ribbons of steel were recorded in Concannon's private notebook, provided to me in the spring of 2007.

Biographical information on producer Kirk Wolfinger, and the reconstruction of his inciting phone call with Chatterton, are from several interviews in fall 2006 and winter 2007.

Biographical information on Richie Kohler is from several interviews in the fall of 2006 and the winter of 2007.

CHAPTER TWO. RIBBONS OF STEEL

The financial arrangements for the charter are from interviews with Chatterton and Kohler, winter 2007.

The technical details about the *Mir* submersibles are from a brochure on the subs, published by Deep Ocean Expeditions, the company that brokers *Keldysh* and *Mir* charters.

The dialogue in *Mir-1* and *Mir-2* during the first dives is from digital audio and video recordings.

CHAPTER THREE. TITANIACS

The planning of the second day's diving by Chatterton and Kohler is from interviews with them in the winter of 2007.

Roger Long's biography and his recollection of events surrounding his decision to join the 2005 expedition are from interviews in the fall of 2006 and subsequent conversations over the course of the following year.

Edward Kamuda's story about his fascination with *Titanic*, and the founding of the Titanic Historical Society are from interviews with him in the fall of 2006. Other information about the society's magazine, Web site, and online store is from those sources.

The conspiracy theories are summarized in the preface to Olympic *and* Titanic: *The Truth Behind the Conspiracy*, by Steve Hall and Bruce Beveridge.

CHAPTER FOUR. THE EYES OF BILLY LANGE

The account of Bill Lange's participation in the discovery of *Titanic* in 1985 is from interviews with him and from Robert D. Ballard's *The Discovery of the* Titanic, pp. 79–84.

The summary of the history of manned submersibles and the story of William Beebe and Otis Barton are from Beebe's book *Half Mile Down* and interviews with many submersible engineers and pilots over the past twenty years.

The history of the search for the wreck of *Titanic* is from Ballard's *The Discovery of the* Titanic, pp. 37–43; and Titanic: *Triumph and Tragedy*, by John P. Eaton and Charles A. Haas, pp. 301–24.

The decision by Chatterton and Kohler to search to the east of the wreck, as suggested by Bill Lange, is from audio and video recordings of the planning meeting, some of which was part of the Lone Wolf Documentary Group production Titanic*'s Final Moments: Missing Pieces.*

Accounts of the third day of diving, conversations in the *Mir*s, and the discovery of the bottom pieces are from the audio and video recordings made at the time

CHAPTER FIVE. PIRRIE

The description of William Pirrie by W. T. Stead is reported in Herbert Jefferson's biography *Viscount Pirrie of Belfast*, p. 311, and quoted from Stead's character sketch in the March 1912 edition of *Review of Reviews.*

The account of Cheiro's reading of Pirrie's hand is from Jefferson, p. 317, describing Cheiro's remembrance of their meeting and quoting a letter Pirrie wrote to the palmist on August 14, 1899. In the letter, Pirrie admitted that he had been skeptical of Cheiro's abilities but that Cheiro had amazed and convinced him that "I was wrong in my estimation of this science."

The description of J. P. Morgan's creation of International Mercantile Marine is from Jean Strouse's *Morgan: American Financier*, pp. 457–59.

Pirrie's concern about the downturn in the shipbuilding industry is confirmed in his remarks to the Harland and Wolff board of directors in October 1901, as reported in *Shipbuilders to the World*, by Michael Moss and John R. Hume, pp. 105–06.

Edward Harland's talent as a shipbuilder and his observant management style are documented in Moss and Hume, pp. 15–16.

The deed of agreement of original partnership signed by Edward Harland and Gustav Wolff is in the Harland and Wolff corporate archives in the custody of the Public Record Office of Northern Ireland, access to which was granted by Titanic Quarter Ltd. in February 2007.

The details of the launching of *Catalonian* are derived from the list of ships and launch dates in Moss and Hume, pp. 506–83.

A note on the tonnage of ships, from Frank E. Dodman's *The Observer's Book of Ships* and from *Principles of Naval Architecture*, edited by John P. Comstock:

There are two methods used to calculate a ship's weight:

1. By the volume of water displaced, with 35 cubic feet of displacement equaling 1 ton;
2. The amount of space enclosed in the ship, with 100 cubic feet equaling 1 ton.

There are six ways to express the tonnage of a ship:

1. *Net register tonnage* is the capacity of the enclosed space used for cargo and passengers, representing the earning potential of a ship.
2. *Gross register tonnage* is the total capacity of all enclosed spaces on a ship. *Titanic* was calculated at 46,328 gross register tons.
3. *Displacement tonnage* is the total weight of the ship and everything on board. *Titanic's* displacement tonnage was 52,310 tons.
4. *Standard displacement tonnage* is a variation usually used only for warship tonnage in which the weight of coal or other fuel is excluded from the calculation.
5. *Deadweight tonnage* is the weight of the cargo, fuel, and passengers carried by a merchant ship when loaded to

capacity. This is equal to displacement tonnage less the weight of the ship itself. *Titanic*'s deadweight tonnage was 13,550 tons.

6. *Lightweight tonnage* is the actual weight of the ship itself, including hull, machinery, and rigging. *Titanic*'s lightweight tonnage was 38,760 tons.

Unless otherwise noted, the tonnages given for ships mentioned in this book are gross register tons.

The account of the meeting between Pirrie and Morgan in the autumn of 1901 is derived from accounts in many books, including Strouse; Jefferson; Moss and Hume; and Paul Louden-Brown's *The White Star Line*; and an interview with Louden-Brown in winter 2007 in which he related the story of Morgan's intense dislike for Cunard. Pirrie and Morgan met at about that time, and though the specifics of their conversation are lost, the outcome and details of the White Star purchase and guarantees to Harland and Wolff are precise.

The text of the builder's agreement Pirrie worked into Morgan's syndicate agreement is taken from the *Journal of Commerce and Commercial Bulletin* (London), February 1902, as reported in Jefferson's biography of Pirrie, pp. 266–69.

CHAPTER SIX. ISMAY

The description of White Star's James Street building and its history are from "White Star Building 30 James Street, Liverpool," by Paul Louden-Brown in the spring 1998 issue of the Titanic Historical Society's Titanic *Commutator* magazine and also from a visit, in the winter of 2007, to the site where the building still stands.

The coat-rack story is well known. This version comes from an interview in February 2007 with Paul Louden-Brown, who is an authority on J. Bruce Ismay and the White Star Line, and from Bruce Ismay's granddaughter, Pauline Matarasso, who related the incident in her book *A Voyage Closed and Done*, p. 16. Matarasso's book also adds dimension to Ismay's nature as an outwardly arrogant yet inwardly insecure man.

Bruce Ismay's introduction to William Randolph Hearst in New York is related by Paul Louden-Brown in *The White Star Line*, p. 22.

The story of Bruce Ismay's proposal to Florence Schieffelin and her father's extraction of Ismay's promise to remain in New York is from an interview with Paul Louden-Brown in February 2007 and an unpublished article by Clifford Ismay, a surviving relative who maintains a family archive.

The story about Ismay reprimanding one of his captains about the windows in his wheelhouse is from an interview with Paul Louden-Brown in February 2007.

The story about Captain William Marshall's referring to Ismay as the Big White Chief in a letter to his wife is from *The Ismay Line*, by Wilton J. Oldham, p. 37.

The meeting between Pirrie and Ismay at Downshire House in London in the summer of 1907, during which they agreed to build the *Olympic*-class liners, is from an interview with Paul-Louden Brown in February 2007 and from his history of the White Star Line. The conversation at that meeting is derived from its outcome, the decision to build *Olympic* and *Titanic*, and is not verbatim.

CHAPTER SEVEN. ANDREWS

The epigraphs are from Shan Bullock's paean to Thomas Andrews, written shortly after the shipbuilder's death aboard *Titanic* in 1912, *A Titanic Hero*, pp. 56 and 44.

Pirrie's marriage to Margaret Carlisle and his relationship with Alexander Carlisle are documented in several sections of Jefferson; and Moss and Hume.

The description of Lady Pirrie's White Star–themed gown at Dublin Castle is from Jefferson, p. 90.

Andrews's childhood nickname, Admiral, is confirmed in Bullock, p. 4.

Majestic on the launchways when Andrews went to work on his first day at the shipyard is from the complete list of Harland and Wolff ships in Moss and Hume, pp. 506–83.

Pirrie's opinion that Tommy Andrews was a good boy with a promising future, which he expressed to his wife, Margaret, is from Jefferson's biography, pp. 77–78.

Thomas Andrews is celebrated as the perfect man and a slaughtered innocent in countless accounts of the *Titanic* disaster. Here, his biography and his record at Harland and Wolff are drawn from Moss and Hume; and Shan Bullock; but the descriptions and opinions of Andrews are informed by many other sources.

The meeting with Andrews, Carlisle, and Wilding that Pirrie called is confirmed by Harland and Wolff archivist Tom McCluskie in *Anatomy of the* Titanic, p. 12.

Pirrie's quote in the *Ulster Echo* that he would build a 1,000-foot ship was passed on by Paul Louden-Brown in an interview in February 2007, and confirmed in a search of that paper's archive at the Public Record Office of Northern Ireland. "The 1,000-foot ship was Pirrie's moon landing, his Mount Everest," Louden-Brown said.

The description of Pirrie's original sketches of *Olympic* and *Titanic* in the summer of 1907 is from Mark Chirnside's *The* Olympic *Class Ships*, pp. 18–19, and Eaton and Haas, Titanic: *Triumph and Tragedy*, pp. 20–21.

The decision by Ismay to build *Olympic* and *Titanic* with four funnels for aesthetic and public relations reasons is from Paul Louden-Brown's *The White Star Line*, pp. 80–93; and Tom McCluskie's *Anatomy of the* Titanic, p. 67.

The Blue Riband for the fastest crossing of the North Atlantic was first awarded to the steamer *Sirius* in April 1838, crossing between Cork, Ireland, and Sandy Hook, New Jersey, in 18 days, 14 hours, and 22 minutes. *Sirius* had set the eastbound record of 18 days flat in early May of the same year. In July 1952, *United States* crossed westbound between roughly the same two points in 3 days, 12 hours, and 12 minutes, a record that still stands. *United States* had crossed eastbound the week before in 3 days, 10 hours, and 40 minutes, but the record for that crossing was set in July 1998, by *Cat Link V*, a catamaran ferryboat, which made the crossing in 2 days, 20 hours, and 9 minutes. Cunard dominated the 160-year competition for the Blue Riband, with White

Star always on its heels. For a complete listing of the Blue Riband ships, records, and dates, see Arnold Kludas's *Record Breakers of the North Atlantic: Blue Riband Liners, 1838–1952.*

Andrews's comment that Pirrie had never looked happier in his life is from Bullock, p. 55.

According to Herbert Jefferson's assessment of Carlisle's character in *Viscount Pirrie of Belfast*, pp. 98–104, he would not have waited long after the order for *Olympic* and *Titanic* to tell Pirrie that he was retiring. In addition to Jefferson, Moss and Hume, pp. 149–50, confirm that Carlisle didn't care much for Pirrie's management style and that it played a role in his early retirement. Jefferson also relates that in retirement, Carlisle's life revolved around his autograph collection and his bicycle. He later became controversial because of his relationship with Wilhelm II, the former kaiser of Germany, who lived in exile in Doorn, Holland, after Germany's defeat in World War I.

Pirrie's record of pragmatic relationships with his workers and managers is described in Jefferson, pp. 204–05.

The construction details and specifications produced by Thomas Andrews are from the Harland and Wolff 1:360 scale plans for *Titanic* from the Ulster Folk and Transportation Museum in Belfast; McCluskie's *Anatomy of the* Titanic, pp. 22–48; Chirnside, pp. 18–36; and Rod Green's *Building the* Titanic, pp. 84–90.

The scene under the gantry in July 1908 is from Bullock, p. 46.

The date of Ismay's visit to Harland and Wolff to receive the plans for *Olympic* and *Titanic* is from Eaton and Haas, Titanic: *Triumph and Tragedy*, p. 20.

The original dimensions Andrews specified for the steel plating and iron rivets are greater than those that were used to build the ship. They were reduced by Bruce Ismay. This scaling down of the dimensions was confirmed in interviews with former Harland and Wolff archivist Tom McCluskie and with historian David G. Brown, in February 2007, and in a rivet table and list of steel specifications from the Harland and Wolff archive in the Public Record Office of Northern Island.

In *Viscount Pirrie of Belfast,* Jefferson refers to the preliminary plans to overbuild the ships in his chapter on Andrews.

The final specifications and details of the two ships are from Chirnside; McCluskie's *Anatomy of the* Titanic; Moss and Hume; Michael McCaughan's *The Birth of the* Titanic; and the Harland and Wolff 1:360 plans.

The price of £3 million (about $15 million), plus overruns and extras for the two ships, is from *Shipbuilder* magazine, cited in McCluskie's *Anatomy of the* Titanic, p. 13. The price for the two ships today would be about £150 million ($300 million), using a multiplier of 20 for the difference between historic and modern dollars.

Hull No. 400 for *Olympic* and Hull No. 401 for *Titanic* were confirmed in the general ledgers of Harland and Wolff at the Public Record Office of Northern Ireland.

CHAPTER EIGHT. A THOUSAND DAYS

The order dates for steel and castings for Hull Nos. 400 and 401 are from the ledger titled "Nov. 1883–Jan. 1919, Contracts (#7) Iron and Steel," in the Harland and Wolff archives at the Public Record Office of Northern Ireland.

The details of steelmaking, circa 1908, and its relationship to the shipbuilding industry are from David Pollock's *The Shipbuilding Industry.*

The dates on which work began on the various stages of *Olympic* and *Titanic* are from Moss and Hume, pp. 518–19; and McCaughan, p. 67.

Descriptions of the riveters and other workmen laying the keel are from McCaughan, pp. 66–85; Green, pp. 39–43; and an interview with Harland and Wolff archivist Tom McCluskie in February 2007.

The location of the sheds surrounding the slipways are from a plan of the shipyard, circa 1910, in the Harland and Wolff archives at the Public Record Office of Northern Ireland.

The details and implications of the *Republic* disaster to Andrews, and Harland and Wolff are from Chirnside, pp. 32–33; Louden-

Brown, *The White Star Line*, p. 77; and an interview with Louden-Brown in February 2007.

Una Reilly of the Belfast Titanic Historical Society described the Harland and Wolff timekeeping system, which was in use through the 1960s. Tom McCluskie, who worked at the yard, still has his board, number 155314, which he produced during an interview in Belfast in February 2007. His number is also confirmed in his book *No Place for a Boy*, p. 33.

The description of the plating shed is from photographs in the Harland and Wolff archives at the Public Record Office of Northern Ireland.

Confirmation of Helen Andrews's pregnancy in 1910 and her visit to the shipyard to view *Titanic* and *Olympic* with Halley's comet overhead is from Bullock, p. 27.

The details of the launching of *Olympic*, including the ticket receipts from the grandstand sales and the donation to the ambulance fund, are from Chirnside, pp. 36–37; and Moss and Hume, pp. 144–45.

The details of *Olympic*'s departure from Belfast are from Chirnside, pp. 40–41; and Moss and Hume, p. 144.

Confirmation that the sides of *Olympic* were "panting" is from an interview with Tom McCluskie in February 2007: "The hull panting was recorded by Thomas Andrews in his design notebook, which he carried with him at all times, and he also made reference to it on the shell drawing which he modified for *Titanic* to include extra stiffening. The panting and hull cracking found on *Olympic* is widely documented in the White Star papers held by the Public Record Office in Kew, London." In an interview in January 2007 David Brown, an expert on the structure of the *Olympic*-class ships, also agreed that Andrews and others observed panting, because the repairs made to strengthen *Olympic* after the *Titanic* disaster focused on seams above the double bottom and on the top deck of the superstructure, which would have endured the most stress from a panting hull. At the British Board of Trade inquiry following the *Titanic* disaster, Edward Wilding refers to the panting of the hulls of *Olympic*-class liners in his testimony.

CHAPTER NINE. *TITANIC*

Author and seaman Joseph Conrad was an outspoken critic of the giant new White Star and Cunard ships. Like many, he believed the "monster ships" would concentrate too much life and wealth in a single bottom. Conrad's statement in the epigraph is quoted in Wyn Craig Wade's *The Titanic: End of a Dream*, p. 16.

The scathing description of J. P. Morgan is quoted in the *New York Times*, April 13, 1910.

The description of Pirrie's office suite is from a visit to the Harland and Wolff main building, which is still standing, along with a photograph taken of the office in 1911, which is in the archive at the Public Record Office of Northern Ireland.

The details of *Titanic*'s launching are from McCaughan, pp. 87–97; and accounts from the *Belfast News-Letter*, and the *Irish News*, June 1, 1911.

The details of the deaths and casualties during the construction of *Olympic* and *Titanic* are from safety reports submitted to the Harland and Wolff directors at monthly meetings, found in the company archives at the Public Record Office of Northern Ireland.

The details of fitting out are from McCaughan, pp. 110–29; and photographs from the Harland and Wolff archive held at the Ulster Folk and Transport Museum in Belfast.

The best article on *Titanic*'s engines, boilers, and generators is "*Titanic*'s Prime Mover: An Examination of Propulsion and Power," by Samuel Halpern, *Encyclopedia Titanica*, July 2007.

A note on *Titanic*'s power plants: There were five rows of five boilers, and one row—nearest the bow—of four boilers. In the bottom of each boiler were three furnaces. They could be stoked from either end, except for the five boilers nearest the stern, which had single-ended furnaces. From the coal fires in the furnaces, flames and smoke flowed upward into bundles of steel tubes surrounded by water. The heat turned the water to steam. The steam drove the engines. The smoke went up and out the funnel.

Each of *Titanic*'s matched pair of four-cylinder, reciprocating engines was as high as a three-story house and weighed a thousand tons. When the engines were running, steam drove a piston down, released its pressure through the exhaust valve, and the piston came back up. Six-foot-long steel rods connected the pistons to a cam that turned the propeller shaft. Together, the two reciprocating engines produced 30,000 horsepower to turn their propellers at 75 revolutions per minute when the ship was at cruising speed.

The third engine was a turbine that was something like a windmill. Instead of the five or six blades of the farmer's tool, it had hundreds of polished steel blades in a steel housing. After the steam drove the pistons of the reciprocating engines, it would travel through pipes to the turbine, turn its blades at 165 revolutions per minute, and produce 16,000 horsepower. The turbine could run in only one direction. It was stopped when the reciprocating engines were reversed.

"Yamsi" was the way Ismay always signed telegrams, as confirmed by Paul Louden-Brown in correspondence in June 2007. Ismay's famous telegrams after the *Titanic* disaster were not the first time he used "Yamsi"; nor did he use that signature to deceive anyone. Variations on a person's name were then in vogue as telegram signatures.

The collision between RMS *Olympic* and HMS *Hawke* is documented by Simon Mills in his *RMS Olympic*, pp. 15–29; and Chirnside, pp. 65–77.

Captain E. J. Smith's comments on the collision and his assessment of the strength of *Olympic* are from Charles Pellegrino's *Her Name* Titanic, p. 246; and a conversation with Smith reported by a passenger on *Olympic* in the *New York Times* on April 17, 1912, two days after *Titanic* sank.

The discovery of cracks in the forward section of *Olympic* in November 1911 is deduced from the location of the additional steel Andrews and Pirrie put into *Titanic*. They reinforced the seam above the bottom in the bow by simply doubling the plates—a questionable repair by modern shipbuilding standards because it allowed a space between the plates where corrosion could form. They also enclosed *Titanic*'s upper promenade from the bridge back to the middle of the ship, which would have stiffened the superstructure and the bow section. Evidence of these differences between *Titanic* and *Olympic* are from Harland and Wolff photographs held at the Ulster Folk and Transport Museum; and from surveyors' reports on *Olympic* that led to the installation of additional steel, held at the British National Archives. Whether or not these weaknesses contributed to the breakup of *Titanic* is not certain, but they do indicate that Pirrie and Andrews were not sure of the strength of the *Olympic*-class hulls. Later, they would finish *Britannic* with a full double hull, instead of just a double bottom.

This surveyor's note on *Titanic*, from the British National Archives, dated February 13, 1912, confirms that *Olympic*'s hull was cracking and had been reinforced:

> *In connection with the scantlings of this vessel now in dry dock here, I beg to report that the builders are fitting a strap 1″ thick over the landings at the upper turn of the bilge, at both sides in the following positions: Forward. In way of No. 6 boiler room & extending three frame spaces forward of the W.T. bulkhead at the forward end of the boiler room, viz: from frame 63 to 81 at the landing of J & K strakes. Aft. In way of the turbine room & extending two frame spaces into the reciprocating room, viz: from frame 50 to 73 at the landing of K & L strakes. An extra row of holes has been drilled in the plate above the landing, making it a quadruple riveted landing. I am informed that this strengthening is in consequence of observation made on board the* Olympic *during a recent heavy passage across the Atlantic.*

The order, keel-laying date, and changes to the original plans for *Olympic* and *Titanic* are confirmed in Harland and Wolff archives, held at the Public Record Office of Northern Ireland, and the White Star papers at the British National Archives.

Olympic's second trip into the dry dock, in March 1912, after losing a propeller blade, is reported in Mills's *RMS* Olympic, p. 23, and confirmed in the White Star papers at the British National Archives.

The surveyor's note, dated March 6, 1912, is from the British National Archives:

> *This vessel has been in dry dock here for the purpose of having a propeller blade fitted, and the opportunity was taken for making an inspection of the hull, upon which I now beg to submit the following report. No signs of undue stress were found in the upper parts of the vessel, from the water line upwards, excepting in the side plating of the deck houses on the Bridge deck, where there are a number of fractures starting from the edges of the windows. Below the water line. Starboard side forward in way of No. 6 Boiler room in the shell landing of J and K strakes from frame 63 to 74 about 160 rivets were slack and were drilled out and removed. About 4 ft. below this landing in the tank bar, from frame 71 to 75, about 50 loose rivets were drilled and replaced. Port side fwd in the tank bar from about frame 71 to 78, about 90 rivets were showing a little slack and caulked.*

The work on *Olympic*'s bow plates is also confirmed in a diagram of damaged shell plating submitted by Harland and Wolff and reproduced in Hall and Beveridge, p. 21.

CHAPTER TEN. MILLIONAIRE'S CAPTAIN

Smith's quips about retiring are from an interview he gave to the *Shipbuilder* in March 1912, when he left *Olympic* in Southampton to take command of *Titanic*.

That Edward J. Smith was known as "the Millionaire's Captain" was confirmed in an interview with White Star historian Paul Louden-Brown in February 2007.

Captain Smith's remarks after RMS *Adriatic*'s maiden voyage are quoted in Chirnside, p. 46, from an article in the *Shipbuilder* in May 1907.

The details, timing, and crew for the sea trials on April 2, 1912, are confirmed in Chirnside, pp. 135–36; McCaughan, pp. 152–58; and Green, pp. 121–24.

Andrews's note to his wife on the evening of April 2, 1912, is from the papers of Helen Andrews, quoted in Bullock, pp. 56–57.

Miners voted to end the coal strike on April 6, 1912. Coal started flowing to the docks a week later but was not up to prestrike supplies for a month. Details are confirmed in the *New York Times*, April 7, 1912, April 12, 1912, and April 23, 1912.

The details about provisioning and loading of cargo are from McCaughan, pp. 158–65; Tom McCluskie's *The Wall Chart of the* Titanic; and the Manifest and Cargo records from the White Star papers at the British National Archives.

The details about the reorganization of the senior officers and the thoughts of Lightoller and Wilde before sailing are from Chirnside, pp. 136–37.

Violet Jessop's biography and her thoughts on arrival aboard *Titanic* are from her book, Titanic *Survivor*, pp. 56–68, and pp. 116–18.

The composition of *Titanic*'s string band is from the White Star papers at the British National Archives.

The observations of the reporters on sailing day are from the *Shipbuilder* and the *London Standard*, April 1912. The *Shipbuilder* devoted forty pages to *Titanic* that month.

The newspaper headlines and observations of monster ships in the *Economist* and *Engineering News* are reported in Wade, p. 16.

Jean Strouse explains J. P. Morgan's absence from *Titanic*'s maiden voyage in Strouse, pp. 642–44.

The timing of the surgery to ease Pirrie's prostate disease and Margaret Pirrie's suggestion that he recuperate aboard *Valiant* are confirmed in Jefferson, pp. 88–89. The symptoms of the disease and the comparative risk of prostate surgery in 1912 were confirmed in correspondence with Harry W. Herr, M.D., Department of Urology, Memorial Sloan-Kettering Cancer Center, and Cornell University Medical College, and in Dr. Herr's article "The Enlarged Prostate: A Brief History of Its Surgical Treatment," *British Journal of Urology International*, vol. 5 (1998), pp. 947–52.

The description of the steam yacht *Valiant* is from Jefferson, pp.

248–51; Moss and Hume, pp. 154–55; and photographs in the Harland and Wolff archive at the Public Record Office of Northern Ireland.

The quotes from the Master's Report and the Report of Survey are from Chirnside, p. 139, and from the British Wreck Commission's inquiry into the *Titanic* disaster, available as a searchable database at http://titanicinquiry.org.

The SS *New York* incident is well reported in many sources, including books by Chirnside; Wade; and McCluskie.

CHAPTER ELEVEN. 41° 46' NORTH, 50° 14' WEST

The chronology of events on the night of April 14–15, 1912, is the work of historian and mariner David G. Brown, author of many articles on *Titanic* and of the book *The Last Log of the* Titanic, for all of which I am grateful. Brown cites work by another highly regarded *Titanic* historian, Sam Halpern, as having contributed to the chronology. The chronology in this book is also informed by John Eaton and Charles Haas in Titanic: *A Journey Through Time.*

Ismay's stateroom, his dinner with Dr. O'Loughlin, and his leaving his bed when he heard the engines change pitch are confirmed in his testimony at the American and British inquiries.

Violet Jessop describes her reaction to the iceberg impact in her book, Titanic *Survivor*, pp. 125–28. The book was compiled from Jessop's notes twenty-six years after she died by editor John Maxtone-Graham. In her manuscript, for unknown reasons, Jessop obscured the identities of *Titanic*'s passengers and crew with pseudonyms, many of which Maxtone-Graham was able to decipher. In the book, Jessop's cabin companion is named Ann Turnbull; according to Maxtone-Graham, she was probably stewardess Elizabeth Leather, who escaped in the same lifeboat as Jessop.

Anna Turja's experience on *Titanic* is chronicled by her grandson, John Randolph; presented at http://www.webcom.com/jrudolph/turja/mumma.html; and confirmed in the records of survivors in the reports of the American and British inquiries.

Olaus Abelseth told his story to the American inquiry, from

which this account is taken. More detail came from "Olaus Jorgensen Abelseth" by Terry Newton, which appeared in the Titanic *Commutator*, fall 2006.

The medley of reactions of passengers to the moment of impact is drawn from the transcripts of the American and British inquiries.

The whereabouts of Thomas Andrews were constructed using accounts by surviving crew members who saw him at various times around the ship, as reported in the transcripts of the American and British inquiries.

Andrews selected a guarantee party of eight men to sail on *Titanic*'s maiden voyage and inspect and repair the ship under way: Roderick Chisholm, ship's draftsman; Anthony Frost, outside foreman engineer; Robert Knight, leading hand engineer; William Campbell, joiner apprentice; Alfred Cunningham, fitter apprentice; Frank Parkes, plumber apprentice; Ennis Watson, electrician apprentice; and William Parr, electrician. None survived.

The descriptions of the boiler rooms and of the life of stokers, trimmers, and engineers is from Art Braunschweiger's article "Feeding the Fires: Boilers, Firemen, and Trimmers," for the Titanic Research and Modeling Association, August 2005.

The location of Barrett and Hesketh in either Boiler Room 6 or the forward coal bunker at the moment of impact is a matter of debate and is the subject of some of the investigation of this book. The descriptions of the alarms, doors closing, and water rushing in are from Barrett's testimony at the American and British inquiries. Hesketh, along with all twenty other engineers, died on *Titanic*.

The telegrams warning about ice are well documented in both the American and the British inquiries; here, they are taken from reproductions in Eaton and Haas's Titanic: *A Journey Through Time*, pp. 55–60; and McCaughan, p. 171.

Murdoch's reply to Smith is from testimony given by Lightoller and others on the bridge, from "British Wreck Commissioner's Inquiry: Report of the Loss of the *Titanic*," July 30, 1912, found at http://ti tanicinquiry.org.

The Marconi transmissions to and from *Titanic* are documented in the transcripts of the American inquiry, including the testimony of telegrapher Harold Bride, who survived the sinking.

The names of passengers in the various lifeboats are from the White Star papers at the British National Archives, reported by Tom McCluskie in his *The Wall Chart of the* Titanic. The order of departure of the lifeboats from the ship is from David G. Brown's unpublished chronology; and Eaton and Haas, Titanic: *A Journey Through Time*, pp. 64–73.

CHAPTER TWELVE. YAMSI

Ismay was in shock when he boarded *Carpathia*, as confirmed by testimony in the transcripts of the American and British inquiries. Ismay's conversation with the ship's doctor upon boarding *Carpathia* is from his own recollection given as testimony in Washington, D.C., on April 30, 1912.

The *New York Times* coverage of *Titanic* is from several daily editions throughout April and May. Carr Van Anda told his story many times in the months following the disaster. However, according to investigation by historian Patrick Leary and filmmaker Rushmore DeNooyer, it is unlikely that the headline appeared anywhere except on the bulletin board in Times Square.

The record of the wireless transmissions after *Titanic* sank, David Sarnoff's receipt of the first confirmation of the sinking from *Olympic*, and the subsequent confusion about the names of survivors are documented in many places, including the papers of the White Star Line in the British National Archives; the reports of the American and British inquiries; Eaton and Haas, Titanic: *A Journey Through Time*, pp. 86–103; and Wade, pp. 28–58. Sarnoff went on to found the Radio Corporation of America, and the National Broadcasting Company.

For the chronicle of events that revolved around Senator William Alden Smith, his biography, and the formation of his investigative committee, I am indebted to the research and reporting of Wyn Craig

Wade and his book *The* Titanic: *End of a Dream,* which is required reading for anyone seeking a deeper understanding of the *Titanic* disaster.

The members of Smith's investigative committee were: Senators
George Perkins, of California; Jonathan Bourne Jr., of Oregon;
Theodore Burton, of Ohio; Furnifold Simmons, of North Carolina;
Francis Newlands, of Nevada; and Duncan Fletcher of Florida.
Secretary of Commerce Nagel and steamship inspector George Uhler
heard testimony and gave advice to the committee.

J. P. Morgan's reaction to the *Titanic* disaster and the cable from his
son are from Strouse, p. 643.

The Harland and Wolff board of directors meeting on the morning of April 16 is confirmed by the original minutes of that meeting,
held at the Public Record Office of Northern Ireland in Belfast.

Margaret Pirrie's withholding the news about *Titanic* until April 20
is confirmed in Jefferson, p. 78.

CHAPTER THIRTEEN. INVESTIGATION

The account of Senator Smith's meeting in Ismay's cabin aboard
Carpathia and his observations of the joy and sorrow in the crowd
below the ship as survivors debarked were recounted by Smith in several newspaper interviews and reported in Wade, pp. 98–100.

The quoted dialogue in this chapter is from the transcripts of
The Titanic *Disaster Hearings Before a Subcommittee of the Committee on
Commerce, Pursuant to Senate Resolution 283 Directing the Committee on
Commerce to Investigate the Causes Leading to the Wreck of the White Star
Liner* Titanic, U.S. Senate, 62nd Congress, 2nd session (Washington,
D.C., Government Printing Office, 1918). In certain cases, I left some
questions and answers out of a line of inquiry, without diminishing the
accuracy of the witness's testimony. The details of the hearing room,
the audience, and the textures of the testimony are from newspaper
accounts and photographs.

Smith's actions during the hearings in New York, including his
work with Sheriff Joe Bayliss to stop the steamship *Lapland* at Sandy

Hook, are from Wyn Craig Wade's research and from his book, pp. 134–35.

Pirrie's note to his sister, Thomas Andrews's mother, is from Bullock, p. 78. His cable to Wilding is not verbatim but was drawn from the May 1912 minutes of the Harland and Wolff board of directors meeting and from letters in the company archive that indicate that Wilding began an internal investigation into the *Titanic* disaster within a week after it occurred.

CHAPTER FOURTEEN. ROGER WRONG, ROGER RIGHT

The description of Roger Long's analysis of *Titanic*'s bottom pieces with the help of Ken Marschall's drawings is from interviews with Long in 2006 and 2007.

Roger Long spent hours explaining to me his low-angle, top-down breakup theory and its implications for what the world understands about the *Titanic* disaster. He reviewed this manuscript many times, offering suggestions for accuracy and clarity.

The paper to which Roger Long referred is "The *Titanic* and *Lusitania*: A Final Forensic Analysis, by William H. Garzke Jr., David K. Brown, Arthur D. Sandiford, John Woodward, and Peter K. Hsu, published in *Marine Technology*, a journal of the Society of Naval Architects and Marine Engineers, October 1996, pp. 241–89.

The account of the December 2005 meeting at Woods Hole is from interviews with the participants and audio and video recordings.

The Associated Press story on the new evidence and Long's theory appeared in hundreds of newspapers around the world, beginning with the afternoon editions of East Coast American papers on December 5. It contained errors of fact and nuance but initiated discussions on Internet forums and among *Titanic* theorists, as well as clarifications in several publications.

The *New York Times* editorial celebrating the new evidence and criticizing Robert Ballard's reaction to it appeared in all editions of the paper on December 8, 2005. Ballard responded to the criticism in a letter to the members of the Titanic Historical Society, which appeared in the winter 2005 edition of the Titanic *Commutator*.

CHAPTER FIFTEEN. WEE MAN

The biographical details of Tom McCluskie's life at Harland and Wolff are from interviews with him in February 2007, his many generous e-mail responses to my lists of questions, and his own account of his career at Harland and Wolff in his book *No Place for a Boy*.

The quote by Per Nielsen after he canceled McCluskie's gala at the shipyard following the screening of *Titanic* is from the *Belfast Telegraph*, July 17, 2006.

McCluskie's statements at dinner with Roger Long were recollected in interviews with both men. McCluskie's statements the following day at Woods Hole are taken verbatim from audio and video recordings.

CHAPTER SIXTEEN. *BRITANNIC*

The construction records for Hull No. 433, which would become *Britannic*, are from the Harland and Wolff ledger of ships in the archives held at the Public Record Office of Northern Ireland.

Descriptions of the Greek coast, the island of Kéa, and the shipping channel where *Britannic* sank are from visits to the site by the author.

Accounts of the sinking are from Simon Mills's book *Hostage to Fortune*, pp. 125–37; Paul Louden-Brown's *The White Star Line*, pp. 92–93; and Chirnside, pp. 217–74.

Violet Jessop's account of surviving the sinking of *Britannic* is from Jessop, pp. 171–87.

The accounts of the aborted dives in the firemen's tunnel in 1998 and 2006 are from interviews with Chatterton and Kohler in September 2006.

The account of Cousteau's discovery and exploration of *Britannic* is from Axel Madsen's *Cousteau: An Unauthorized Biography*, pp. 178–81; and Richard Munson's *The Captain and His World*, pp. 168–72.

The account of Kohler and Barnette on the promenade deck and the bridge of *Britannic* is from interviews with them in September 2006.

NOTES

Cover-Up

During his tenure as the Harland and Wolff archivist, Tom McCluskie came across internal engineering notes and memoranda that clearly indicate that Wilding and Pirrie, and perhaps other engineers, knew that there was an 80 percent chance that *Titanic* had broken on the surface before it sank. The subsequent fitting of *Olympic* and *Britannic* with full double hulls was not for protection from puncture by icebergs but to stiffen the ship. Wilding and Pirrie were not at all sure that *Titanic*, as built, had been strong enough to resist not only massive damage from an iceberg but the stresses of normal service in all weather and sea conditions.

Harland and Wolff redesigned the expansion joints to include a radius corner at the base of the joint rather than the simple square section or V notch as on *Olympic* and *Titanic*. When Wilding looked at the hull design and, in particular, the degree of hull cracking on *Olympic*, he determined that the shear forces at the joint corners were far in excess of the structure's capabilities. As a result, they completely redesigned these joints and increased the number to three on *Britannic* simply in an attempt to relieve the hull stresses. Harland and Wolff was aware that the hull form and strength were deficient in many respects and attempted a number of quick fixes, in addition to the major addition of steel to the hulls.

Two passionate *Titanic* researchers, Rob Ottmers and Bill Wormstedt, created the *Titanic* Inquiry Project, http://www.titanicinquiry.org/. For anyone interested in reading the transcripts of the American and British inquiries into the disaster, this site is a priceless gift. Questions, testimony, and biographies of the participants are fully searchable by keyword, and navigation on the site is a snap. There is no charge for using it.

Wilding's letter to the Harland and Wolff managing directors is from the company's archive, held at the Public Record Office of Northern Ireland.

8418 GERRARD
Telegrams
HARLANDIC, LONDON

June 29, 1912
Managing Directors, Harland and Wolff
Dear Sirs,

I confirm sending from the court this morning a telegram to the effect that the big model can now go back to Belfast, and that as the hall is required for an examination on Monday we should begin the removal first thing that morning to avoid delays and risk of damage. The model makers should be there at 6:30 and the same assistance as before will be provided.

I only learnt this morning that Monday's sitting is to be at the Caxton Hall, where I there learnt the other things. The sittings of the Inquiry will I think finish on Monday, but not till late.

I am therefore arranging to see Lloyd's on Tuesday morning re: No. 433 plans and correspondence.

If not required here on Wednesday for consultation on Olympic *and* Hawke *I propose to return to Belfast for that day, but will have to come back on Wednesday evening.*

The Commissioner's speech has indicated so far no attack on the builders of Titanic, *and did begin with a note of thanks for the assistance and full information given. It may therefore be stated I think that neither the firm nor any of the staff will be under any imputation as we succeeded in forcing the withdrawal of the only material charge made by an outside counsel that we had not submitted our strength calculations to the board of trade.*

Yours faithfully,
Ed. Wilding

Pirrie's bitterness toward Wilding is documented in the minutes of the managing directors meetings for June, July, and August 1912, which are held at the Public Record Office of Northern Ireland. In several other accounts, Pirrie immediately fired Wilding, but those could not be confirmed in primary sources. In the minutes, however, it is obvious that Pirrie marginalized Wilding at the shipyard. In one instance, the minutes reveal that the directors castigated Wilding for abusing his right to entertain guests in the executive dining room.

From "British Wreck Commissioner's Inquiry: Report of the Loss of the *Titanic*," July 30, 1912:

> *The Court, having carefully inquired into the circumstances of the above mentioned shipping casualty, finds, for the reasons appearing in the annex hereto, that the loss of the said ship was due to collision with an iceberg, brought about by the excessive speed at which the ship was being navigated.*

From the wreck commissioner's replies to the questions asked by the British Board of Trade:

> *25. When the "Titanic" left Queenstown on or about the 11th April last was she properly constructed and adequately equipped as a passenger steamer and emigrant ship for the Atlantic service?*

Answer:

Yes.

From "Description of the Damage to the Ship and Its Gradual Final Effect":

> *The collision with the iceberg, which took place at 11.40 p.m., caused damage to the bottom of the starboard side of the vessel at about 10 feet above the level of the keel, but there was no damage above this height. There was damage in: The forepeak, No. 1 hold, No. 2 hold, No. 3 hold,*

No. 6 boiler room, No. 5 boiler room. The damage extended over a length of about 300 ft.

The later stages of the sinking cannot be stated with any precision, owing to a confusion of the times which was natural under the circumstances. From "Description of the Damage to the Ship and Its Gradual Final Effect: Final Effect of the Damage":

Her stern was gradually rising out of the water, and the propellers were clear of the water. The ship did not break in two; and she did eventually attain the perpendicular. . . . Before reaching the perpendicular when at an angle of 50 or 60 degrees, there was a rumbling sound which may be attributed to the boilers leaving their beds and crashing down on to or through the bulkheads. She became more perpendicular and finally absolutely perpendicular, when she went slowly down. After sinking as far as the after part of the Boat deck she went down more quickly. The ship disappeared at 2.20 a.m.

ENDINGS

White Star historian Paul Louden-Brown described Bruce Ismay's life after *Titanic* to me in interviews in February 2007 and in subsequent correspondence.

The numbers of passengers carried by White Star and Cunard in 1913 are from an article, "The White Star Line and the International Mercantile Marine Company," by William B. Saphire on the Internet site of the Titanic Historical Society at http://titanichistoricalsociety .org/articles.

The details of J. P. Morgan's death and the failure of International Mercantile Marine are from Strouse, pp. 680–83 and 457–81.

The details of Pirrie's life after *Titanic* and his death at sea are from Jefferson, pp. 283–99; and Moss and Hume, pp. 208–44.

In the winter of 2007, Chatterton and Kohler commissioned a naval architect to do a computer simulation of *Titanic*'s last hours. It proved conclusively that Roger Long's low-angle breakup theory was correct. It also proved that while *Titanic*'s hull and the steel with which the giant ship was built had many flaws that contributed to it sinking so quickly, the main hull girder was probably strong enough for normal service on the North Atlantic.

BIBLIOGRAPHY

BOOKS

Ballard, Robert D. *The Discovery of the* Titanic. Toronto: Madison Press Books, 1987.

Beebe, William. *Half Mile Down.* New York: Harcourt Brace, 1934.

Beesley, Lawrence. *The Loss of the* S.S. Titanic: *Its Story and Its Lessons.* New York: Houghton Mifflin, 1913.

Brewster, Hugh, and Laurie Coulter. *882½ Amazing Answers to Your Questions About the* Titanic. Toronto: Scholastic Canada, Ltd., 1998.

Brown, David G. *The Last Log of the* Titanic: *What Really Happened on the Doomed Ship's Bridge.* New York: International Marine/McGraw-Hill, 2001.

Bryceson, Dave. *The* Titanic *Disaster as Reported in the British National Press, April–July, 1912.* New York: Norton, 1997.

Bullock, Shan F. *A* Titanic *Hero: Thomas Andrews, Shipbuilder.* 1912. Reprint, Ludlow, Mass.: Titanic Historical Society/7 C's Press, 1995.

Butler, Daniel Allen. *Unsinkable: The Full Story.* Mechanicsburg, Penn.: Stackpole Books, 1998.

Chernow, Ron. *The House of Morgan: An American Banking Dynasty and the Rise and Fall of Modern Finance.* New York: Grove Press, 2001.

Chirnside, Mark. *The* Olympic *Class Ships:* Olympic, Titanic, Britannic. Gloucestershire, U.K.: Tempus Publishing, 2004.

Comstock, John P., ed. *Principles of Naval Architecture.* Revised edition.

New York: Society of Naval Architects and Marine Engineers, 1967.

Cousteau, Jacques-Yves, with Frederic Dumas. *The Silent World*. New York: Harper and Row, 1953; reprinted by the National Geographic Society, 2004.

Dodman, Frank E. *The Observer's Book of Ships*. London: Warne, 1958.

Eaton, John P., and Charles A. Haas. Titanic*: A Journey Through Time*. New York: Norton, 1999.

———. Titanic*: Triumph and Tragedy*. 2nd ed. New York: Norton, 1995.

Goldsmith, Frank J. W. *Echoes in the Night: Memories of a* Titanic *Survivor*. Springfield, Mass.: Titanic Historical Society, 1991.

Gracie, Archibald. *The Truth About the* Titanic. New York: Michael Kennerly, 1913.

Green, Rod. *Building the* Titanic*: An Epic Tale of the Creation of History's Most Famous Ocean Liner*. New York: Reader's Digest, 2005.

Gruber, Michael. *The Book of Air and Shadows*. New York: William Morrow, 2007.

Hall, Steve, and Bruce Beveridge. Olympic *and* Titanic*: The Truth Behind the Conspiracy*. Haverford, Penn.: Infinity, 2004.

Jefferson, Herbert. *Viscount Pirrie of Belfast*. Belfast: William Mullan and Son, 1948.

Jessop, Violet. Titanic *Survivor: The Newly Discovered Memoirs of Violet Jessop Who Survived Both the* Titanic *and* Britannic *Disasters*. Dobbs Ferry, N.Y.: Sheridan House, 1997.

Kludas, Arnold. *Record Breakers of the North Atlantic: Blue Riband Liners, 1838–1952*. London: Chatham Publishing, 2000.

Kuntz, Tom. *The* Titanic *Disaster Hearings: The Official Transcripts of the 1912 Senate Investigation*. New York: Pocket Books, 1998.

Kurson, Robert. *Shadow Divers: The True Adventure of Two Americans Who Risked Everything to Solve One of the Last Mysteries of World War II*. New York: Random House, 2004.

Lightoller, Charles H. Titanic *and Other Ships*. London: Ivor, Nicholson and Watson, 1935.

Lord, Walter. *A Night to Remember.* New York: Holt, Rinehart, and Winston, 1955.

Louden-Brown, Paul. *The White Star Line: An Illustrated History, 1869–1934.* Kent, Eng.: Ship Pictorial Publications, 1991.

Lynch, John. *Forgotten Shipbuilders of Belfast: Workman, Clark, 1880–1935.* Belfast: Friar's Bush Press, 2004.

———. *An Unlikely Success Story: The Belfast Shipbuilding Industry, 1880–1935.* Belfast: Belfast Society, 2001.

MacInnis, Joseph. Titanic *in a New Light.* Charlottesville, Va.: Thomasson-Grant, 1992.

Madsen, Axel. *Cousteau: An Unauthorized Biography.* New York: Beaufort Books, 1986.

Marschall, Ken. *Ken Marschall's Art of* Titanic. Toronto: Madison Press, 1998.

Matarasso, Pauline. *A Voyage Closed and Done.* Norwich, Eng.: Michael Russell Publishing, 2005.

Matsen, Brad. *Descent: The Heroic Discovery of the Abyss.* New York: Pantheon, 2005.

McCaughan, Michael. *The Birth of the* Titanic. Montreal: McGill–Queen's University Press, 1998.

McCluskie, Tom. *Anatomy of the* Titanic. San Diego: Thunder Bay Press, 1998.

———. *No Place for a Boy: A Life at Harland & Wolff.* Gloucestershire: Tempus Publishing, 2007.

———. *The Wall Chart of the* Titanic. San Diego: Thunder Bay Press, 1998.

Mills, Simon. *Hostage to Fortune: The Dramatic Story of the Last Olympian HMHS* Britannic. Chesham, Eng.: Wordsmith Publications, 2002.

———. *RMS* Olympic: *Old Reliable.* London: Waterfront Publications, 1995.

Moss, Michael, and John R. Hume. *Shipbuilders to the World: 125 Years of Harland and Wolff, Belfast, 1861–1986.* Belfast: Blackstaff Press, 1986.

Mowbray, Jay Henry, ed. *Sinking of the* Titanic: *Eyewitness Accounts.* Harrisburg, Penn.: Minter Company, 1912.

Munson, Richard. *The Captain and His World.* New York: Paragon House, 1991.

Oldham, Wilton J. *The Ismay Line.* Liverpool: Journal of Commerce, 1961.

Pellegrino, Charles. *Her Name* Titanic*: The Untold Story of the Sinking and Finding of the Unsinkable Ship.* New York: Avon Books, 1990.

Pollard, Sidney, and Paul Robertson. *The British Shipbuilding Industry, 1870–1914.* Cambridge: Harvard University Press, 1979.

Pollock, David. *The Shipbuilding Industry: Its History, Practice, Science and Finance.* London: Methuen, 1905.

Reade, Leslie. *The Ship That Stood Still: The* Californian *and Her Mysterious Role in the* Titanic *Disaster.* New York: Norton, 1993.

Strouse, Jean. *Morgan: American Financier.* New York: Random House, 1999.

Tuchman, Barbara W. *The Proud Tower: A Portrait of the World Before the War, 1890–1914.* New York: Random House, 1962.

Wade, Wyn Craig. *The* Titanic*: End of a Dream.* New York: Rawson, Wade, 1979.

Ward, Ralph T. *Ships Through History.* New York: Bobbs-Merrill, 1973.

Winocour, Jack, ed. *The Story of the* Titanic *as Told by Its Survivors.* New York: Dover, 1960.

PAMPHLETS

Dodge, Washington. *The Loss of the* Titanic*: An Address by Washington Dodge, May 11, 1912.* Reprinted, Springfield, Mass.: 7 C's Press and Titanic Historical Society, n.d.

Rostron, Arthur H. *The Loss of the* Titanic. 1931. Reprinted, Springfield, Mass.: 7 C's Press and Titanic Historical Society, n.d.

Thayer, John B. *The Sinking of the S.S.* Titanic. 1940. Reprinted, Springfield, Mass.: 7 C's Press and Titanic Historical Society, n.d.

PERIODICALS

Ballard, Robert D. "A *Titanic* Tract." *Titanic Commutator*, vol. 29, no. 172 (fall 2005).

BIBLIOGRAPHY

Bride, Harold. "Thrilling Tale by *Titanic*'s Surviving Wireless Operator." *New York Times*, April 28, 1912.

Chatterton, John; Richie Kohler; et al. "The *Titanic* Puzzle: Two More Pieces." *Wreck Diving Magazine*, spring 2006.

Halpern, Samuel. "*Titanic*'s Prime Mover: An Examination of Propulsion and Power." *Encyclopedia Titanica*, July 2007.

Louden-Brown, Paul. "White Star Building 30 James Street, Liverpool." Titanic *Commutator*, vol. 21, no. 4 (spring 1998).

Mills, Simon. "*Titanic*'s Final Moments, Missing Pieces: More Questions Than Answers." *Titanic Commutator*, vol. 29, no. 172 (fall 2005).

Newton, Terry. "Olaus Jorgensen Abelseth: A Fortunate Titantic Survivor." Titantic *Commutator*, vol. 30, no. 175 (fall 2006).

FILMS

A Night to Remember. Rank Organization, 1958.

Titanic. A James Cameron Film, Twentieth Century Fox, 1997.

Titanic. Twentieth Century Fox, 1953.

Titanic*'s Achilles Heel.* Lone Wolf Documentary Group, for the History Channel, 2007.

Titanic*'s Final Moments: Missing Pieces.* Lone Wolf Documentary Group, for the History Channel, 2006.

INDEX

INDEX

INDEX

INDEX

INDEX

INDEX

INDEX

ABOUT THE AUTHOR

Brad Matsen has been writing about the sea and its inhabitants for thirty years, in books, film scripts, essays, and magazine articles. He is the author of *Descent: The Heroic Discovery of the Abyss*, which was a finalist for the *Los Angeles Times* Book Prize in 2006; *Planet Ocean: A Story of Life, the Sea, and Dancing to the Fossil Record*; and the award-winning Incredible Deep Sea Adventure series for children. He was a creative producer for *The Shape of Life*, an eight-hour *National Geographic* television series on evolutionary biology, and wrote the accompanying book of the same name. He has written on marine science and the environment for *Mother Jones, Audubon, Natural History*, and many other magazines. His coverage of depleted ocean resources in *Mother Jones* won the Project Censored Award as one of the ten best underreported stories of 1999. His essays have been included in *The Book of the Tongass* as part of the influential Literature for a Land Ethic series, the Smithsonian Institution's *Ocean Planet*, and other anthologies. Brad Matsen has twice been awarded residencies at the MacDowell Colony. He lives on Vashon Island in Washington.

ABOUT TWELVE

MISSION STATEMENT

TWELVE was established in August 2005 with the objective of publishing no more than one book per month. We strive to publish the singular book, by authors who have a unique perspective and compelling authority. Works that explain our culture; that illuminate, inspire, provoke, and entertain. We seek to establish communities of conversation surrounding our books. Talented authors deserve attention not only from publishers but from readers as well. To sell the book is only the beginning of our mission. To build avid audiences of readers who are enriched by these works—that is our ultimate purpose.

For more information about forthcoming TWELVE books, you can visit us at www.twelvebooks.com.